What Makes Windows 98 Special?

The most exciting feature of Windows 98 is its seamless integration of Internet Explorer 4, Microsoft's Web browser. **This integration makes possible several exciting new features through its Active Desktop.**

As this book was going to·press, there was a legal injunction pending to prevent Microsoft from integrating Internet Explorer 4 with Windows 98. If this injunction prevails, the copy of Windows 98 you purchase may not have Internet Explorer 4 built in.

Without Internet Explorer 4, you will miss out on many of the exciting features described in this book, so we recommend that you get and install Internet Explorer 4 right away. It's easy–*and free!* Just visit Microsoft's Web site (http://www.microsoft.com) and download your free copy of Internet Explorer 4. Run the installation program, and you're ready to go.

Even if you choose not to use Internet Explorer 4, Windows 98 still has many great new features to offer, including more powerful utilities and easier-to-use file management, all of which are covered in this book.

Congratulations on choosing Windows 98! It can be a great tool for making your computer work harder and smarter. Now, sit back and relax, and let this book teach you how to harness the power of Windows 98 for your own PC productivity.

How to Order:

For information on quantity discounts contact the publisher: Prima Publishing, P.O. Box 1260BK, Rocklin, CA 95677-1260; (916) 632-4400. On your letterhead include information concerning the intended use of the books and the number of books you wish to purchase. For individual orders, turn to the back of this book for more information.

Windows® 98

fast & easy™

Diane Koers

PRIMA PUBLISHING

Prima Publishing and colophon are registered trademarks of Prima Communications, Inc. Fast & Easy is a trademark of Prima Communications, Inc. Prima Publishing, Rocklin, California 95677.

Publisher: Matthew H. Carleson
Managing Editor: Dan J. Foster
Acquisitions Editor: Jenny L. Watson
Senior Editor: Kelli R. Crump
Assistant Project Editor: Kevin W. Ferns
Editorial Assistant: Kim V. Benbow
Technical Reviewer: Emily Kim
Copy Editor: Theresa Mathias
Interior Layout: Marian Hartsough
Cover Design: Prima Design Team
Indexer: Katherine Stimson

Microsoft and Windows are registered trademarks of Microsoft Corporation.

Important: If you have problems installing or running Microsoft Windows 98, notify Microsoft at (425) 635-7056 or on the Web at www.microsoft.com. Prima Publishing cannot provide software support.

Prima Publishing and the author have attempted throughout this book to distinguish proprietary trademarks from descriptive terms by following the capitalization style used by the manufacturer.

Information contained in this book has been obtained by Prima Publishing from sources believed to be reliable. However, because of the possibility of human or mechanical error by our sources, Prima Publishing, or others, the Publisher does not guarantee the accuracy, adequacy, or completeness of any information and is not responsible for any errors or omissions or the results obtained from the use of such information. Readers should be particularly aware of the fact that the Internet is an ever-changing entity. Some facts may have changed since this book went to press.

ISBN: 0-7615-1006-0
Library of Congress Catalog Card Number: 97-69603
Printed in the United States of America

98 99 00 01 02 HH 10 9 8 7 6 5 4 3 2 1

To the Drewster,
Grandma's little buddy

Acknowledgments

I am deeply thankful to the many people at Prima Publishing who worked on this book. Thank you for all the time you gave and for your assistance.

To Jenny Watson, for the opportunity to write this book and for her confidence in me. To Theresa Mathias and Emily Kim, for helping make this book technically correct, and to Kelli Crump, for all her assistance in the development of this book. Also, thanks to Elaine Marmel for helping me stay on track.

Lastly, to my husband. Thank you again Vern, for all your support and never-ending faith in me. For thirty years, you've believed in me.

About the Author

Diane Koers owns and operates All Business Service, a software training and consulting business formed in 1988 that services the central Indiana area. Her area of expertise is in the word processing, spreadsheet, and graphics area of computing as well as providing training and support for Peachtree Accounting software.

Diane's authoring experience includes Prima's *Lotus 1-2-3 97 Fast & Easy, WordPerfect 8 Fast & Easy,* and *The Essential Windows 98 Book.* She has also developed and written software training manuals for her clients' use.

Active in her church and civic activities, Diane enjoys spending her free time traveling and playing with her grandson and her three Yorkshire Terriers.

Contents at a Glance

Contents

PART II
WORKING WITH THE ACCESSORIES 57

Introduction

This new Fast & Easy book from Prima Publishing will help you unleash the power of Windows 98—the newest release of the world's most popular operating system. Microsoft has long had a reputation of delivering the type of products consumers have asked for, and Windows 98 is no exception.

Windows 98 Fast & Easy shows you how to accomplish the most common Windows tasks in the quickest and easiest manner possible. Fast & Easy guides use a step-by-step approach and are written in an easy to understand manner. Each step is accompanied by a color visual representation of your screen, so you can follow along on your screen to make sure you are on the right track.

This book provides you with the tools you need to successfully learn to use Windows 98. You will quickly be able to tap into the power of the user-friendly program.

Windows 98 Fast & Easy will not teach you everything you can do with Windows 98, nor will it give you all the different ways to accomplish a task. What it does do is provide you with the fastest and easiest method to get things done.

WHO SHOULD READ THIS BOOK?

This book can be used as a learning tool or as a step-by-step task reference. The easy-to-follow, highly visual nature of this book makes it the perfect learning tool for a beginning computer user or a seasoned computer user new to this version of

Windows. By using *Windows 98 Fast & Easy*, a user can look up steps for a task quickly, without having to plow through pages of descriptions.

ADDED ADVICE TO MAKE YOU A PRO

You'll notice that this book focuses on the steps necessary for a task and keeps explanations to a minimum. Included in the book are elements that provide some additional information to help you master the program, without encumbering your progress through the steps:

✦ **Tips** offer shortcuts when performing an action and describe features that can make your work in Windows quicker and easier.

✦ **Notes** give you a bit of background or additional information about a feature; they also give advice about how to use the feature in your day-to-day activities.

As an added bonus, an installation appendix is included to help you upgrade to Windows 98.

This book is the fastest and easiest way to learn Windows 98. Enjoy!

PART I

Understanding Basic Windows Operations

1 Getting Started with Windows 98

Using your computer has just become easier than ever. If you're upgrading from Windows 3.1 to Windows 98, you'll find Windows 98 a faster, more logical environment. If you're upgrading from Windows 95, you'll notice a faster response time from your computer. Also, making choices will require less effort on your part due to fewer buttons to click and less mouse movement. In this chapter, you'll learn how to:

✦ Start Windows 98

✦ Make a selection with the mouse

STARTING WINDOWS 98

By default, most computers start Windows 98 when you turn on the computer. Also, several diagnostics are run at the same time to make sure certain components of your computer are performing correctly. Depending upon the speed and processor of your computer, this process may take a couple of minutes.

After Windows 98 has loaded, you see a large area called the *desktop*. You can customize the desktop by adding shortcuts to your favorite programs, documents, and printers, and by changing its look to fit your mood and personality.

NOTE

If your computer was not shut down properly during the previous session of Windows, you will see a message prompting you to run ScanDisk when you start your machine. It would be wise to run this diagnostic tool. The Windows program will then continue to load. ScanDisk is covered in more detail in Chapter 11, "Using Windows System Tools."

TIP

If you haven't installed Windows 98 yet, go to the Appendix.

Using Windows 98 on a Network

If you are on a network, you may be prompted for your user name and network password.

1. **Type** the **password**. A series of asterisks will appear.

2. **Press** the **Enter key**. The Windows 98 desktop will appear.

TOURING THE WELCOME TO WINDOWS 98 DIALOG BOX

If your computer has sound capabilities, you will hear music accompanying the Welcome to Windows 98 dialog box. It allows you to register the Windows 98 product, tour the new features of Windows 98, and optimize the performance of your computer.

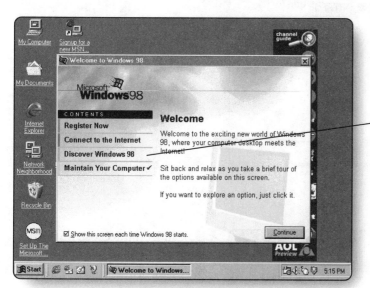

1. Pause your **mouse** over each of the choices. Different information will appear depending on your selection.

2. Click on an **option**. A new screen will appear.

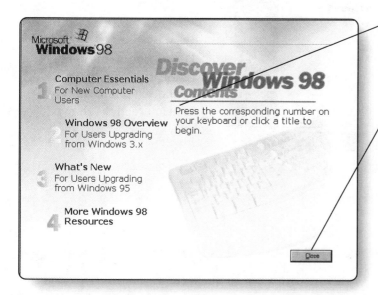

3a. Follow the **instructions** onscreen to continue with the demonstration.

OR

3b. Click on the **Close button** to exit the demonstration. A dialog box will open, asking whether you are sure you want to quit.

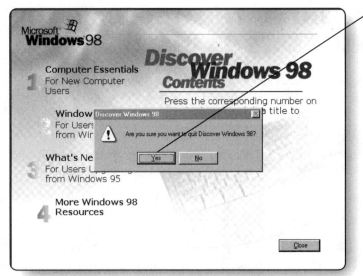

4. **Click** on **Yes**. The dialog box will close, and you will return to the Welcome to Windows 98 dialog box.

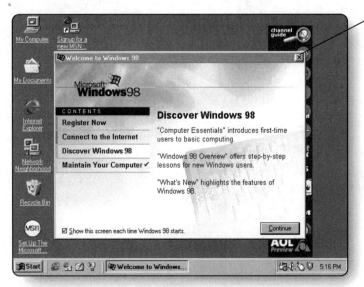

5. **Click** on the **Close button** ([X]). The Welcome to Windows 98 dialog box will close, and you will return to the Windows 98 desktop.

NOTE

Depending on the configuration of your computer, your desktop may not appear exactly as shown.

TIP

If you do not want the Welcome to Windows 98 dialog box to display each time you start your computer, click on the check box by Show this screen each time Windows 98 starts. The ✔ will be removed and the Welcome dialog box will not appear the next time you start Windows.

If you want to see the Welcome to Windows 98 dialog box at another time, you can access it by clicking on the Start menu, and then Programs, Accessories, System Tools, and Welcome to Windows.

NOTE

With a standard mouse, your index finger should rest on the left button while the middle finger should rest on the right button.

MAKING SELECTIONS WITH THE MOUSE

There are several varieties of computer mouses available. The most common mouse is the standard type that rolls across the desktop, usually on top of a foam pad. Other types of mouse devices include trackballs or touchpads. No matter which type of mouse you have, there are at least two buttons for you to use with the mouse. Some have three buttons and some have a wheel on the top.

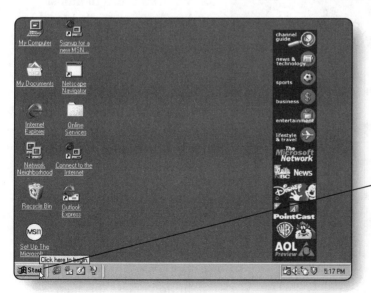

The left mouse button is the most frequently used of the buttons. It is used to make selections or choices from the Windows 98 menus or icons. When you make selections with the mouse, you do one of several things:

✦ **Click on the left mouse button once**. A single click activates the Start menu, launches a program, or selects an item for modification.

✦ **Click on the left mouse button twice** (this is called a *double-click*). A double-click is the process of pushing the buttons twice (click, click) in rapid succession without moving the mouse while you click. Double-clicking the mouse is often used as a shortcut. Many new features of Windows 98 eliminate the need to double-click.

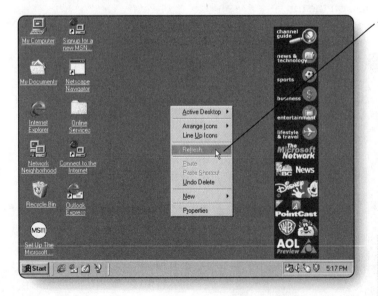

✦ **Click on the left mouse button and drag the mouse**. Performed by pointing the mouse pointer at an object, clicking on the left mouse button, and then moving the mouse while keeping the button pressed. This process can be used to select several items at a time or to move an object.

✦ **Click on the right mouse button** (this is called a *right-click*). Right-clicking opens a shortcut menu, which allows you to select common features quickly and easily. Although you make a shortcut menu appear by right-clicking, selections from the shortcut menu are made with the left mouse button.

TIP

All references in this book will refer to the left mouse button unless specified otherwise.

2 Recognizing Parts of the Desktop

There are several pictures or icons displayed on your computer desktop. It is necessary to recognize these icons in order to operate many of the Windows 98 features. In this chapter, you'll learn how to:

✦ Open the My Computer icon

✦ Browse the Network Neighborhood

✦ Work with the Taskbar

✦ Look at other desktop components

OPENING THE MY COMPUTER ICON

The My Computer icon is used to quickly and easily see everything on your computer. You can also customize your Windows 98 program through the My Computer icon.

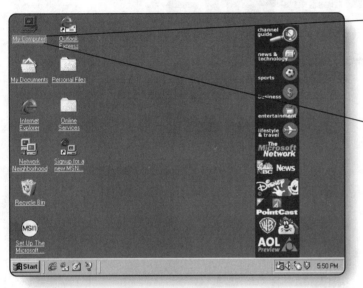

1. Click on the **My Computer icon**. The My Computer window will appear.

TIP

If the words "My Computer" are not underlined, your Windows 98 is configured with the Classic Style Desktop. You will need to double-click on icons to open them. In Chapter 17, "Having Fun with the Control Panel," you'll learn how to switch from the Classic Style Desktop to the Web Style Desktop.

When a window is open, a button appears at the bottom of the screen in an area called the *Taskbar*. (The Taskbar is discussed later in this chapter.)

NOTE

The configuration of your machine will probably be different from the setup shown in the figures.

Although you will learn about the different parts of a window in the next chapter, take a look at the contents of the My Computer window. From the My Computer window, you can see each disk drive on your computer and whether it is a floppy disk drive, a hard disk drive, or a CD-ROM drive. From each of these disk drives you will be able to browse through your files and folders.

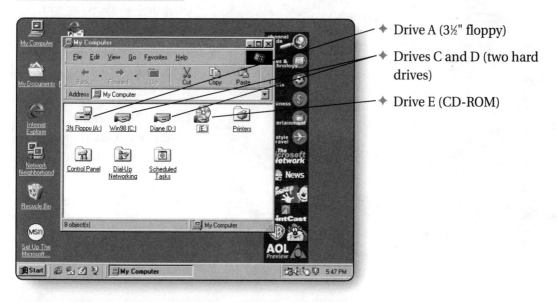

✦ Drive A (3½" floppy)

✦ Drives C and D (two hard drives)

✦ Drive E (CD-ROM)

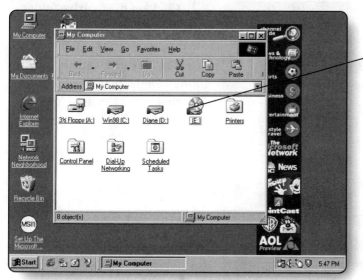

NOTE

If a disk drive has a little hand underneath it, it means that disk drive is shared across a network. Other people can access the information on that disk drive. If there is no hand, the drive is not shared.

There are more than disk drives displayed in the My Computer window. Other items that can be accessed from My Computer include:

✦ Control Panel (discussed in Chapter 16, "Tinkering with the Control Panel")

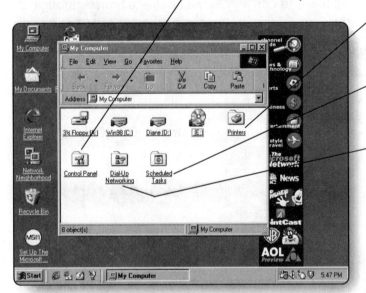

✦ Printers (discussed in Chapter 18, "Working with Printers")

✦ Scheduled Tasks (discussed in Chapter 11, "Using Windows System Tools")

✦ Dial-Up Networking (discussed in Chapter 19, "Connecting to the Internet")

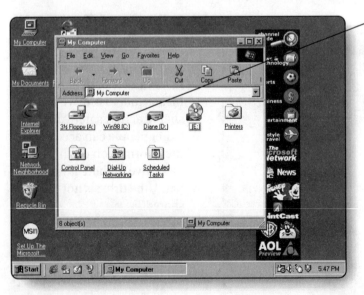

2. Click on the **C: drive folder**. The C: drive window will appear. It shows a listing of all the folders (formerly called *directories*) along with any files located in the top level folder of your hard drive.

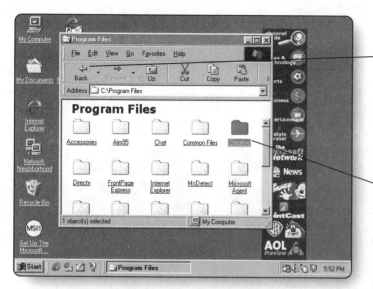

TIP
If you click on the wrong folder, click on the Back button to return to the previous window so you can try again.

3. **Click** on a **folder** to open it. The window for that folder will appear, and you can view any files (or other folders) in it.

When you are finished looking at the folders, you need to close the windows.

4. **Click** on the **Close buttons** (⌧) located in the upper right corner of the windows. You will return to the Windows 98 desktop.

BROWSING THE NETWORK

If you are using a network, the Network Neighborhood icon appears on your desktop. You'll use it to browse through the computers in your workgroup and the computers on your entire network.

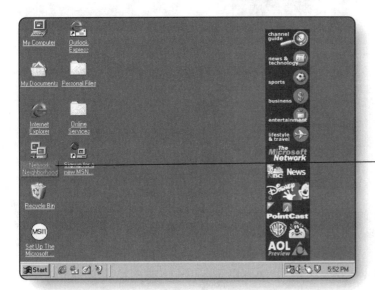

NOTE

Depending upon the features installed with Windows 98, you may not see this icon.

1. Click on the **Network Neighborhood icon**. The Network Neighborhood window will appear. You'll see a listing of each computer in every workgroup to which you are connected.

TIP

Instead of using the mouse to click on an icon, you can use the arrow keys on your keyboard to maneuver to the appropriate icon, and then press the Enter key to activate it.

NOTE

A *workgroup* is the group of computers that your computer is in. They are generally the computers with which you most likely need to communicate or share resources. An example of a workgroup might be "Accounting."

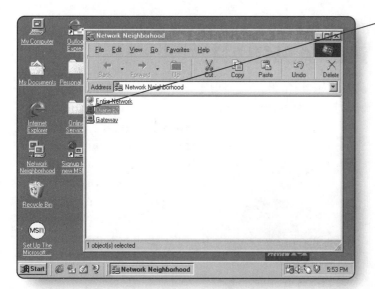

2. **Click** on the **computer** you want to access. A listing of all shared folders or disk drives as well as any shared printers on that computer will appear.

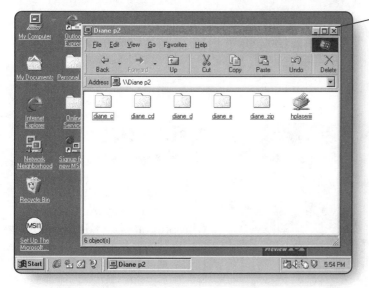

3. **Click** on the **Close button** ([**X**]). The window will close, and you will return to the Windows 98 desktop.

WORKING WITH THE TASKBAR

The Taskbar is the bar located across the bottom of your screen. It represents several different components. The Taskbar displays the button representing the main Start menu, buttons for each application you have open and running on your computer, and the System Tray to help you monitor your computer.

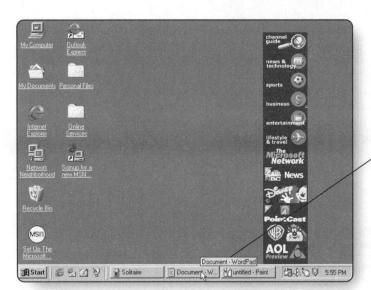

As you move your mouse pointer across any of the buttons on the Taskbar, a yellow tool tip appears indicating the name of each button.

Using the Start Button

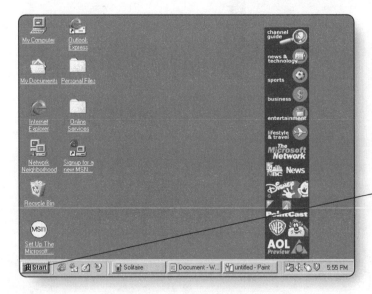

The Start button is the button you will generally use to access your programs and documents. It is located on the lower left side of your screen.

1. **Click** on the **Start button**. The Start menu will appear.

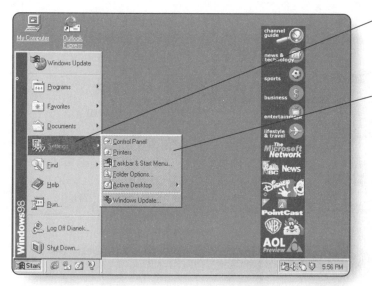

2. Click on the **desired option**. One of three things will happen next:

✦ If you selected Programs, Favorites, Documents, Settings, or Find, a submenu will appear allowing you to make another selection. Notice these items have a small right-facing arrow next to the options. The arrow indicates a cascading submenu will appear.

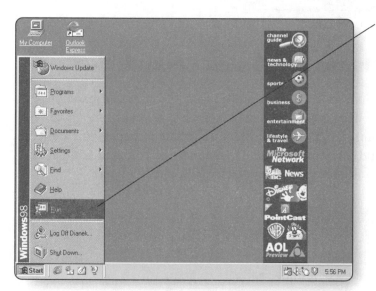

✦ If you selected Run, Log Off, or Shut Down, a dialog box will open asking you for more information. Dialog boxes are discussed in Chapter 4, "Using Windows Menus and Dialog Boxes." Notice these items have three dots displayed after the menu choice. The dots are called *ellipses* and indicate a dialog box will open.

♦ If you selected Help, the Help system will open. Help is discussed in Chapter 10, "Using Windows Help."

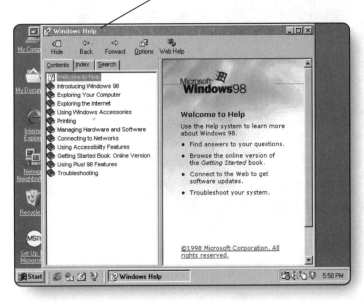

TIP

If you have one of the newer keyboards, you probably have a key on the keyboard between the Ctrl key and the Alt key that has the Windows logo (a flying window) on it. This is the Windows key. You can also open the Start menu by pressing this key.

Using the Quick Launch Bar

Windows 98 allows you to add any of four ready-made toolbars to the Taskbar. One of these toolbars is the Quick Launch bar, which provides a shortcut to display your desktop and shortcuts to several frequently-used programs, including Internet Explorer, Outlook Express, and Channels.

TIP

Position the mouse pointer on top of each button to see a description of that feature.

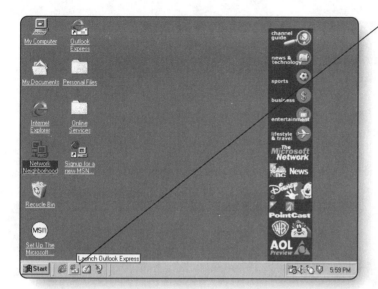

1. **Click** on any **button** on the Quick Launch bar. The selected program will open.

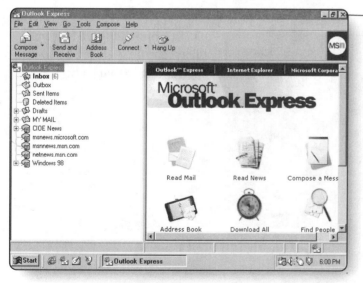

2. **Click** on the **Close button** ($\boxed{\times}$). The activated program will close.

Using the System Tray

The System Tray is located on the right side of the Taskbar. It displays a series of icons to help you see what is going on in your system. Items such as the current time, antivirus programs, and volume control can be modified from the System Tray.

The System Tray can also manage power options. This is particularly helpful if you are using a laptop computer.

NOTE

Similar to the Quick Launch bar, you can position the mouse pointer on top of each button in the System Tray to see a description of that feature.

1. Double-click on a **System Tray feature**. A dialog box pertaining to that feature will open.

2. Make any desired **changes** in the dialog box.

3. Click on the **Close button** ([X]). The dialog box will close.

LOOKING AT OTHER DESKTOP ITEMS

There are also a couple of other icons on the desktop. (Most of these will be covered in detail in later chapters.)

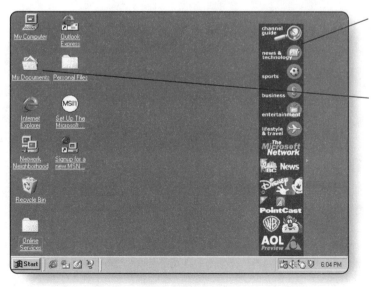

◆ **Channel bar**. The Channel bar lists many Web site channels to which you can subscribe.

◆ **My Documents folder**. The My Documents folder is a convenient place to store documents or files that you may need to access quickly and easily.

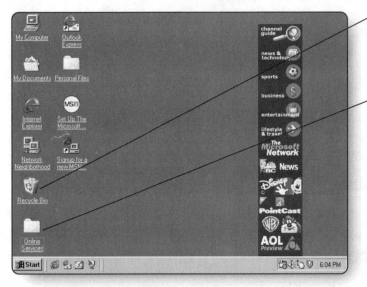

✦ **Recycle Bin**. This icon represents the place where your files go after they are deleted.

✦ **Online Services folder**. This folder provides shortcuts to several of the major Internet Servicce Providers.

3 Recognizing Parts of a Window

There are several common components to Windows 98 windows. Each component of a window has a purpose to assist you in one way or another. Some components change the view of the document on the screen; other components speed up a process, such as closing a window. In this chapter, you'll learn how to:

✦ Identify window components

✦ Use the scroll bars

✦ Resize and move a window

✦ Maximize and minimize a window

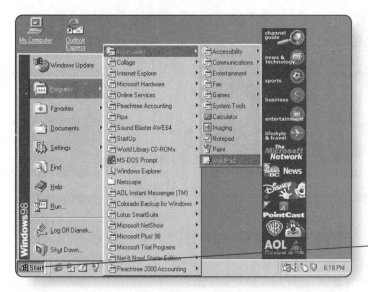

IDENTIFYING WINDOW COMPONENTS

Most of the features listed in this section will appear whether a window is from a program or a folder. An example of a typical window and its components is the WordPad window.

1. **Click** on the **Start button**. The Start menu will appear.

2. **Click** on **Programs**. The Programs submenu will appear.

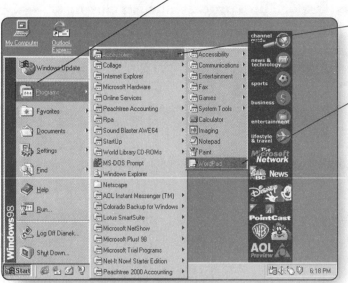

3. **Click** on **Accessories**. The Accessories submenu will appear.

4. **Click** on **WordPad**. The WordPad program will open.

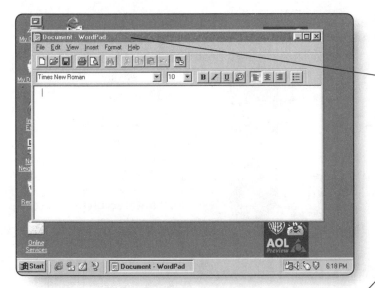

Items usually present in a window include the:

◆ **Title bar**. The title bar displays the name of the open window or program.

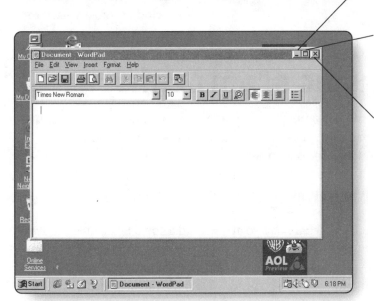

◆ **Minimize button**. The Minimize button ([_]) temporarily hides a window.

◆ **Maximize button**. The Maximize button ([□]) enlarges a window to its largest size.

◆ **Close button**. The Close button ([X]) closes the active window.

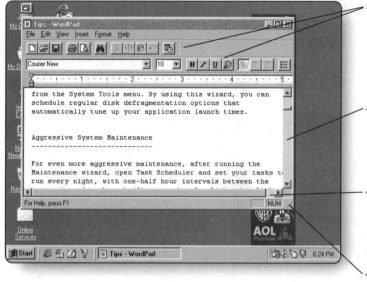

Toolbars. While not all windows have a toolbar, most program windows do. Toolbars are shortcuts to menu selections.

Vertical scroll bar. The vertical scroll bar allows you to view a window from top to bottom.

Horizontal scroll bar. The horizontal scroll bar allows you to view a window from left to right.

Window borders. Window borders frame the perimeter of a window and are used to resize a window.

USING SCROLL BARS

Scroll bars appear on a window when there is more to see than can be displayed in the window. Depending on the window, you may see one or two scroll bars. The horizontal scroll bar will appear at the bottom of the window and the vertical scroll bar will appear on the right side of the window.

Each scroll bar has two arrows and a small box called the *scroll box*. Picture the scroll box as an elevator. If the scroll box is at the top of the bar, this is like being on the top floor. The only direction you can go is down—so the down arrow is used to scroll down through the window. If you are in a word processing window, for example, clicking on the down arrow will display one or two lines at a time—sort of like stopping at each floor in the elevator.

NOTE

All of the options listed in this section apply to both the vertical and horizontal scroll bar.

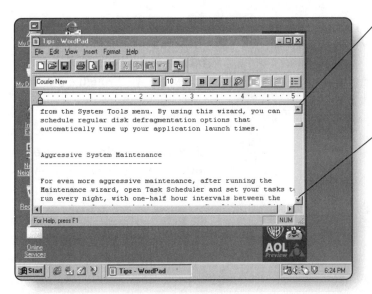

1. **Click** on the **up arrow** (▲) of the vertical scroll bar. The next row of text or objects located farther up in the window will appear.

2. **Click** on the **down arrow** (▼) of the vertical scroll bar. The next row of text or objects located farther down in the window will appear.

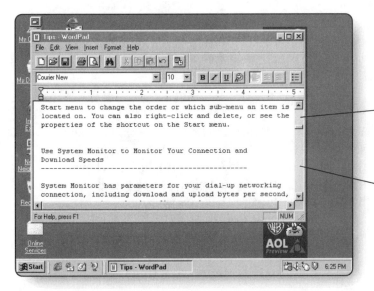

Another method is to move the screen up or down one "page" at a time—with a "page" being a window size at a time.

3. **Click** on the **scroll bar** just above the scroll box. The screen will move up one page at a time.

4. **Click** on the **scroll bar** just below the scroll box. The screen will move down one page at a time.

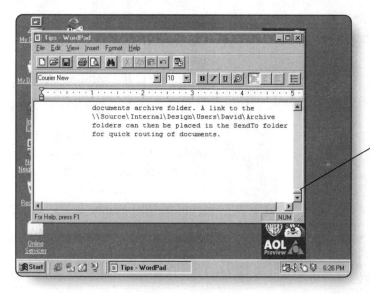

A third method of moving with the scroll bar is to drag the scroll box up or down the bar to quickly move through a window. (Sort of like an "express" elevator.)

5. **Press** and **hold** the **mouse button** and **drag** the **scroll box** to the bottom of the scroll bar.

6. **Release** the **mouse button**. The text or objects located at the bottom of the window will appear.

7. **Press** and **hold** the **mouse button** and **drag** the **scroll box** to the top of the scroll bar.

8. **Release** the **mouse button**. The text or objects located at the top of the window will appear.

TIP

You can also drag the scroll box to any point in the scroll bar. The scroll bar is relative to the length of the document or window. For example, if you have a 10-page report and you drag the scroll box about halfway down the scroll bar, you will stop at approximately page five.

MANUALLY RESIZING WINDOWS

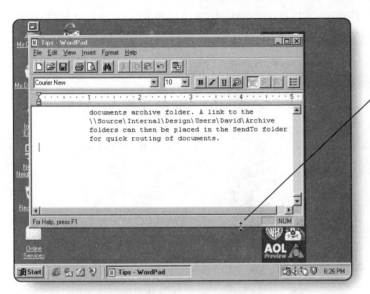

If a window is too small or too large, you can resize it by using your mouse.

1. **Position** the **mouse pointer** on an outside edge of a window. The mouse pointer will become a double-headed arrow.

2. **Press** and **hold** the **mouse button** while moving the mouse. The window will be resized in the direction you move the mouse.

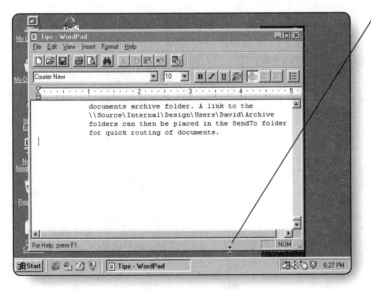

3. **Release** the **mouse button** when the window is the desired size.

MAXIMIZING A WINDOW

Although you can manually resize a window, a favorite choice for many users is to *maximize* the window. To maximize is to make it as large as possible—as large as your screen will allow. The Maximize button is the middle of the three buttons located in the upper right corner of the window.

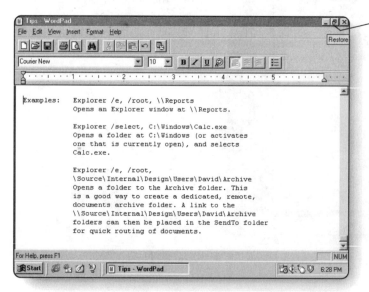

1. **Click** on the **Maximize button** (□). The window will be enlarged.

Notice that the appearance of the Maximize button has changed. When a window is already maximized, the button is called the *Restore* button.

2. **Click** on the **Restore button** (⧉). The window will return to its previous size.

TIP

You can also double-click on the title bar of a window to maximize it. Double-click on the title bar again to restore it.

MINIMIZING A WINDOW

Occasionally a window may be on top of something else you need to see on your desktop. You can move a window as covered in the next section, or you can *minimize* it. Minimizing a window does not close it, but simply sets it aside for later use. The Minimize button is the first of the three buttons located in the upper right corner of the window.

1. **Click** on the **Minimize button** (⊟). The window will temporarily disappear from your screen.

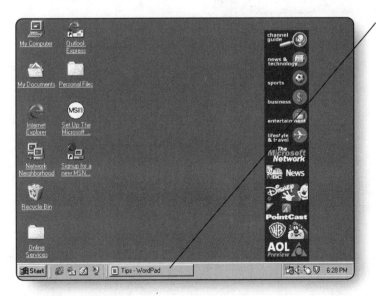

2. **Click** on the **program button** on the Taskbar to restore it to its previous size.

MOVING A WINDOW

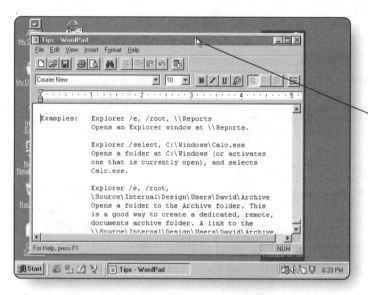

Besides resizing a window, you can also move a window to a different location on the desktop.

1. **Position** the **mouse pointer** on the title bar of the window to be moved.

2. **Press** and **hold** the **mouse button** on the title bar while moving the mouse.

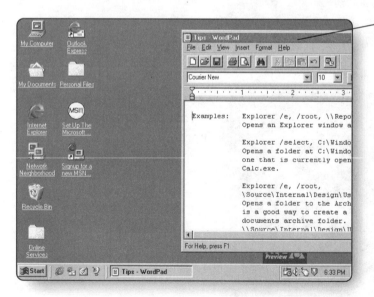

3. **Release** the **mouse button**. The window will move to the new location.

4. **Click** on the **Close button** ([**X**]). WordPad will close.

4

Using Windows Menus and Dialog Boxes

When you go into a restaurant, you make selections from a menu. So it is with a Windows program. Windows programs use the concept of a *menu* to make choices. In this chapter, you'll learn how to:

✦ Make menu choices with your mouse and keyboard

✦ Work in a Windows dialog box

✦ Learn common Windows 98 menu commands

MAKING MENU CHOICES WITH THE MOUSE

When you open an application, the main menu options appear at the top of the window. Selecting a choice from the main menu with your left mouse button leads you to another menu selection. Occasionally that second menu leads to a third menu. This is called a *submenu* or a *cascading menu*.

Most Windows applications have several menu selections in common. The first one is usually File, the second is Edit, the third is View, and the last one is usually Help. The menu selections in between View and Help vary from application to application. An example of a typical application and its components is the Windows Paint program.

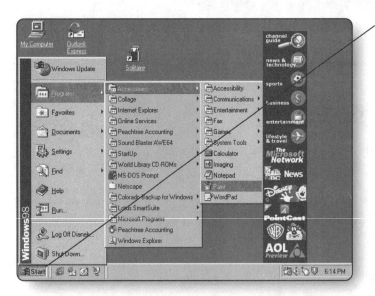

1. **Click** on the **Start button**. The Start menu will appear.

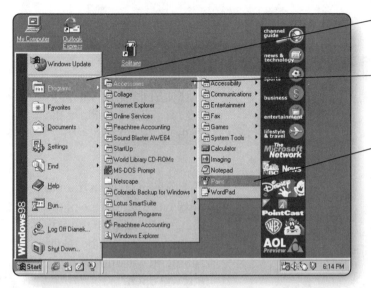

2. **Click** on **Programs**. The Programs submenu will appear.

3. **Click** on **Accessories**. The Accessories submenu will appear.

4. **Click** on **Paint**. The Paint program will open.

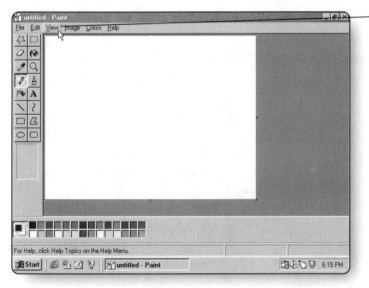

5. **Position** the **mouse pointer** over the desired menu. The menu will become three-dimensional in shape.

6. Click on the **mouse button**. The menu will appear.

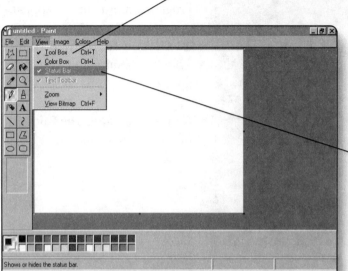

7. Click on an **item** from the displayed menu. One of three things will happen: the action you requested will be taken, a submenu will appear, or a dialog box will open.

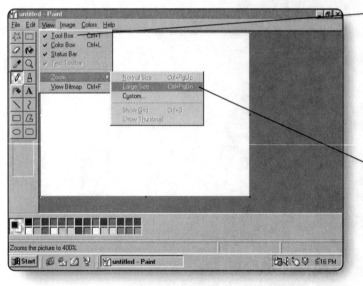

If you choose an item with a check mark beside it, the feature will be turned off. Check-marked items are like toggle switches—a ✔ means the item is active while no check mark means the item is not active.

If you choose a menu item with a submenu, you will need to select another choice from that menu.

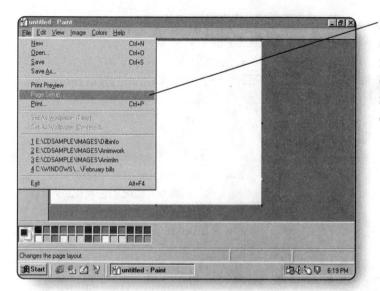

If you choose a menu item with an ellipses (. . .) following the menu selection, a dialog box will open, prompting you for further information. Dialog boxes are discussed later in this chapter.

Using Shortcut Menus

Many programs now offer a menu when you click on the right mouse button. This is called a *shortcut menu*. A shortcut menu is a variable collection of frequently-used choices that are relative to your mouse pointer position. For example, if you are using Microsoft Word and your mouse pointer is positioned over a word and you click with the right mouse button, the shortcut menu shows items that are pertinent to working with text, such as fonts or paragraph choices. However, if your mouse pointer is positioned on the toolbar and you click with the right mouse button, your choices are pertinent to working with different toolbars.

1. **Position** the **mouse pointer** at the desired location in a document.

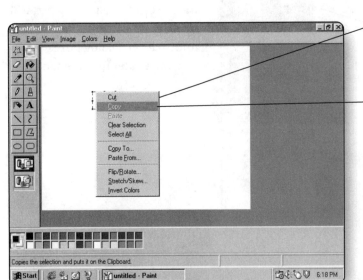

2. **Click** on the **right mouse button**. A shortcut menu will appear.

3. **Make** a **selection** from the shortcut menu with the left mouse button. The requested action will be taken or a dialog box will open.

4. **Click** on the **Minimize button** (☐). The Paint window will be minimized.

MAKING MENU CHOICES WITH THE KEYBOARD

Many programs offer shortcut keys, such as pressing Ctrl+B to bold a selection or pressing the F1 key for help. The disadvantage of these types of shortcuts is that you must rely on your memory for them. I don't know about you, but the older I get, the shorter my memory gets. However, sometimes it's very cumbersome to take your hands from the keyboard to the mouse, from the mouse to the keyboard, and back and forth.

Fortunately, you do not have to use the mouse to make a selection from a menu. You can use the keyboard to access all menu selections. Notice that each menu selection has an underlined letter. Using the Alt key and the underlined letter gives you control of the menu from your keyboard. Again, the magic key to remember is the Alt key.

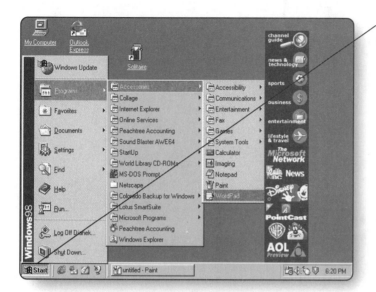

1. Click on the **Start button**. The Start menu will appear.

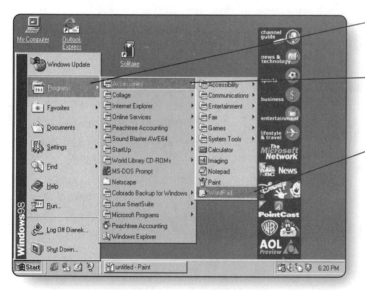

2. Click on **Programs**. The Programs submenu will appear.

3. Click on **Accessories**. The Accessories submenu will appear.

4. Click on **WordPad**. The WordPad program will open.

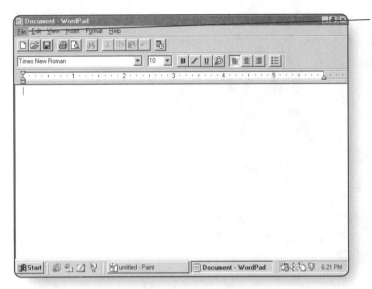

5. Press and **release** the **Alt key**. The first menu will be selected with a three-dimensional box around it.

6. Type the **mnemonic underline letter** for the menu you want to select. The menu will appear and the first item will be selected.

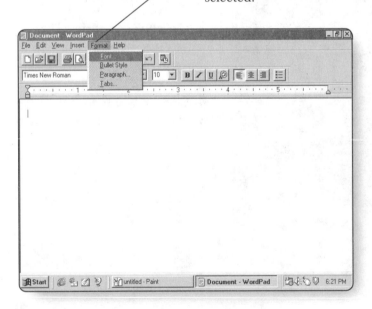

7. Type the **underlined letter** for the item you want to select from the menu. (You do not need to press the Alt key again because you are already in the menu.) One of three things could happen: the action you requested will be taken, a dialog box will open, or a submenu will appear.

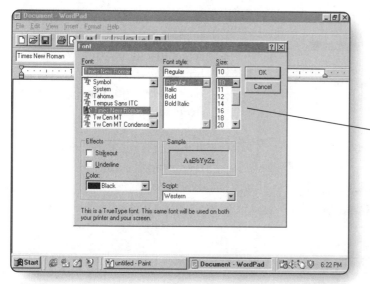

8a. Repeat step **6** for your next menu selection if a submenu appears.

OR

8b. Make any necessary selections if a dialog box appears.

WORKING IN A DIALOG BOX

Menu selections that have three dots after it, called ellipses (. . .), indicate that a dialog box will open if you choose that menu item. A *dialog box* prompts you for additional information. Many menu selections open a dialog box. Although each dialog box is different than the next one, there are common types of selections that can be made from a dialog box.

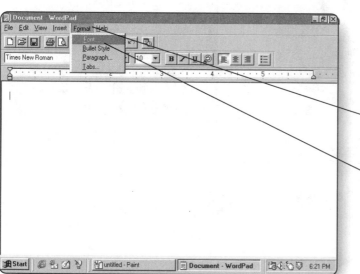

1. Click on **Format**. The Format menu will appear.

2. Click on **Font**. The Font dialog box will open.

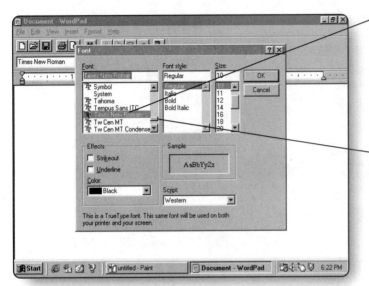

3. Click on the **desired choice** in a scroll box. The item you selected will be displayed in the box at the top of the list. *Scroll boxes* allow you to select an item from a displayed list.

If the list is too large to be displayed, a scroll bar will be available.

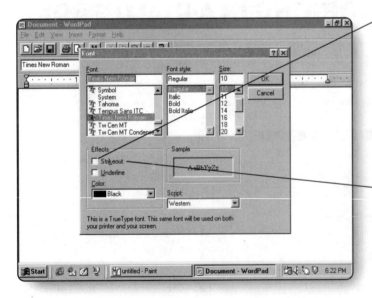

4. Click on the **check boxes** next to your desired choices. *Check boxes* allow you to choose multiple selections. When you select a check box, a ✔ will appear in the box.

TIP

You can also make a choice in a check box by clicking on the words next to the box.

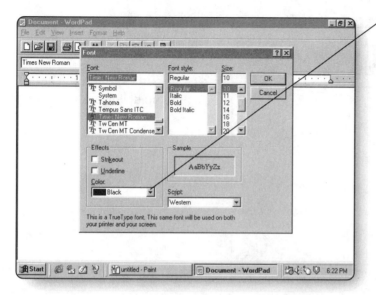

5. **Click** on the **down arrow (▼)** next to a list box. A list of possible selections will appear. These *list boxes* allow you to select an item from a list that appears. List boxes have a small down arrow (▼) to the right of the current selection.

6. **Click** on the **desired choice**. The list of possible selections will close and the selected choice will appear in the list box.

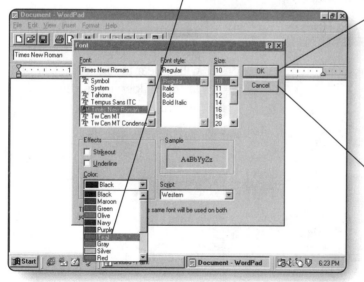

7a. **Click** on the **OK button**. The dialog box will close and your selections will be accepted. The *OK button* allows you to accept your selections from a dialog box.

OR

7b. **Click** on the **Cancel button**. The dialog box will close and your selections will be ignored. The Cancel button allows you to reject your selections from a dialog box.

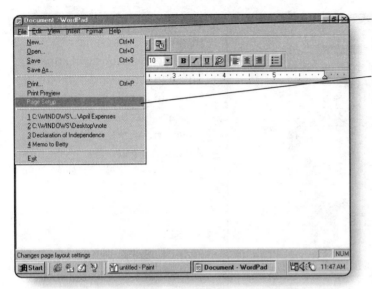

8. **Click** on **File**. The File menu will appear.

9. **Click** on **Page Setup**. The Page Setup dialog box will open.

10. **Type** the **desired information** in a text box. *Text boxes* allow you to type specified information in a box.

11. **Click** on the **circle** next to your desired choice. A small dot will appear in the circle. *Option buttons* allow you to choose one of several selections.

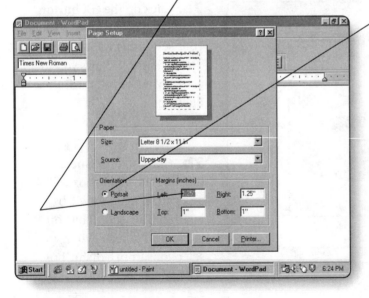

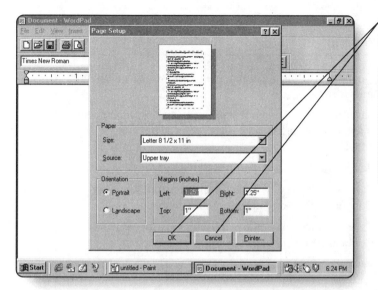

12. **Click** on **OK** or **Cancel**. The dialog box will close.

TIP

You can also choose an option button by clicking on the words next to the circle.

NOTE

If you want to use your keyboard to select from a dialog box, use the Tab key to move from section to section of the dialog box. You can then use your down arrow key to select from a scroll box, list box, or option buttons; or you can use the space bar to select/deselect choices with check boxes. Press the Enter key at an OK button to accept the choices or press the Esc key to cancel your selections.

LEARNING COMMON WINDOWS COMMANDS

There are certain conditions software developers conform to in order to designate their products as Windows products. Part of these conditions are common commands that Windows programs can use, whether you're using your word processing program, spreadsheet, or Internet browser program. The following table illustrates some of the common commands, along with their descriptions and common shortcut keys. Many, but not all, software programs use the same shortcut keys.

Feature	Shortcut	Description
Open	Ctrl+O	Opens an existing document or file. You will be prompted for a filename.
Save	Ctrl+S	Saves the current document or file. If it is the first time the document or file has been saved, you will be prompted for a filename.
Select All	Ctrl+A	Selects the entire text of a document or all files in a folder.
Cut	Ctrl+X	Takes selected text or file and copies it to the Windows Clipboard. The original text or file is removed.
Copy	Ctrl+C	Takes selected text or file and copies it to the Windows Clipboard. The original text or file remains in place.
Paste	Ctrl+V	Places the text or file from the Clipboard to the current location in the document or folder.
Undo	Ctrl+Z	Reverses the last action you took in the current program.
Print	Ctrl+P	Prints the current document.
Close	Ctrl+W	Closes the current document, but leaves the program open.
Exit	Alt+F4	Closes the current document and closes the program.
Help	F1	Starts the Help program. The type of help may vary according to the specific software you are using.

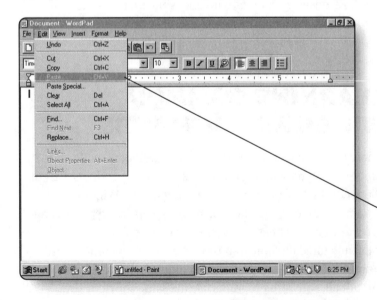

TIP

When a shortcut key begins with Ctrl or Alt, you need to press and hold the Ctrl or Alt key down, and then tap the second required key.

NOTE

Many menus list keyboard shortcuts on the right of a menu selection.

5 Multitasking and Shutting Down Windows

Windows 98 has the capability to manage several jobs at one time. This means you can jump to a different program without having to exit the first one, and then return to it later. Sometimes, however, programs or even Windows itself can "lock up" and won't allow you to proceed. In this chapter, you'll learn how to:

✦ Open and close a Windows program

✦ Switch between open programs

✦ Handle a "locked up" program

✦ Shut down Windows the right way and when your computer locks up

OPENING A WINDOWS PROGRAM

You can have as many programs open as you have memory for in your computer. In this section, where I refer to opening a second program, bear in mind that the same information applies whether it is the first, third, fourth, or thirteenth program you want to open. There are several ways to open additional programs while another one is currently open. It just depends on the location of the shortcut to the second program.

Opening with the Start Menu

Most programs can be accessed from the Start button. Your selections may vary from the following picture.

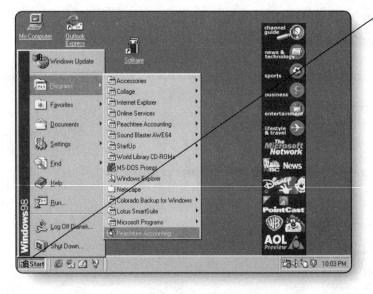

1. **Click** on the **Start button**. The Start menu will appear.

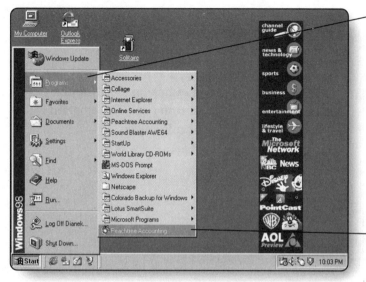

2. **Click** on **Programs**. The Programs submenu will appear.

> **NOTE**
> Your program may be buried in one or more additional levels. Continue clicking on the cascading submenus until you reach the item for which you are looking.

3. **Click** on the **program** you want to use. The program will open.

Opening from the Desktop

Suppose you have a shortcut to one of your favorite programs on the Windows 98 desktop. If you had several other programs open and needed to access that shortcut, you would normally need to minimize each of the other programs to get to the desktop. Windows 98 includes a Show Desktop button on the Quick Launch bar to allow you easy access to your desktop. This eliminates the need to do all that minimizing.

1. **Click** on the **Show Desktop button** on the Quick Launch bar. All current programs will be hidden and your desktop will be displayed.

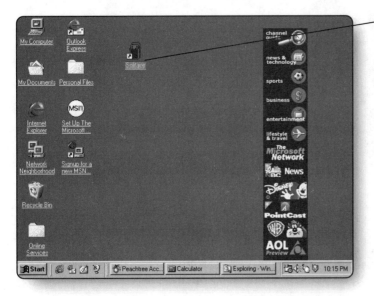

2. **Click** on the **shortcut** for the program you want to use. The program will open.

3. **Click** on the **Minimize button** (⎯). The program will be minimized.

SWITCHING BETWEEN PROGRAMS

A button appears on the Taskbar for each and every program you have open. When you have multiple programs open, it is very easy to switch back and forth between them.

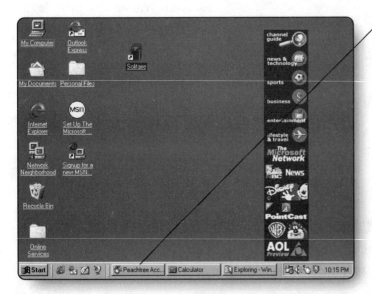

1. **Click** on the **button** on the Taskbar for the program you want to make active. The window for that program will return to the front of the screen.

TIP

You can also press Alt+Tab to switch between open programs.

CLOSING A WINDOWS PROGRAM

When you are finished using a Windows program, you should close the program. Keeping it open uses computer resources that you may need for another application.

1. Click on **File**. The File menu will appear.

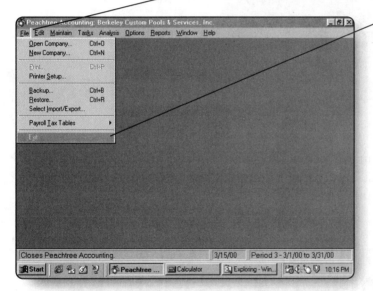

2. Click on **Exit**. The program will close.

OR

1. Click on the **Close Button** (⊠) of the application window. The program will close.

If you are using an application that has data that may need to be saved, you will be prompted to save that information.

HANDLING A LOCKED UP APPLICATION

As much as you try to avoid it, sometimes application programs simply crash and quit responding. The reasons are varied and far too numerous to mention. The real question is, "How do I get out of it?" If a program locks up and quits responding, you can try to "unfreeze" Windows.

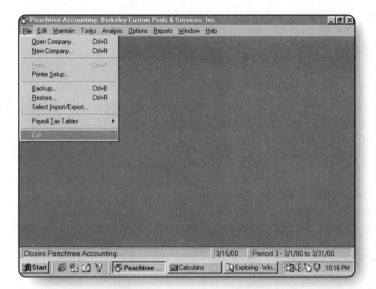

1. **Press** and **hold** the **Ctrl key**, while **pressing** the **Alt** and **Delete key**. (All at the same time.) The Close Program dialog box will open.

2. **Click** on the **program name** giving you problems. It will be selected.

3. **Click** on the **End Task button**. The selected program will shut down.

TIP

A quick way to restart your computer is to press Ctrl+Alt+Del twice.

You can try restarting the application again. Occasionally, you will have to restart your computer to get the application to launch again.

SHUTTING DOWN WINDOWS THE RIGHT WAY

There is a series of steps that Windows takes when it is time to shut down the computer. One thing you should not do (if at all possible) is just turn off the power. This can cause errors on the hard drive of the computer. It's best to let Windows "do its thing" and shut down using normal procedures.

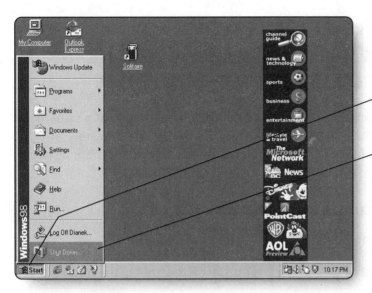

1. Close any **open programs**, saving any documents if necessary.

2. Click on the **Start button**. The Start menu will appear.

3. Click on **Shut Down**. The Shut Down Windows dialog box will open.

4. Click on the **Shut down option button**. The option will be selected.

5. Click on **OK**. The computer will begin its shut down procedure. You may see a message advising you "It is now safe to shut off your computer."

6. Turn off the **power** to your computer and monitor.

TIP

Some computers have their own power off device. After running its shut down procedure, the power of the machine automatically turns off.

SHUTTING DOWN WINDOWS WHEN YOUR COMPUTER LOCKS UP

When the computer gremlin gets into your machine and the Windows 98 program crashes, you can try closing the individual programs. If that doesn't help, there's nothing else you can do but restart your machine.

1a. **Turn off** the **power** to the computer.

OR

1b. **Press** the **restart button** on the front of the computer.

2. Count slowly to **10**. This will give the fans and components time to stop.

3. Turn on the **computer**. The rebooting process will begin again. You will be prompted to run ScanDisk, a Windows utility used to repair errors on a hard drive.

4. Click on **Yes** to run ScanDisk. After the utility has completed its job, Windows 98 will continue to load.

PART I REVIEW QUESTIONS

1. **What character is displayed when you type a password?** *See "Starting Windows 98" in Chapter 1*

2. **What is another word for the little pictures that appear on your desktop?** *See the introduction in Chapter 2*

3. **What does it mean when a disk drive icon has a hand underneath it?** *See "Opening the My Computer Icon" in Chapter 2*

4. **What is the bar called that is displayed at the bottom of your screen?** *See "Working with the Taskbar" in Chapter 2*

5. **What does the Minimize button do?** *See "Identifying Window Components" in Chapter 3*

6. **What is usually the first menu choice in a Windows application?** *See "Making Menu Choices with the Mouse" in Chapter 4*

7. **How do you access a shortcut menu?** *See "Using Shortcut Menus" in Chapter 4*

8. **How many choices can be selected from a dialog box with option buttons?** *See "Working in a Dialog Box" in Chapter 4*

9. **What does pressing Ctrl+S usually do in a Windows application?** *See "Learning Common Windows Commands" in Chapter 4*

10. **What steps should you take before you turn off your computer?** *See "Shutting Down Windows the Right Way" in Chapter 5*

PART II
Working with the Accessories

Outlook
Express

Network
Neighborhood

6 Using the Calculator

Have you ever needed to quickly add something up but couldn't locate your pocket calculator? It does have a way of getting buried beneath papers. Windows 98 allows you to have a calculator available at your fingertips. In this chapter, you'll learn how to:

✦ Start and use the Calculator

✦ Identify Calculator buttons

✦ Copy values from the Calculator to another program

✦ Change the style of the Calculator program

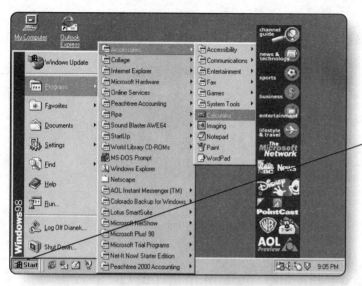

STARTING THE CALCULATOR

The Calculator program is located in the Accessories folder.

1. **Click** on the **Start button**. The Start menu will appear.

2. **Click** on **Programs**. The Programs submenu will appear.

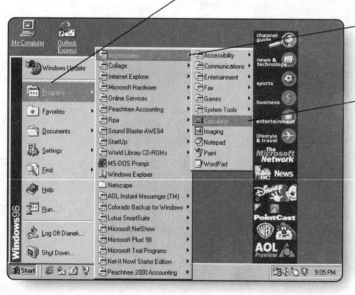

3. **Click** on **Accessories**. The Accessories submenu will appear.

4. **Click** on **Calculator**. The Calculator will appear.

IDENTIFYING CALCULATOR BUTTONS

The Calculator program by default is a standard 10-key calculator used to perform basic mathematical functions. Besides the normal 0–9 numeric buttons, there are several other important buttons to know:

✦ + Addition

✦ - Subtraction

✦ / Division

✦ * Multiplication

✦ % Displays the result of multiplication as a percentage

✦ . Adds decimal point

✦ = Total

USING THE CALCULATOR

You can use the keyboard or the mouse to enter values into the Calculator. If you are already proficient with a 10-key calculator, you may prefer to use the numeric keypad on the right side of your keyboard. When entering values, be sure to use the decimal point if the value you are entering is not a whole number. For example, to enter the price of a new shirt, type 29.95, not 2995.

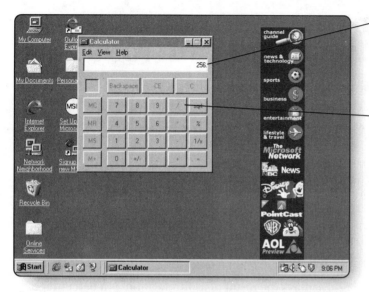

1. **Type** or **click** on the **first value** in the calculation. The number will appear in the display box of the Calculator.

2. **Type** or **click** on the **operator** needed. When typing, use + (plus) for addition, - (hyphen) for subtraction, * (asterisk) for multiplication, and / (backslash) for division.

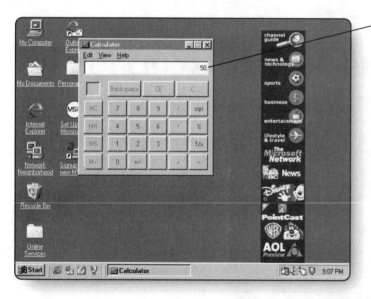

3. **Type** or **click** on the **second value** in the calculation. The number will appear in the display box of the Calculator.

4. **Type** or **click** on another **operator** and **value**, if needed.

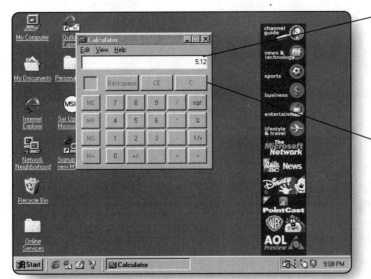

5. Press the **Enter key** or **click** on the = **button**. The result will appear in the display box of the Calculator.

Copying Values from the Calculator

Windows 98 includes a feature called the *Clipboard*. The Clipboard is a special holding area to assist you with transferring information from one document to another or from one program to another. This can be accomplished by using two features of Windows called *copy* and *paste*.

The Windows copy-and-paste function works with the Calculator. After you get the results of the calculation, you can copy it and then paste it into another document.

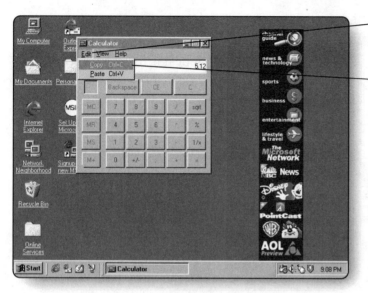

1. Click on **Edit**. The Edit menu will appear.

2. Click on **Copy**. The information will be copied to the Clipboard.

3. Start or **switch** to your **word processing** or other **program**. The Calculator may be temporarily hidden from view.

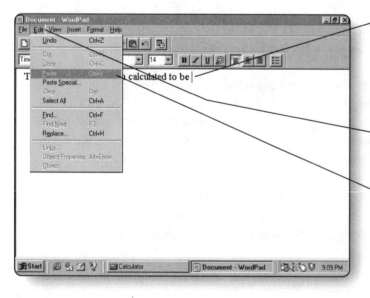

4. Click on the **mouse button** at the location you want the data to appear. A blinking insertion point will appear at the location you clicked.

5. Click on **Edit**. The Edit menu will appear.

6. Click on **Paste**. The Edit menu will close.

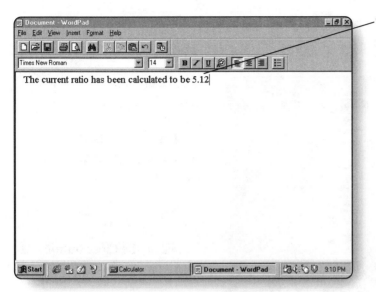

The value from the Clipboard is inserted into your document.

CHANGING THE STYLE OF THE CALCULATOR

Besides the standard 10-key Calculator, Windows 98 also gives you the option to use a scientific Calculator. This Calculator will calculate most trigonometric and statistical functions. The basics of this Calculator operate the same as the standard Calculator.

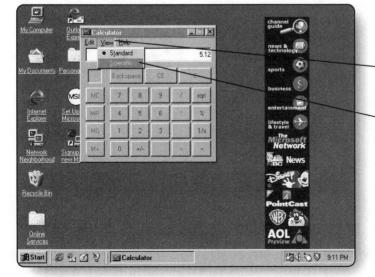

1. Click on **View**. The View menu will appear.

2. Click on **Scientific**. The Calculator will change to the scientific style.

NOTE

The selection on the View menu with a bullet beside it is the current view.

Returning to the Standard Calculator

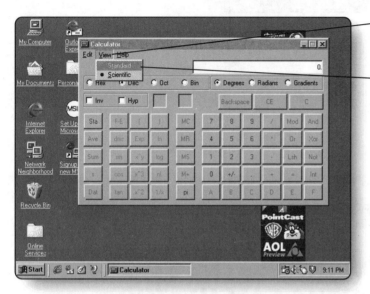

1. **Click** on **View**. The View menu will appear.

2. **Click** on **Standard**. The Calculator will change to the standard style.

TIP

Click on the Close button ([X]) to close the Calculator.

7 Using WordPad

One of the basic uses of a computer is word processing. Windows 98 includes a small word processing program called *WordPad*. It's a simple program that includes most of the basic features of many popular word processing programs. In this chapter, you'll learn how to:

✦ **Start WordPad**

✦ **Enter and edit text**

✦ **Insert the current date**

✦ **Change the appearance of text**

✦ **Add bullet points to a list**

✦ **Save and print a document**

✦ **Open other WordPad documents**

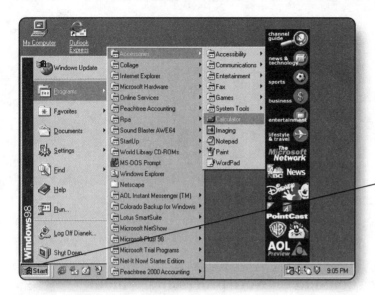

STARTING WORDPAD

WordPad is similar to Microsoft Word. The WordPad program is included with the Windows 98 program as an accessory.

1. **Click** on the **Start button**. The Start menu will appear.

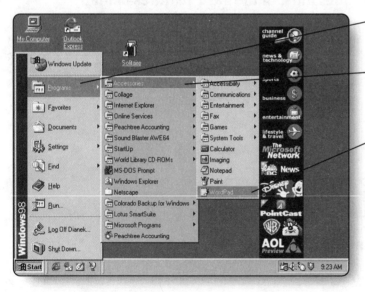

2. **Click** on **Programs**. The Programs submenu will appear.

3. **Click** on **Accessories**. The Accessories submenu will appear.

4. **Click** on **WordPad**. The WordPad program will open. A blank document will appear, ready to use.

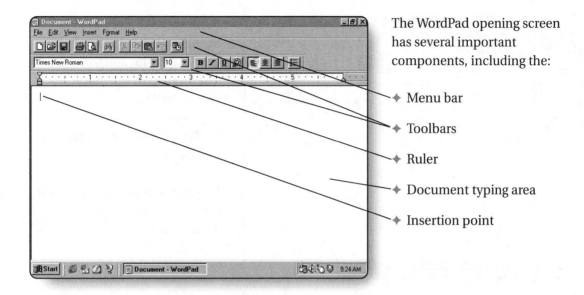

The WordPad opening screen has several important components, including the:

✦ Menu bar

✦ Toolbars

✦ Ruler

✦ Document typing area

✦ Insertion point

ENTERING TEXT

When typing a document, WordPad monitors the lines within a paragraph. If the word you are typing will not fit entirely on the current line, WordPad will go to the next line. This feature is called *word wrap*. Press the Enter key only when you get to the end of a paragraph. You can press the Enter key twice if you want an extra blank line between paragraphs. A short line of text—a date or greeting, such as "Dear Mr. Jones"—counts as a paragraph all by itself.

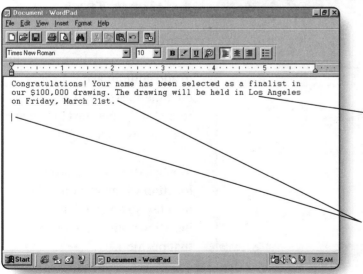

1. Type the desired **text**. The text will appear at the location of the insertion point. Do not press the Enter key until you have completed the entire paragraph.

2. Press the **Enter key**. The insertion point will move down one line.

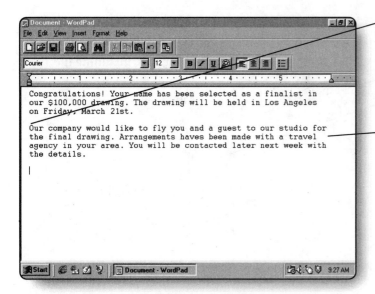

3. **Press** the **Enter key again.** A blank line will appear between the paragraphs, and the insertion point will move down one line.

4. **Type** the **next paragraph** of the document.

5. **Repeat steps 2** through **4** for each paragraph of the document.

EDITING TEXT

We all make mistakes. Errors are easy to correct with WordPad, whether you need to add something you forgot or delete something you didn't mean to type.

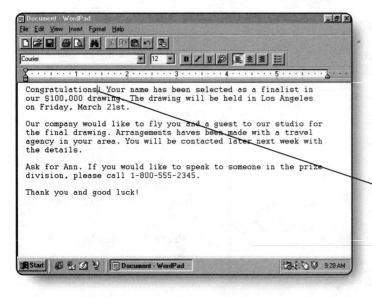

Adding Text

WordPad begins in *insert mode.* This means that when you want to add additional text to your document, WordPad will make room for the new text by moving existing text to the right.

1. **Click** directly in **front of the location** where you want the next text to appear. The insertion point will move to that position.

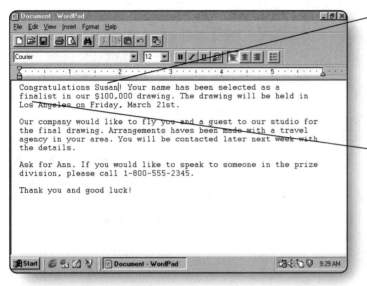

2. Type any new **word** or **phrase**, adding a space before or after as necessary. The additional words will be inserted at the position of the insertion point.

Notice how the words that were previously at the end of the line on which you began typing no longer fit on the first line and have dropped down to the second line.

Deleting Text

Text can be deleted one character, one word, or even one paragraph at a time. You can use one of two keys to delete a single character: the Backspace key or the Delete key. The Backspace key will delete a character to the left of the insertion point, while the Delete key will delete a character to the right of the insertion point.

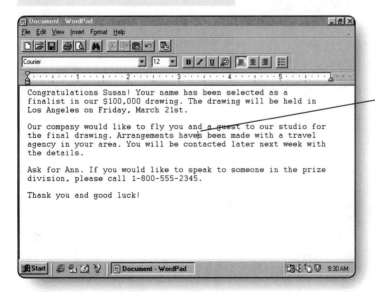

1. Click directly in **front of the character** you want to delete. The insertion point will move to that position.

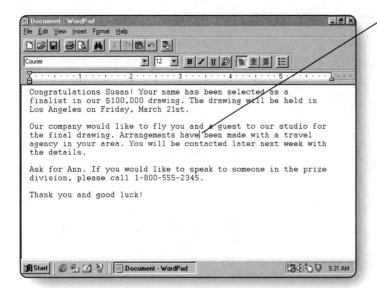

2. Press the **Delete key**. The empty space will be filled by the existing text from the right.

INSERTING THE CURRENT DATE AND TIME

Instead of searching around for a calendar, let WordPad put today's date in your document for you.

1. Position the **insertion point** at the location where you want the date or time to appear.

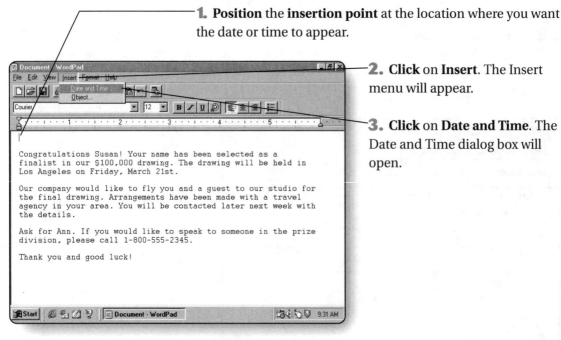

2. Click on **Insert**. The Insert menu will appear.

3. Click on **Date and Time**. The Date and Time dialog box will open.

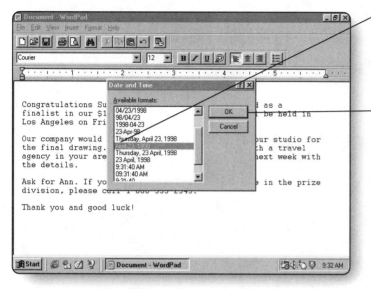

4. Click on the **date** or **time format** you would like to use in your letter. The format will be selected.

5. Click on **OK**. The Date and Time dialog box will close, and the date will be inserted into your document.

SELECTING TEXT

To change formatting, alignment, or to delete an area of text, the text needs to be selected prior to modification. WordPad allows you to select a word, a paragraph, the entire document, or any portion of a document.

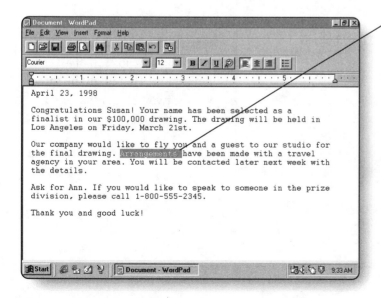

1. Double-click on a **word**. The word will be selected.

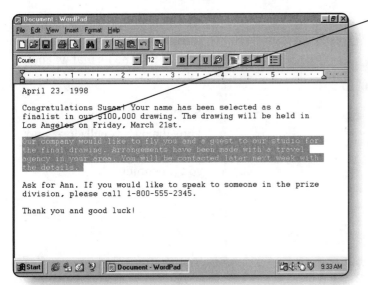

2. **Triple-click** on a **paragraph.** The entire paragraph will be selected.

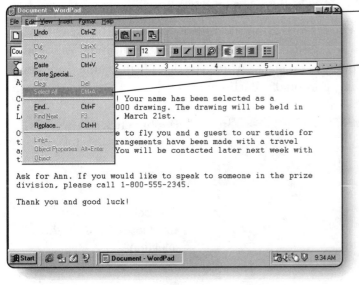

3. **Click** on **Edit**. The Edit menu will appear.

4. **Click** on **Select All**. The entire document will be selected.

You also have the option of selecting any portion of a document. That might be three words, two paragraphs, or six pages of a document.

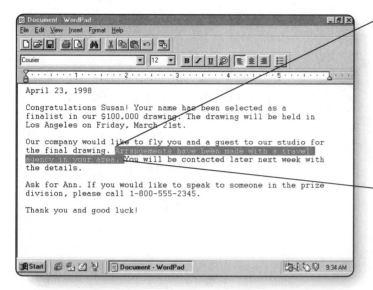

5. **Position** the **mouse pointer** at the beginning of the text to be selected.

6. **Press** and **hold** the **mouse button** and **drag** the **mouse pointer** to the end of the selection.

7. **Release** the **mouse button** when the desired text has been selected.

CUTTING AND PASTING TEXT

If you have mistakenly placed text in the wrong place, don't delete it and retype it, use the Windows Clipboard feature to move it.

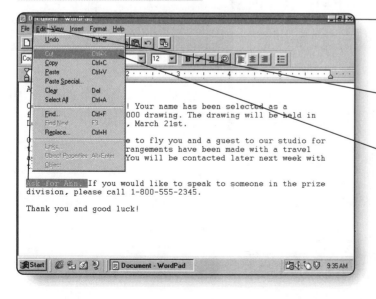

1. **Select** the **text** to be moved to a new location. The text will be selected.

2. **Click** on **Edit**. The Edit menu will appear.

3. **Click** on **Cut**. The selected text will be removed from the document.

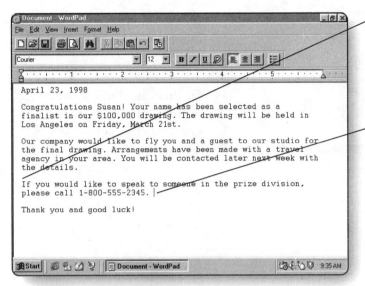

The selected text looks like it disappeared, but it didn't! It was placed on the Windows Clipboard and is waiting for you to tell it where to be placed.

4. **Position** the **insertion point** where you want the text to be placed. The insertion point will move to that location.

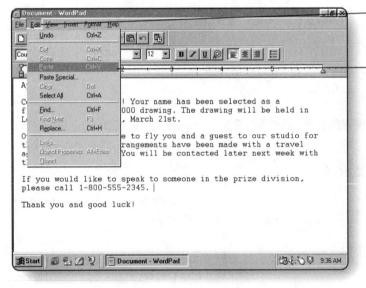

5. **Click** on **Edit**. The Edit menu will appear.

6. **Click** on **Paste**. The text will appear in the new location.

FORMATTING TEXT

Formatting is changing the appearance of text, such as the font, the color, or such attributes as bolding or underlining. Formatting can also include changing the alignment of text.

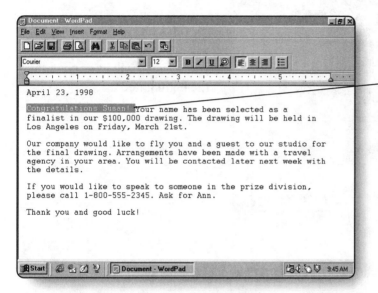

Changing the Font

1. Select the **text** to be formatted.

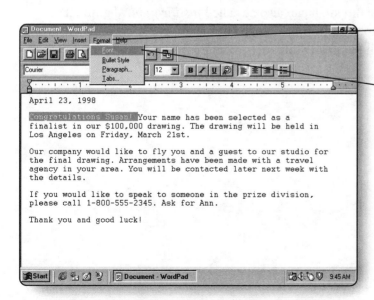

2. Click on **Format**. The Format menu will appear.

3. Click on **Font**. The Font dialog box will open.

From this dialog box you can select the font and the style, size, color, and special effects to be used with your font choice.

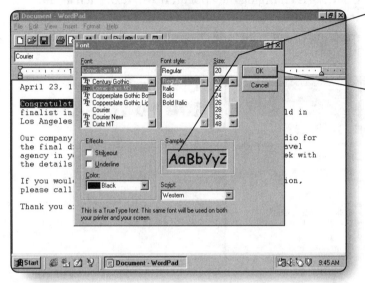

4. **Make** any desired **choices**. The Sample box will display your choices.

5. **Click** on **OK**. The dialog box will close, and the font choices you selected will be applied to the highlighted text.

Modifying the Alignment

Alignment is the arrangement of text to the margins of a document. It can also be called *justification.* Alignment choices are applied to an entire paragraph and are made from the WordPad toolbar.

There are three alignment choices available:

✦ Left-aligned text is even with the left margin and uneven on the right margin.

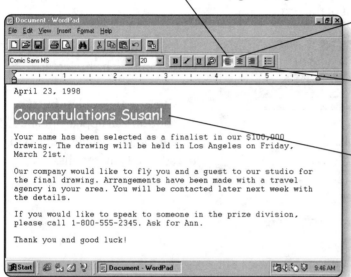

✦ Center-aligned text is centered between the left and right margins.

✦ Right-aligned text is even with the right margin and uneven on the left margin.

1. **Click in** or **select** the **paragraph** to be modified.

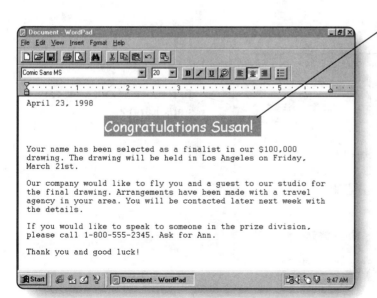

2. **Click** on the desired **alignment button**. The selected button will appear "pushed in" to show the current selection, and the current paragraph will be modified.

ADDING BULLETS

Bullets call attention to specific points in a document. Bulleted items are indented with a small black circle in the front of the text.

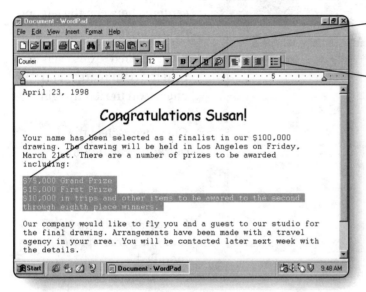

1. **Click on** or **select** the **paragraphs** to be bulleted.

2. **Click** on the **Bullets button**. The button will appear "pushed in" and bullets will be applied to the selected paragraphs.

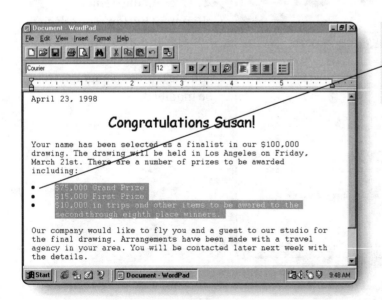

SAVING A WORDPAD DOCUMENT

When you work on a document, the changes you make are stored only in the computer memory. That memory gets erased when you turn the computer off, if the power fails, or if the computer locks up. To avoid losing a document, you should save it to a file.

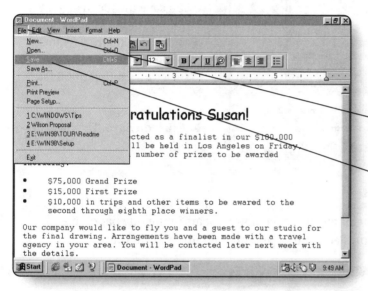

1. **Click** on **File**. The File menu will appear.

2. **Click** on **Save**. The Save As dialog box will open.

3. **Type** a **descriptive name** for the file in the File name: text box.

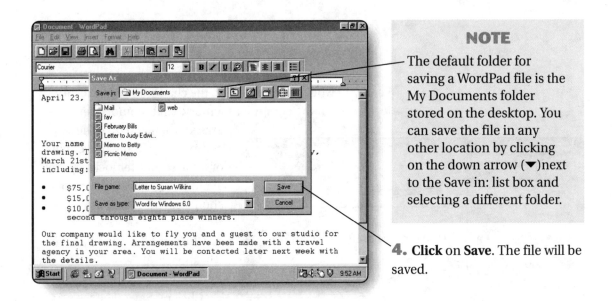

The default folder for saving a WordPad file is the My Documents folder stored on the desktop. You can save the file in any other location by clicking on the down arrow (▼)next to the Save in: list box and selecting a different folder.

4. Click on **Save**. The file will be saved.

The name of the file now appears in the title bar of the WordPad window and on the Windows Taskbar.

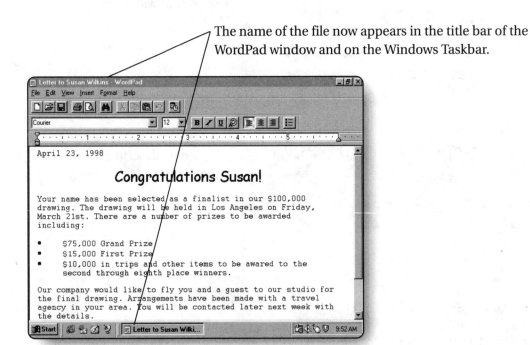

PRINTING A WORDPAD DOCUMENT

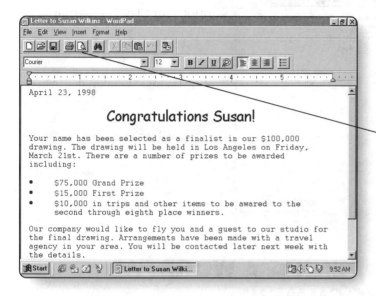

Printing is an expensive process that uses our natural resources. You can use WordPad's Print Preview feature to review the document prior to printing it.

1. Click on the **Print Preview button**. The screen will change to a non-editable bird's eye view of your document.

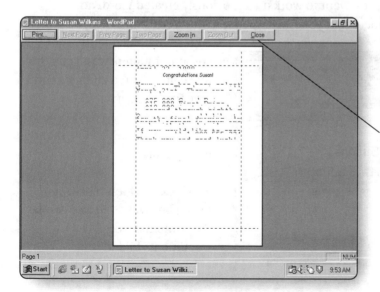

Don't worry if you can't read it very well. You're not supposed to! At this point you are checking out the overall appearance of the document, not the content.

2. Click on the **Close button**. You will return to the document typing area.

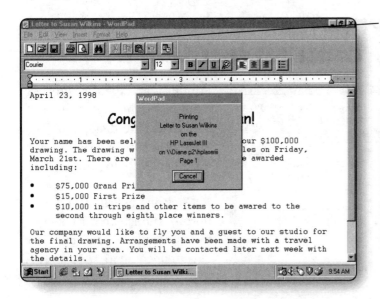

3. **Click** on the **Print button** when you are ready to print the document. The document will print with all default settings.

TIP

If you need to change a print setting, click on File, and then Print. The Print dialog box will appear prompting you for changes.

OPENING A WORDPAD DOCUMENT

If you want to work on a previously created WordPad document you must open it. When you open a file, you pull a copy of that file up into the computer memory. You can then make any desired changes and save the file again.

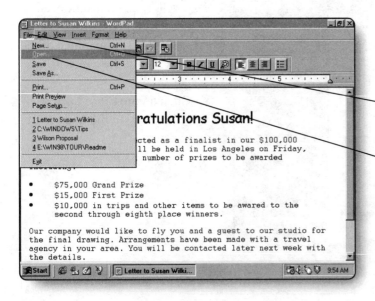

1. **Click** on **File**. The File menu will appear.

2. **Click** on **Open**. The Open dialog box will open and display the contents of the My Documents folder.

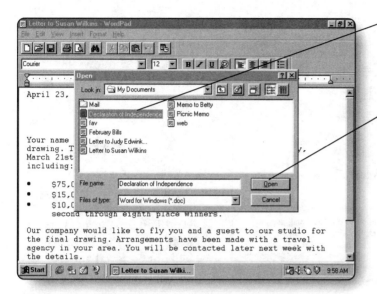

3. **Click** on the **name** of the file you want to open. The filename will be selected and appear in the File name: text box.

4. **Click** on the **Open button**. The Open dialog box will close, and the document will appear onscreen, ready for you to edit.

CLOSING THE WORDPAD PROGRAM

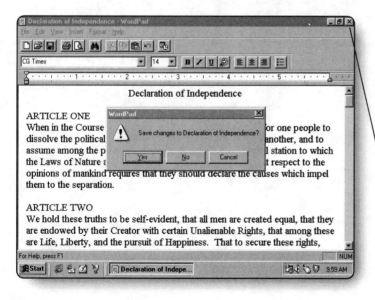

When you are finished using the WordPad program, you should close it. Keeping a program open unnecessarily uses computer resources that you may need for other areas.

1. **Click** on the **Close button** (☒). WordPad will prompt you to save the changes to your document.

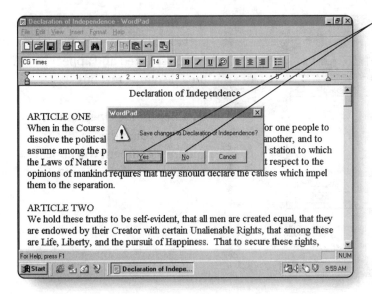

2. Click on **Yes** or **No**. The program will close and you will return to the Windows 98 desktop or to the next open program.

8 Painting with the Paint Program

Most of us don't have a lot of artistic skill, so the Microsoft Paint program is included with Windows 98. This program is designed to assist you with making drawings. In this chapter, you'll learn how to:

✦ Identify the Paint tools

✦ Draw with the brush

✦ Draw a rectangle or circle

✦ Fill in the background color

✦ Flip and skew an object

✦ Select and move an object

✦ Print and save a drawing

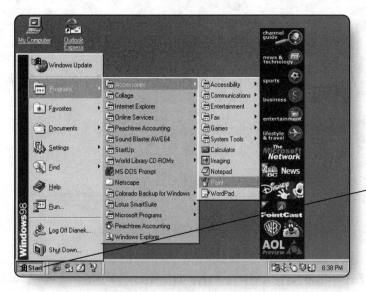

STARTING THE PAINT PROGRAM

The Paint program is one of the Accessories supplied with Windows.

1. **Click** on the **Start button**. The Start menu will appear.

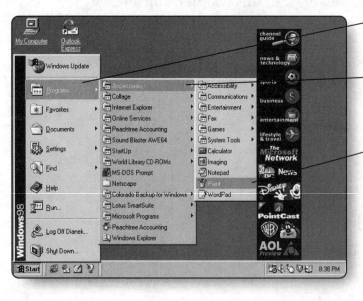

2. Click on **Programs**. The Programs submenu will appear.

3. Click on **Accessories**. The Accessories submenu will appear.

4. Click on **Paint**. The Paint program will open.

DISCOVERING THE PAINT TOOLS

TIP

If the Tool Box does not appear, click on View, and then Tool Box.

A feature called the *Tool Box* appears on the left side of your screen. You will use these 16 tools to create or edit the objects you need for your drawing.

There are many tools available to assist you with your drawing. Some of the tools included are:

✦ **Free-Form Select**. Selects an irregular-shaped area to edit.

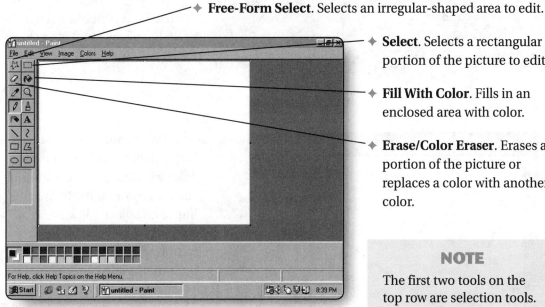

✦ **Select**. Selects a rectangular portion of the picture to edit.

✦ **Fill With Color**. Fills in an enclosed area with color.

✦ **Erase/Color Eraser**. Erases a portion of the picture or replaces a color with another color.

NOTE

The first two tools on the top row are selection tools.

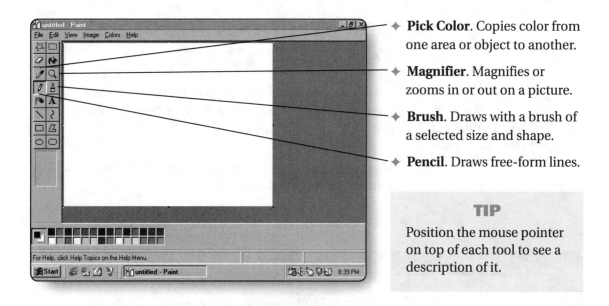

✦ **Pick Color**. Copies color from one area or object to another.

✦ **Magnifier**. Magnifies or zooms in or out on a picture.

✦ **Brush**. Draws with a brush of a selected size and shape.

✦ **Pencil**. Draws free-form lines.

TIP

Position the mouse pointer on top of each tool to see a description of it.

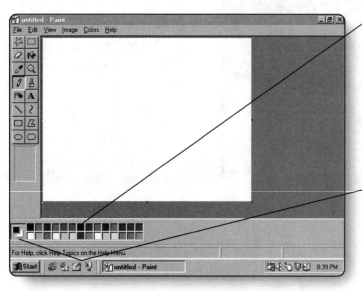

At the very bottom of the screen is the Color Box. Clicking on a color with the left mouse button selects a color for the frame or line of an object. Clicking on a color with the right mouse button selects a color for the interior of a filled object.

The current colors are displayed on the left side of the Color Box.

DRAWING WITH THE BRUSH

The Brush tool is a free-form drawing tool, which means it can have an irregular or asymmetrical shape or design. A tool is selected by clicking once on its designated button. When a tool has been selected, many will display any available options at the bottom of the Tool Box. For example, if you select the Brush, various shapes, thicknesses, and angles will be available for you to choose from. If you select the Rectangle tool, you can choose from a rectangle with a frame only, filled with a frame, or filled only.

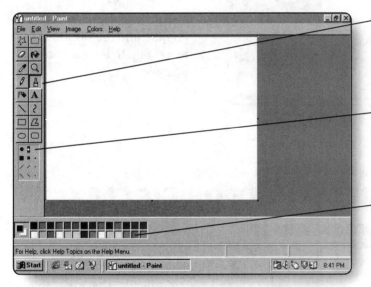

1. **Click** on the **Brush tool**. The Brush button will appear pushed in to indicate the tool is active.

2. **Click** on a **brush shape** from the bottom of the Tool Box. A shaded box will appear around the brush shape.

3. **Click** on a **color** from the Color Box. The color will appear in the top of the two boxes on the left side of the Color Box.

4. **Press** and **hold** the **mouse button** and **drag** the **mouse pointer** on the drawing screen to draw the desired shape or object. The drawing will appear onscreen as you move the mouse.

5. **Release** the **mouse button**. The completed drawn object will appear onscreen.

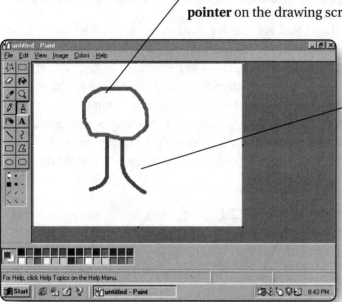

TIP

If you make a mistake, click on Edit, and then Undo to reverse up to the last three actions.

DRAWING A RECTANGLE OR CIRCLE

Unless you are a skilled artist, sometimes getting a good-looking drawing with the Brush tool is difficult. That's why the rectangle and other shapes are available to assist you.

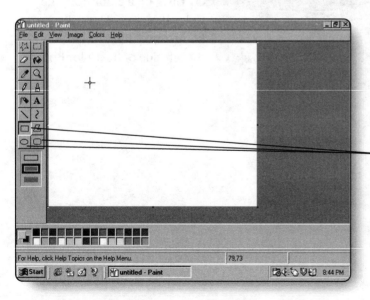

1. **Click** on the **Rectangle tool**, the **Rounded Rectangle tool**, or the **Ellipse tool**. The tool will be selected and the mouse pointer will become a small cross.

2. Click on a **color** from the Color Box for the shape's outline. The selected color will appear in the top of the two boxes on the left side of the Color Box.

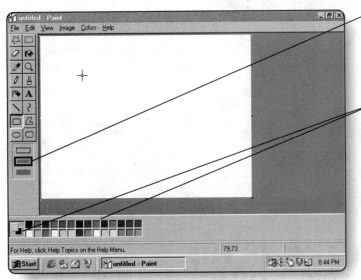

3. Click on a **fill style** from the bottom of the Tool Box. A shaded box will appear around the selection.

4. Optionally, **right-click** on a **color** in the Color Box for the shape's interior (fill) color. The selected color will appear in the bottom of the two boxes on the left side of the Color Box.

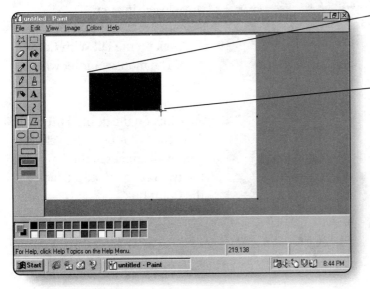

5. Click on **the mouse** at the location where you want the object to begin.

6. Drag the **mouse pointer diagonally**. The object will appear as you move the mouse.

7. Release the **mouse button** when the shape is the correct size. The drawn object will be complete.

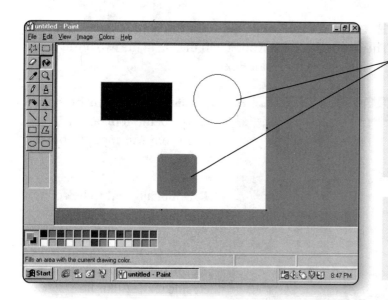

TIP

To draw a perfect square or circle, press and hold the Shift key as you draw the shape. Release the mouse button *before* you release the Shift key.

NOTE

A tool stays selected until a new tool is chosen.

FILLING IN THE BACKGROUND COLOR

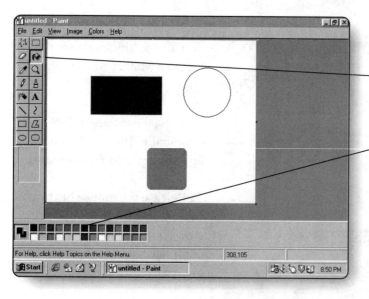

You can change the fill color of any closed-in area.

1. **Click** on the **Fill With Color tool**. The mouse pointer will look like a paint bucket.

2. **Click** on the desired **fill color** from the Color Box. The selected color will appear in the top of the two boxes on the left side of the Color Box.

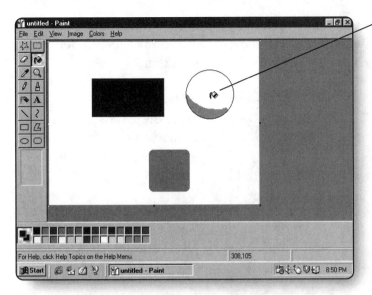

3. **Click** the **mouse pointer** inside the object to be filled. The interior of the object will take on the new color.

TIP

If you click in the background area of the drawing, the background changes to the new color.

SELECTING AND MOVING AN OBJECT

Objects or shapes that have been drawn onscreen can be moved to a new location. The secret to moving an object is to select it first. With Microsoft Paint, you can move all or just part of a drawn object.

1. **Click** on the **Select tool** or the **Free-Form Select tool**. The mouse pointer will become a small white cross.

2. **Select** whether the **background** of the object you're going to move is to be solid in color or transparent.

3. **Click** and **drag** around the area of the object to be moved. A dotted line (called the *selection box*) will appear around the area when you release the mouse button.

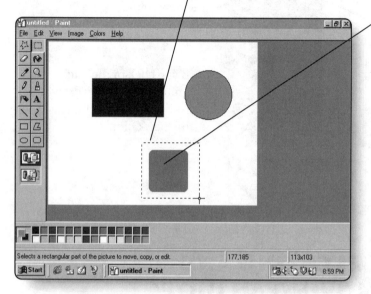

4. **Place** the **mouse pointer** in the middle of the selection box. The mouse pointer will become a small black cross with four arrowheads.

TIP

If you position the mouse pointer over one of the eight small black "handles" on the selection box, it becomes a double-headed arrow. You can resize the object by clicking and dragging the box to the desired size.

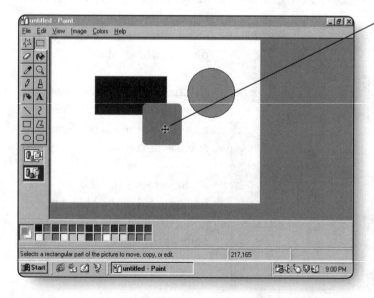

5. **Click** and **drag** the **selection box** to the desired location. The selected object will move.

6. **Release** the **mouse button**. The object will remain selected and be ready for the next editing action.

TIP

To deselect an object, click on any other area of the drawing, or click on another tool.

FLIPPING AND SKEWING AN OBJECT

Webster's dictionary defines the word skew as "to distort." With Microsoft Paint, you have the capability to skew objects to give them a distinctly distorted appearance. You also have the capability to flip or rotate objects.

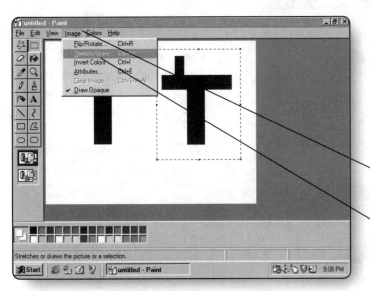

1. **Select** the **object** or **area** to be skewed. A dotted line will appear around the selected object or area.

NOTE

If a specific object or area is not selected, the entire drawing will be skewed.

TIP

Before you skew an object, make sure the transparent background is selected. If not, when the object is skewed, it will pick up the currently selected background color.

2. **Click** on **Image**. The Image menu will appear.

3. **Click** on **Stretch/Skew**. The Stretch and Skew dialog box will open.

4. **Enter** the **number of degrees** to skew the object in either the Horizontal: or Vertical: text boxes. The maximum value is 89.

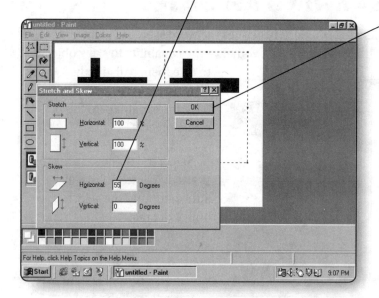

5. **Click** on **OK**. The Stretch and Skew dialog box will close, and the object or area will be redrawn with the new settings.

> **NOTE**
>
> An object can be skewed both horizontally and vertically, but each step must be done separately.

6. **Click** on **Image**, first making sure the object is still selected. The Image menu will appear.

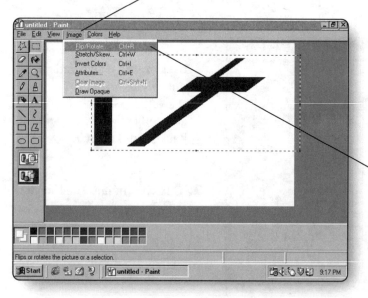

> **NOTE**
>
> If a specific object or area is not selected, the entire drawing will be flipped or rotated.

7. **Click** on **Flip/Rotate**. The Flip and Rotate dialog box will open.

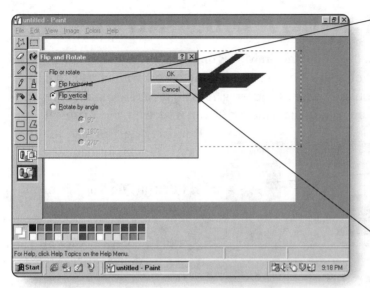

8. **Click** on **Flip horizontal**, **Flip vertical**, or **Rotate by angle**. The option will be selected.

NOTE

If you select Rotate by angle, you must also select by how many degrees to rotate the object.

9. **Click** on **OK**. The Flip and Rotate dialog box will close.

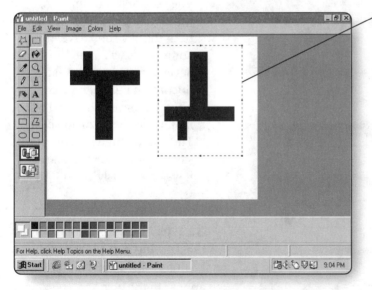

The object or area is redrawn with your selection.

SAVING A DRAWING

At this point, the drawing is only temporarily stored in the computer's memory. If you want to work with or refer to it later, you must save the drawing. Although there are many types of graphic formats Windows 98 can work with, the Microsoft Paint program can save only in a .bmp (bitmap) format.

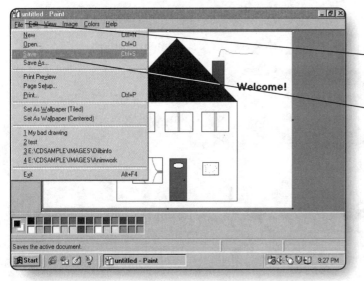

1. **Click** on **File**. The File menu will appear.

2. **Click** on **Save** or **Save As**. The Save As dialog box will open.

NOTE

The very first time an untitled document is saved, both the Save and Save As commands will open the Save As dialog box. After a document has been saved once, the Save command will no longer open a dialog box. The document will simply be saved under the same name it was previously given.

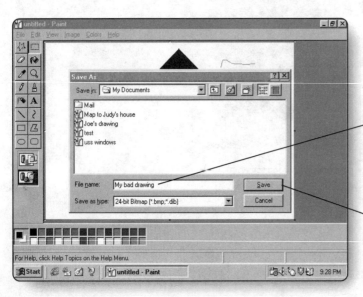

3. **Type** a **descriptive name** for the drawing in the File name: text box. The name you type will appear in the box.

4. **Click** on the **Save button**. The document will be saved and the name will appear in the title bar.

SAVING A DRAWING AS WALLPAPER

Once a drawing has been saved and given a name, you can choose to save the drawing as wallpaper to appear on your Windows 98 desktop. You can select the wallpaper to be tiled or centered.

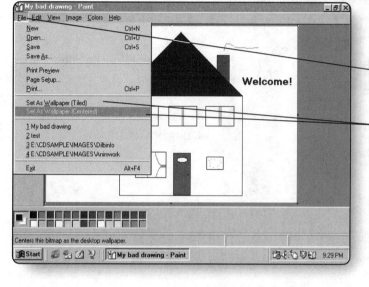

1. **Click** on **File**. The File menu will appear.

2. **Click** on **Set As Wallpaper (Tiled)** or **Set as Wallpaper (Centered)**. The drawing will appear as wallpaper on your desktop.

TIP

To see what the wallpaper looks like, click on the Minimize button (▣).

NOTE

Desktop wallpaper is discussed in more detail in Chapter 17, "Having Fun with the Control Panel."

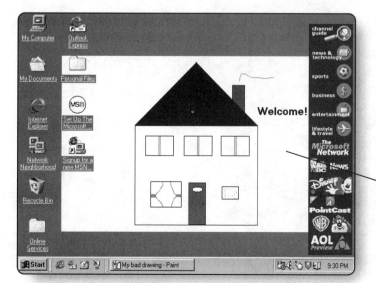

The drawing as it appears on the Windows desktop.

PRINTING A DRAWING

Printing is the final step for many drawing projects. Windows 98 brings more and more consistency between software programs, including the methods used to print. (Printing a drawing is done in the same manner as printing a WordPad document.)

1. **Click** on **File**. The File menu will appear.

2. **Click** on **Print**. The Print dialog box will open.

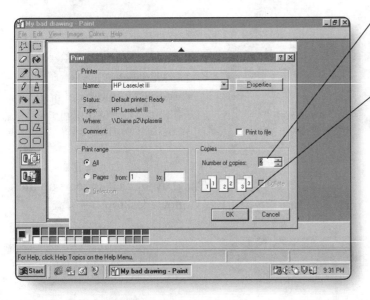

3. **Type** the **number of copies** to print (if more than one) in the Number of copies: box.

4. **Click** on **OK**. The document will print.

9 Playing Around with the Games

I'm sure you've heard the saying, "All work and no play. . . ." Well, Microsoft has included several great games with the Windows 98 software. These games include FreeCell, Hearts, Solitaire, and Mindsweeper. Games serve multiple purposes: one, of course, is to have fun and reduce stress. But more importantly, when you are new to a Windows environment, mastering control of the mouse can be difficult. The Windows 98 games are great tools for learning to use your mouse. In this chapter, you'll learn how to:

✦ Start the Solitaire game

✦ Move a card

✦ Add a card to the stack

✦ Change the Solitaire options

STARTING SOLITAIRE

Solitaire is designed to be played by one player at a time. The objective is to place all the cards of the deck in the top stacks.

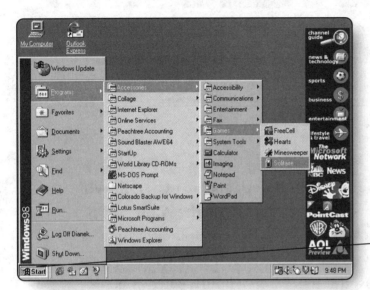

NOTE

The games are located in the Accessories folder but Windows 98 does not install all the games by default. If the games do not show up on your Accessories menu, you'll need to add them (see "Adding and Removing Programs" in Chapter 16).

1. Click on the **Start button**. The Start menu will appear.

2. Click on **Programs**. The Programs submenu will appear.

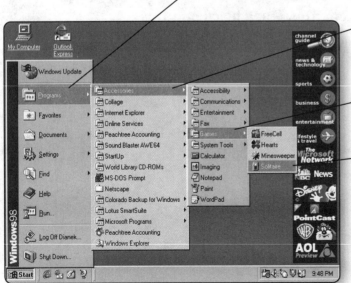

3. Click on **Accessories**. The Accessories submenu will appear.

4. Click on **Games**. The Games submenu will appear.

5. Click on **Solitaire**. The Solitaire game will open and cards will be dealt.

MOVING A CARD

When working with the seven main piles (row stacks) of the Solitaire game, only a card that is one step lower and the opposite color can be placed on another card. For example, the only cards you could place on top of a Queen of Spades would be the Jack of Hearts or Jack of Diamonds.

1. **Click** on and **drag** a **card** to a new location. The card will move with the mouse pointer.

Click the mouse pointer on the bottom card of the stack to move the whole stack.

2. **Release** the **mouse button**. The card will drop into the new location.

NOTE

If you try to make a move that is not permitted, the card will return to its original location.

3. **Click** on the **next card** to be turned over in the row stack. The card will turn face up and be ready for play.

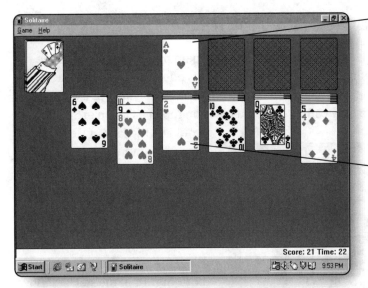

The top row of stacks (suit stacks) are placed in ascending order from Ace to King. All cards must be of the same suit. For example, you can only play a seven of Hearts on a six of Hearts.

4. **Double-click** on a **card** to be placed on the suit stack. The card will jump automatically to the correct stack.

5. **Click** on the **deck** to begin turning over cards to play. The card that is face up on the deck will now be available for play.

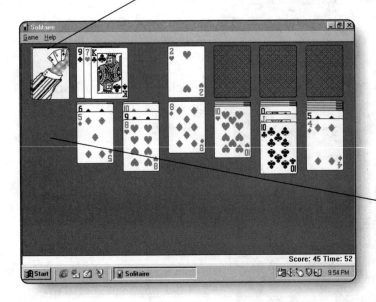

TIP

If you play or turn over a card in error, click on Game, and then Undo to reverse the last card played.

NOTE

Only Kings are allowed to be placed in an empty row stack.

CHANGING SOLITAIRE OPTIONS

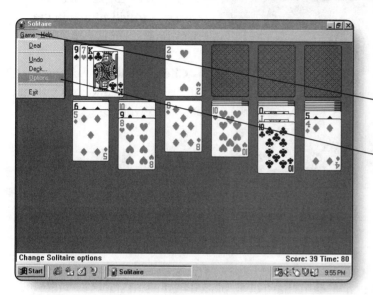

There are several types of Solitaire games and scoring methods from which to choose.

1. **Click** on **Game**. The Game menu will appear.

2. **Click** on **Options**. The Options dialog box will open.

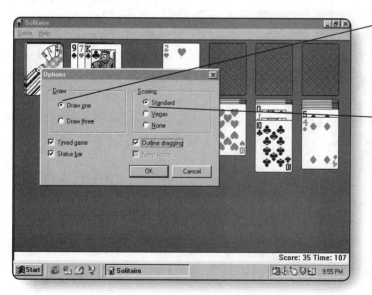

3. **Click** on **Draw one** to turn over one card at a time from the deck. The option will be selected.

4. **Click** on **Standard**, **Vegas**, or **None**.

NOTE

Standard scoring allows you to go through the deck multiple times, while the Vegas method only allows you to go through the deck a single time.

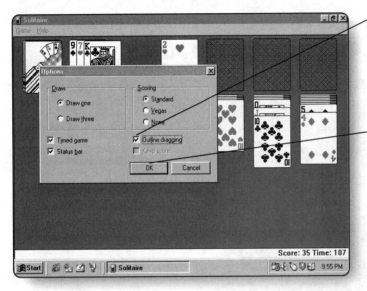

5. **Click** on **Outline dragging**. This feature allows an outline of the card to be displayed as you move it. A ✔ will appear in the check box.

6. **Click** on **OK**. Your choices will be accepted and the Options dialog box will close.

NOTE

A new Solitaire game may start based on changes you made in the Options dialog box.

When all cards have been placed in the suit stacks and the game is finished, the cards start to cascade down the screen.

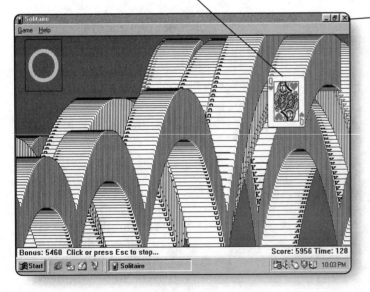

7. **Click** on the **Close button** ([X]). The Solitaire game will close and you will return to the Windows 98 desktop.

PART II REVIEW QUESTIONS

1. What key can be pressed to clear the totals on the Windows calculator? *See the introduction in Chapter 6*

2. What are the two types of Windows Calculators that can be displayed? *See "Changing the Style of the Calculator" in Chapter 6*

3. Where do you go to access the WordPad program? *See "Starting WordPad" in Chapter 7*

4. In WordPad, pressing the Backspace key will delete text in which direction? *See "Deleting Text" in Chapter 7*

5. What are the three alignment choices available in WordPad? *See "Modifying the Alignment" in Chapter 7*

6. What does the Fill With Color tool in Paint do? *See "Discovering the Paint Tools" in Chapter 8*

7. What key can you press to draw a perfect circle in Paint? *See "Drawing a Rectangle or Circle" in Chapter 8*

8. In a Paint drawing, what can you do when you position the mouse over any of the eight handles on a selection box? *See "Selecting and Moving an Object" in Chapter 8*

9. When playing Solitaire, what card can be placed in an empty row stack? *See "Moving a Card" in Chapter 9*

10. How many times can you go through the deck in a Vegas game of Solitaire? *See "Changing Solitaire Options" in Chapter 9*

PART III
Discovering the Windows Tools

10 Using Windows Help

Although I sincerely hope you find many answers to your Windows 98 questions from this book, sometimes you need additional information. Microsoft supplies you with several types of assistance. In this chapter, you'll learn how to:

✦ Use the Help Contents and Index

✦ Use the Troubleshooting Wizards

✦ Get Help on the Web

USING THE HELP CONTENTS

The Help Contents feature is a list of general help topics covering such issues as exploring your computer, connecting to networks, and using the accessibility features. The Help Contents also lists the Troubleshooting Wizards.

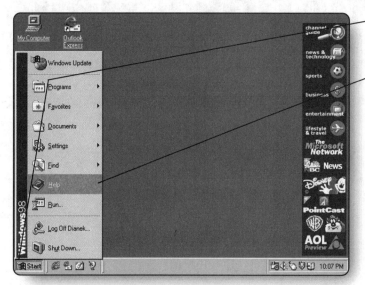

1. **Click** on the **Start button**. The Start menu will appear.

2. **Click** on **Help**. The Windows Help window will appear with a Welcome to Help message on the right side of the screen.

TIP

You can also just press the F1 key to access the Windows Help window.

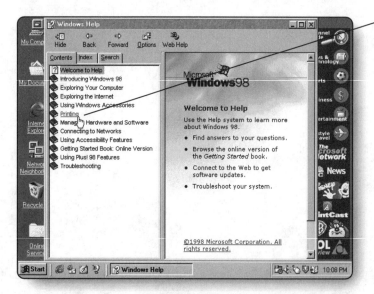

3. **Click** on the **general topic** that you want more information about. The book will open and a list of specific topics will appear.

NOTE

A *general topic* is signified by a small book, while a *specific topic* is indicated by a paper with a question mark on it. Some general topics may have other general topics listed under them.

4. **Click** on a **specific topic**. Information about that topic will appear on the right side of the screen.

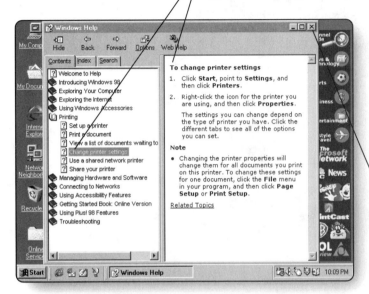

TIP

To print a help topic, click on the help information and then press Ctrl+P. The Print dialog box will appear with available options.

5. **Click** on the **Close button** (X). The Windows Help window will close.

Troubleshooting Wizards

A new addition to Windows 98 is the Troubleshooting Wizard feature. There are 13 wizards included that ask you a series of interactive questions relating to a problem you might be having with your system.

1. **Click** on the **Start button**. The Start menu will appear.

2. **Click** on **Help**. The Windows Help window will appear.

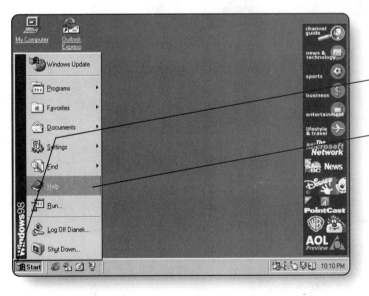

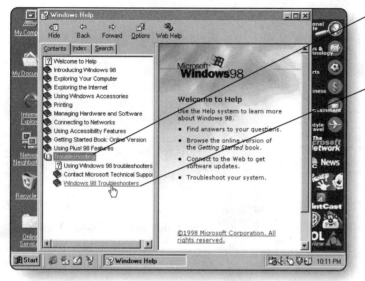

3. **Click** on **Troubleshooting**. The Troubleshooting topic will open.

4. **Click** on **Windows 98 Troubleshooters**. A list of 15 available troubleshooters will appear.

5. **Click** on the **appropriate troubleshooter**. The first question in the Troubleshooter will appear on the right side of the window.

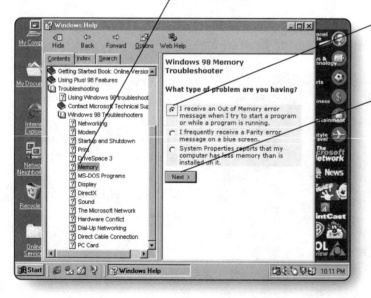

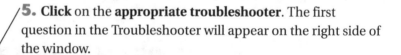

6. **Click** on the **problem** you are having. The option will be selected.

7. **Click** on **Next** to continue.

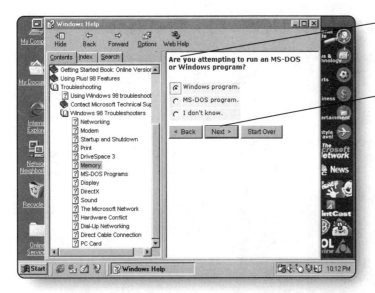

8. **Read** and **try** the possible **solutions** offered or **answer** the next **question**.

9. **Click** on **Next** to continue. The next question or a possible solution will appear, based on your answer to the previous question.

NOTE

The number of questions asked will vary with the problem and your responses to the questions.

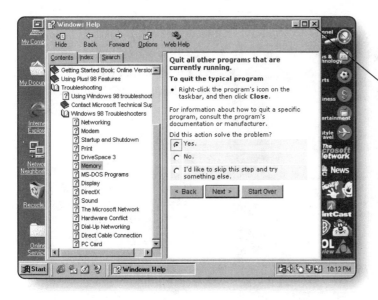

10. **Repeat steps 8** and **9** if necessary.

11. **Click** on the **Close button** (⊠). The Windows Help window will close.

USING THE HELP INDEX

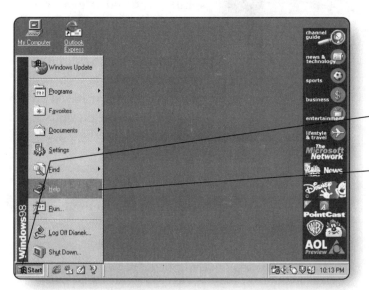

The Windows 98 Help Index is a list of every available topic covered in the Windows 98 Help feature.

1. **Click** on the **Start button**. The Start menu will appear.

2. **Click** on **Help**. The Windows Help window will appear.

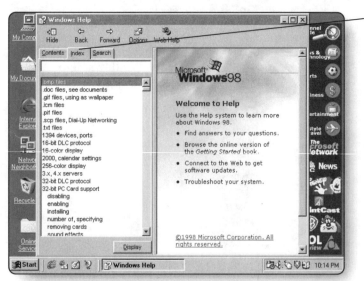

3. **Click** on the **Index tab**. The topics will be listed alphabetically with some topics displaying a list of subtopics.

NOTE

The first time the Index is accessed, it may take a moment to display.

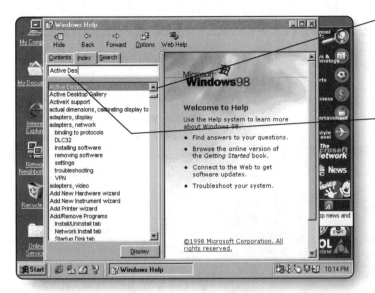

4a. **Scroll through** the **list of topics** until you find the topic you are looking for.

OR

4b. **Type** the **first word** of the topic you are looking for. The topics will jump alphabetically to the word you typed.

5. **Double-click** on the desired **topic**. The information will be displayed on the right side of the screen.

NOTE

Some topics have more than one article of information. Double-click on the article that is most appropriate for your search.

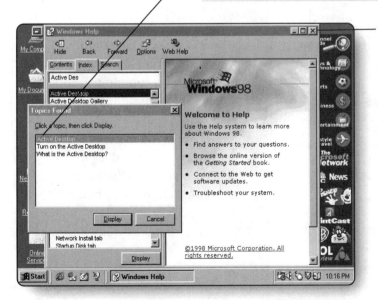

6. **Click** on the **Close button** (⊠). The Windows Help window will close.

FINDING HELP ON THE WEB

There are many sources of assistance supplied with Windows 98. You've already seen several good resources. Another one is the World Wide Web. Microsoft includes technical support for you at its Web site. From the Web site, you can search the entire Microsoft database of information, known as Knowledge Base or Troubleshooting Wizards.

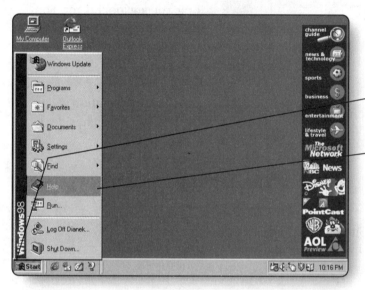

1. **Click** on the **Start button**. The Start menu will appear.

2. **Click** on **Help**. The Windows Help window will appear.

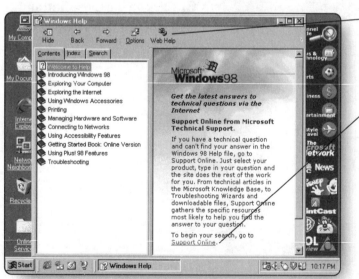

3. **Click** on **Web Help**. Information about Windows Technical support will appear on the right side of the screen.

4. **Click** on **Support Online**. If you are using a dial-up connection to the Internet, your connection dialog box will open.

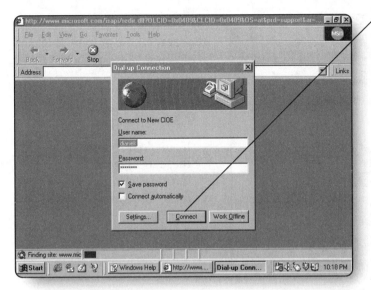

5. **Click** on **Connect**. A connection to the Internet will be established and Internet Explorer will display the Microsoft Support Online page.

> **NOTE**
>
> You may see a Security Alert message about an ActiveX object. Click on Yes to continue.

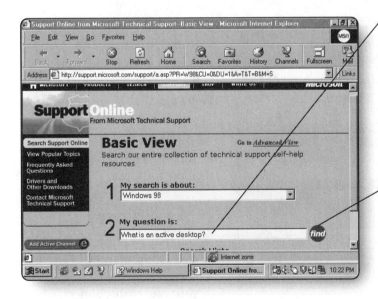

6. **Click** in the **text box** below the My question is: text box. A blinking insertion point will appear.

7. **Type** the **topic** with which you need assistance. This can be a word or phrase.

8. **Click** on **Find**. A Security Alert message box will appear.

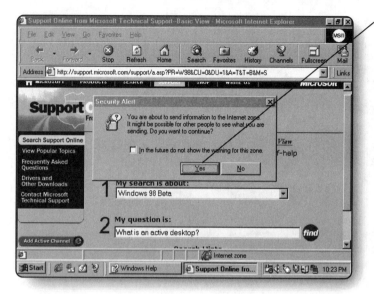

9. **Click** on **Yes** to continue with the search. One or more Internet redirection messages will appear.

TIP

If you do not want to see these messages in the future, click on In the future do not show the warning . . . check box.

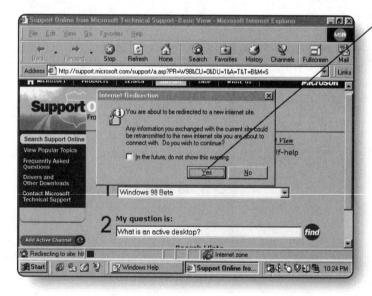

10. **Click** on **Yes** to continue with each message. The information you requested will appear in the form of a Web Page.

11. **Click** on the **Close button** (X). The Internet Explorer window will close.

NOTE

You may be prompted to close your Internet connection. Click on Yes if you want to disconnect.

12. **Click** on the **Close button** (X). The Windows Help window will close.

11 Using Windows System Tools

Windows 98 has added new tools to aid you with the housekeeping and maintenance of your PC. Several of the programs were available in previous versions of Windows but not easily accessible. Windows 98 not only makes them available with just a few clicks of the mouse, but many can also be set to run automatically. In this chapter, you'll learn how to:

✦ Back up your files

✦ Scan your disk for errors

✦ Defragment your hard disk drive

✦ Schedule applications to run automatically

✦ Use the Windows Update Wizard

✦ Convert your disk to FAT32

BACKING UP YOUR WORK

Microsoft Backup is a utility that allows you to copy information from your hard drive to another medium, such as a floppy disk or tape. The copied data can then be stored for safekeeping against catastrophic events, such as hard drive crashes, the theft of your computer, or fire. You can automate the Backup program to back up all or a particular group of files at a preset time.

> **NOTE**
>
> The Microsoft Backup program is not installed by default, so you will need to install it. See "Adding and Removing Programs" in Chapter 16 for information on installing Microsoft Backup.

When you are going to back up files, there are three pieces of information that Microsoft Backup will need.

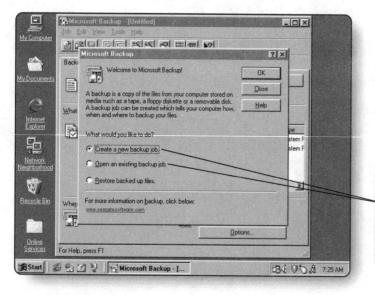

✦ What files do you want to back up?

✦ Where do you want to back them up?

✦ What do you want to call the backup job?

> **TIP**
>
> A *backup job* is the name used to describe the files you are backing up.

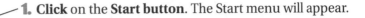

1. Click on the **Start button**. The Start menu will appear.

2. Click on **Programs**. The Programs submenu will appear.

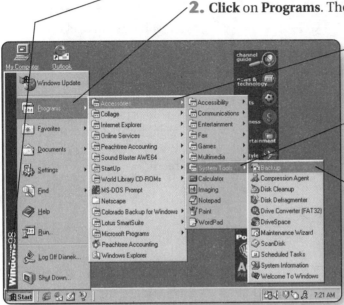

3. Click on **Accessories**. The Accessories submenu will appear.

4. Click on **System Tools**. The System Tools submenu will appear.

5. Click on **Backup**. The Microsoft Backup dialog box will appear, prompting you to create a new backup job, open an existing backup job, or restore backed up files.

NOTE

The first time you run the Microsoft Backup program you may see a message that no backup devices were found. If you have a tape backup click on Yes to install the tape drive, however if you do not have a tape backup click on No and the program will continue.

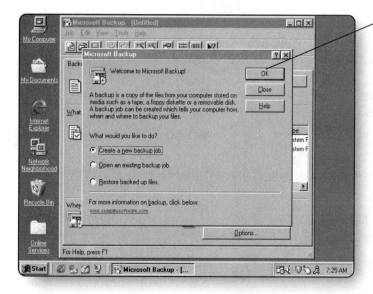

6. **Click** on **OK** to create a new backup job. The Backup Wizard dialog box will open, asking for what you want to backup.

NOTE

If you are backing up *all* the files on your computer to floppy disks, be prepared to have a *big* stack of disks ready!

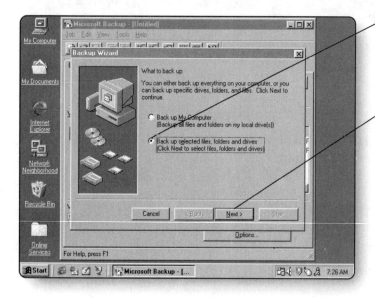

7. **Click** on **Back up selected files, folders and drives** if you want to back up data files. The option will be selected.

8. **Click** on **Next**. The next screen will display a directory tree of your computer, showing all available disk drives and folders.

TIP

Click on the + (plus sign) next to the drive you want to back up. The tree will expand and folders on that particular drive will be displayed. Click on the plus sign next to the folders and the tree will expand farther.

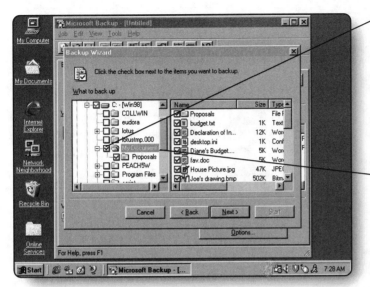

9a. **Click** on the **check box** next to the folder you want to back up. A ✔ will appear, indicating that the folder and all of its subfolders have been selected.

OR

9b. **Click** on the **folder name** if you want to back up selected files from a particular folder. The files in that folder will be indicated on the right side of the window.

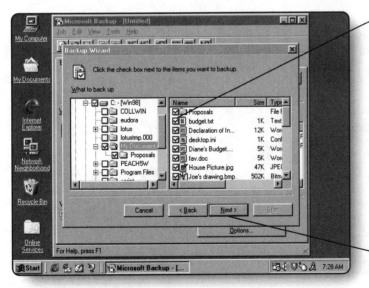

10. **Click** on the **check box** next to the filenames you want to back up. A ✔ will appear, indicating that the files have been selected.

TIP

To deselect a folder or file, click on the check box again to remove the ✔.

11. **Click** on **Next**. You will continue to the next screen.

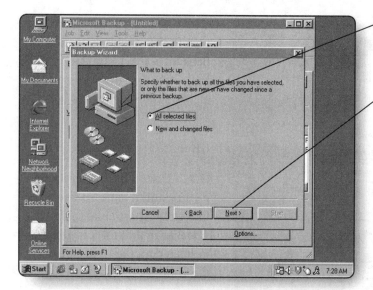

12. **Click** on **All selected files** to back up the files you have selected.

13. **Click** on **Next**. You will continue to the next screen, which may vary, depending on the configuration of your system.

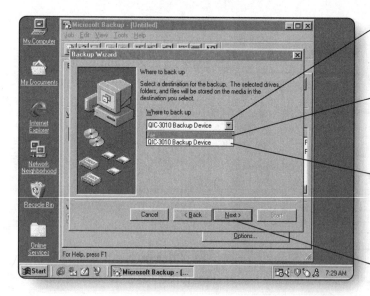

14. **Click** on the **down arrow** (▾) below Where to back up. A list of choices will appear.

15a. **Click** on **File** if you are backing up to floppy disks.

OR

15b. **Click** on your **backup device** (the choice may vary) if you are backing up to a tape drive.

16. **Click** on **Next**. You will continue to the next screen.

17. **Click** in the **second text box**. The insertion point will appear in the text box.

18. **Type** the **drive name** and **location** for this particular backup session. You must enter the drive name for the floppy disks (such as a:), and then a name for the files.

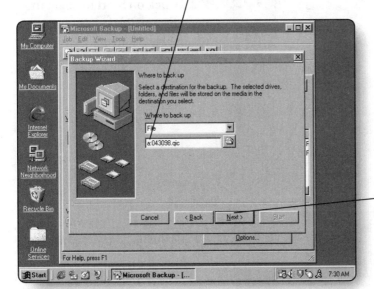

TIP

A common practice is to use the date you are backing up, but don't use any spaces, dashes, or characters. An example might be a:121897.

19. **Click** on **Next**. You will continue to the next screen.

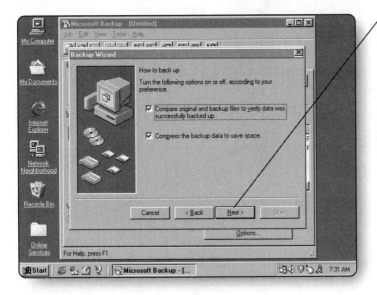

20. **Click** on **Next**. The backup options will be accepted.

The next screen prompts you for an optional name to store these instructions for future use. By doing so, the next time you use the Backup program, you won't have to specify which, where, and how (if you are backing up the same set of information).

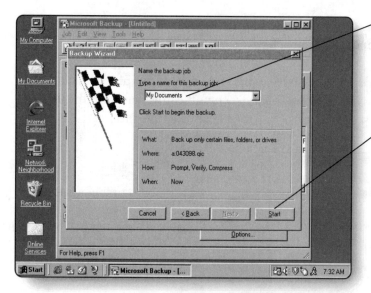

21. **Type** a **name** for the backup job, if desired, in the Type a name for this backup job: list box. The name will appear in the list box.

22. **Click** on **Start** to begin the backup. The Backup Progress window will appear.

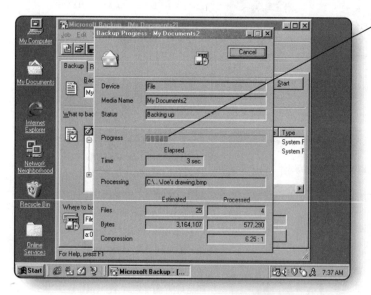

The Backup Progress window details the backup progress.

23. **Click** on **OK** when the backup is completed and the Microsoft Backup message box opens. The message box will close.

24. **Click** on **OK**. The Backup Progress window will close.

25. **Click** on the **Close button** (⊠). The Microsoft Backup window will close, and you can remove the disk or tape.

> **TIP**
> For maximum safekeeping of your data, keep backups stored in a different building than where your computer is located.

SCANNING YOUR HARD DRIVE FOR PROBLEMS

When you shut down your computer normally, several internal checks and operations occur to make sure everything is closed and filed properly. If Windows is not shut down normally, for example, if the computer locks up or if you turned off the power while in Windows, those internal checks don't get the chance to work. This can cause problems with your computer's hard drive. Windows 98 includes a program to

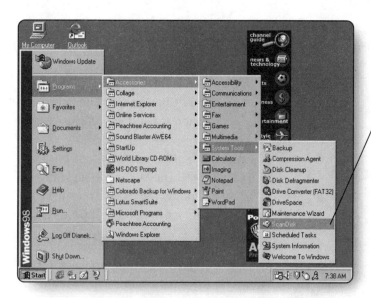

check your hard drive for potential errors.

1. Follow steps 1 through **4** in "Backing Up Your Work." The System Tools submenu will appear.

2. Click on **ScanDisk**. The ScanDisk window will appear.

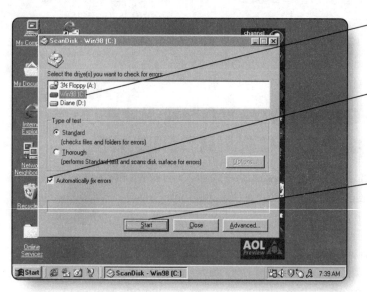

3. Click on the **disk drive** you want to check. The selected drive will be highlighted.

4. Click on the **Automatically fix errors check box,** if it is not already checked. A ✔ will appear in the check box.

5. Click on **Start**. The ScanDisk process will begin. A progress indicator will display at the bottom of the ScanDisk window. When ScanDisk has finished checking the drive, the ScanDisk Results dialog box will open.

TIP

If you have more than one disk to scan, hold down the Ctrl key and click on each subsequent drive to be checked.

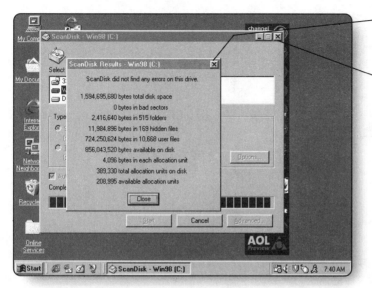

6. **Click** on **Close**. The ScanDisk Results dialog box will close.

7. **Click** on the **Close button** ([X]). The ScanDisk program will close.

DEFRAGMENTING YOUR HARD DRIVE

When a file is stored, the computer puts it in the first available space on the disk drive. If there's not enough room for the entire file, the rest of the file is put into the next available space. A file is fragmented when it is split into more than one location on your hard drive. Defragmenting rearranges the way data is stored on your hard drive. Programs and documents are organized so that the entire program or document you want can be read with a minimum number of physical movements of the disk drive. This can substantially improve the performance of your computer.

TIP

It's a good idea to run this program every couple of months or after you delete large amounts of data or programs from your hard drive.

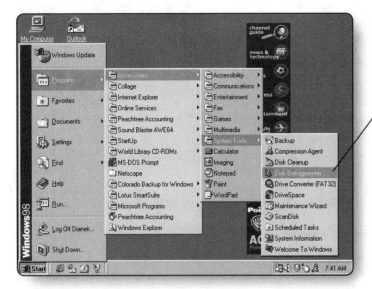

1. **Follow steps 1** through **4** in "Backing Up Your Work." The System Tools submenu will appear.

2. **Click** on **Disk Defragmenter**. The Select Drive dialog box will open.

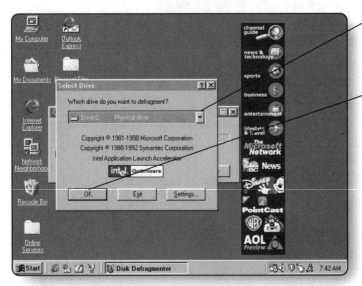

3. **Click** on the **down arrow** (▼), and **click** on the **drive** you want to defragment.

4. **Click** on **OK**. The Defragmenting dialog box will open and show your progress.

TIP

Be patient! The defragmenting process with ScanDisk can take a few hours.

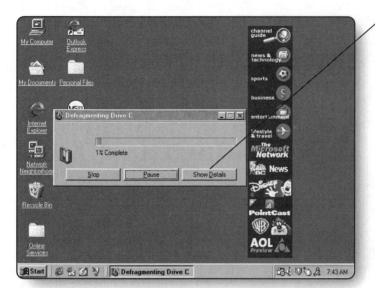

5. **Click** on **Show Details**, if desired. You will be able to see the actual blocks of the hard drive as they are being cleaned up.

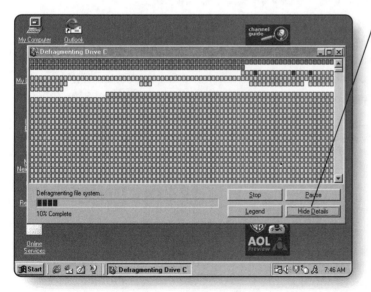

6. **Click** on **Hide Details**. You will return to the Defragmenting dialog box.

NOTE

You can use your computer while the defragment process is working, but all tasks will be slower.

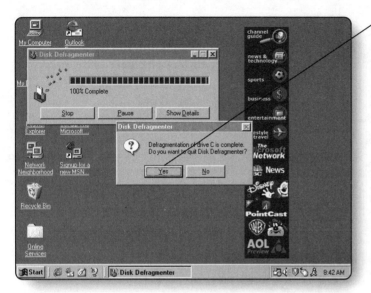

7. **Click** on **Yes** to quit the Disk Defragmenter program. The Disk Defragmenter dialog boxes will close.

AUTOMATICALLY SCHEDULING TASKS

Many system tasks can be scheduled to run automatically at a time when you normally are not using the computer. To enroll these tasks, Windows 98 includes a feature called *Scheduled Tasks*. These can be housekeeping chores, such as ScanDisk or Disk Defragmenting, or they can be opening your favorite software application.

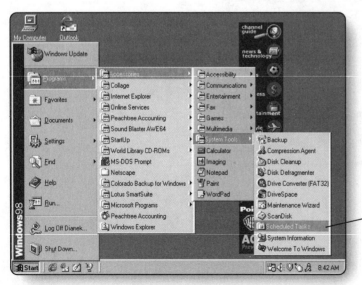

1. **Follow steps 1** through **4** in "Backing Up Your Work." The System Tools submenu will appear.

2. **Click** on **Scheduled Tasks**. The Scheduled Tasks window will appear with a list of all currently scheduled tasks.

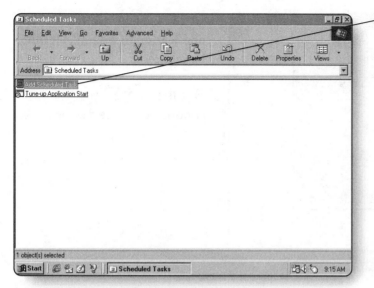

3. Click on **Add Scheduled Task**. The Scheduled Task Wizard will open to assist you in making your selections.

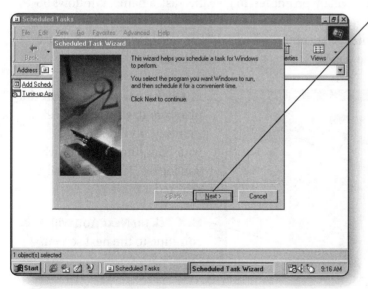

4. Click on **Next**. You will continue to the next screen, which lists the applications your computer has in the Windows 98 Registry.

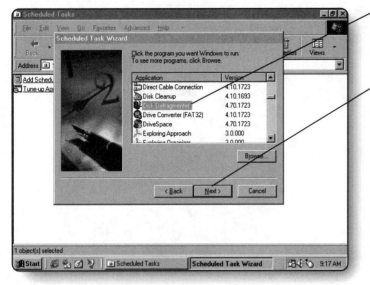

5. Click on the **desired application** to schedule. It will be selected.

6. Click on **Next**. You will continue to the next screen.

You will be prompted to give this task a name. Windows 98 suggests the same name as the program you will be running. You can accept this name or type one of your own choice in the text box.

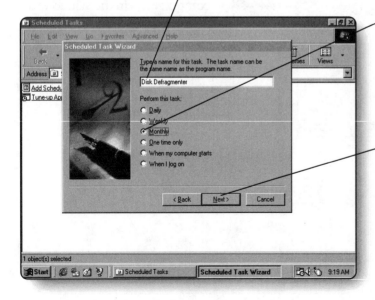

7. Click on **when you want this program to run**: daily, weekly, monthly, one time only, when your computer starts, or when you log on. The option will be selected.

8. Click on **Next**. You will continue to the next screen.

The choices you see next will vary depending on the selection you made. For example, the choices for a task to be performed daily will vary from the choices for a task to be performed monthly.

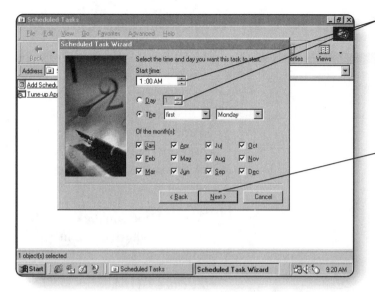

9. Choose the appropriate **start time** as well as which **date** or **day** of the month to run the program. You can also deactivate any month in which you do not want the task to run.

10. Click on **Next**. You will continue to the next screen. The Scheduled Task Wizard will confirm the choices you made for the task you selected.

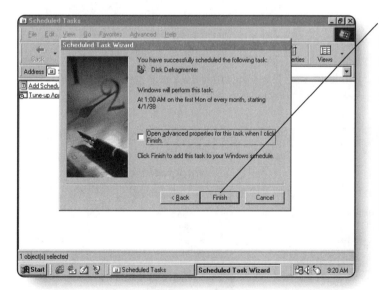

11. Click on **Finish**. The Scheduled Task Wizard will close, and the scheduled task will be listed in the Scheduled Tasks window.

NOTE

Your computer must be powered on for any tasks to run at the designated time.

Deleting a Scheduled Task

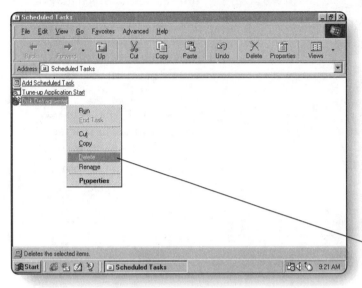

If you decide you no longer want a task to run automatically, you can delete it from the list of scheduled tasks. You are not going to delete the application, only the command that the task be run at the predetermined time.

1. Right-click on the **task** to be deleted. A shortcut menu will appear.

2. Click on **Delete**. The Confirm File Delete dialog box will open, asking for confirmation.

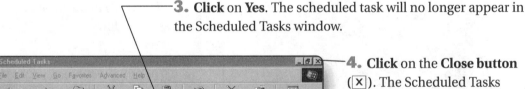

3. Click on **Yes**. The scheduled task will no longer appear in the Scheduled Tasks window.

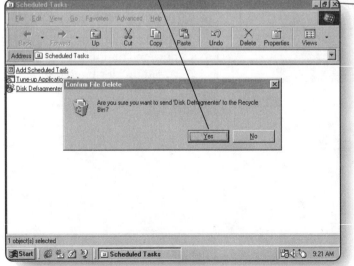

4. Click on the **Close button** ([X]). The Scheduled Tasks window will close.

AUTOMATING SYSTEM UPDATES

The Windows Update Wizard is a Web-based service you can use to update your hardware and system software. The Windows Update Wizard compares your hardware and system software files to a Microsoft database to determine whether there are updated files for you to install. Use this to update device drivers, install software upgrades, get service packs, and copy bug fixes and other software patches to your computer.

Available updates will be listed with descriptions so you can decide whether to install them. You can select which drivers, files, or updates you want to install, and you can remove any updates you choose not to keep.

TIP

Updates change periodically, so you should use the Windows Update Wizard on a regular basis.

1. **Click** on the **Start button**. The Start menu will appear.

2. **Click** on **Windows Update**. If you are not already connected to the Internet, the Dial-up Connection dialog box will open.

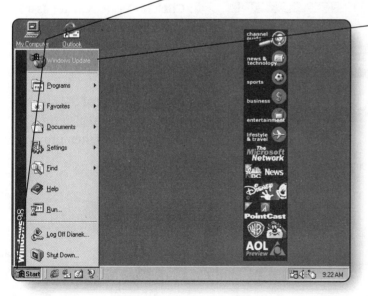

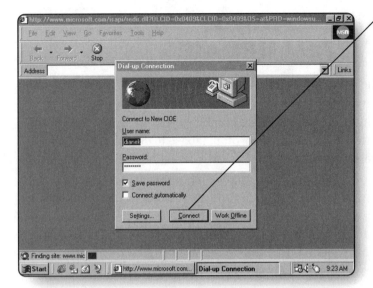

3. **Click** on **Connect**. You will be connected to your Internet Service Provider, and the Windows Update Web page will appear.

If you have not already registered your software, you will be prompted to do so. If you have already registered your software, proceed to step 6.

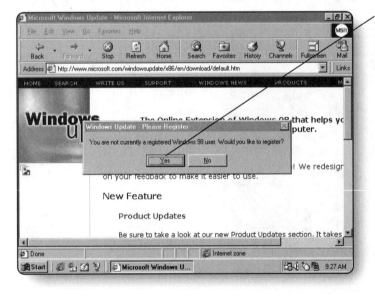

4. **Click** on **Yes** to register as a current Windows 98 user. The first registration screen will appear.

5. **Follow** the **rest of the steps** onscreen to finish registering your software, and then proceed to step 6.

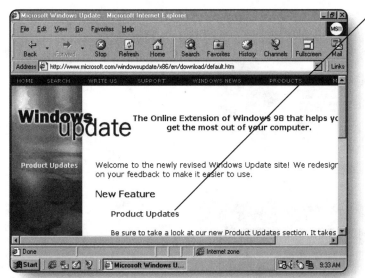

6. **Click** on **Product Updates**. The Active Setup dialog box will open.

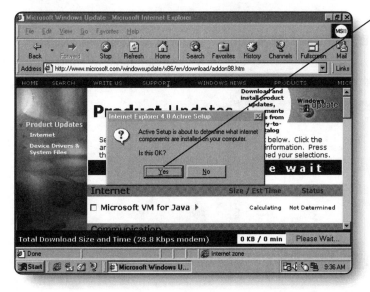

7. **Click** on **Yes**. The Product Updates Web page will appear.

NOTE

How the Windows Update Wizard works: When you visit this site, the Windows Update Wizard will download an index file on to your computer from the Microsoft server. It will compare the available updates from the server with your computer hardware and software. If there are newer versions on the server, you will be prompted to install the most recent drivers and files available specific to your computer system.

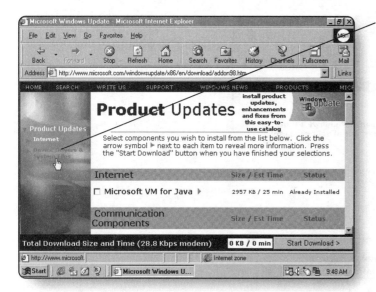

8. **Click** on **Device Drivers & System Files**. The Device Drivers and System Files Web page will appear.

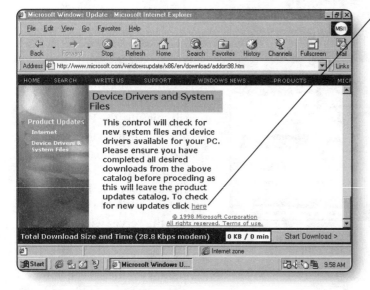

9. **Click** on **here**. The Update Wizard Web page will appear.

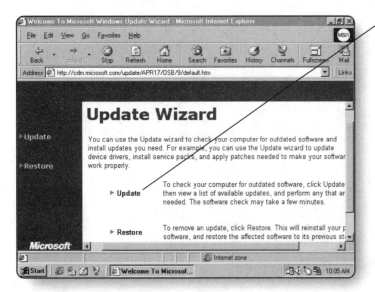

10. **Click** on **Update**. A new window will appear, and the Wizard will scan the computer for updates. A list of available updates will be displayed in the Update Wizard window.

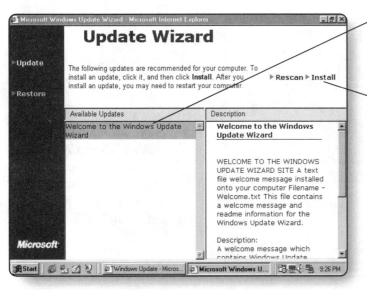

11. **Click** on the **updates** you want to add to your system. They will be selected.

12. **Click** on **Install**. A message box will open.

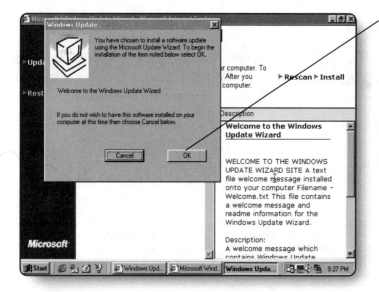

13. **Click** on **OK**. The download process will begin.

A status bar indicates the download progress. When the process is complete and the update is installed, another message box will open.

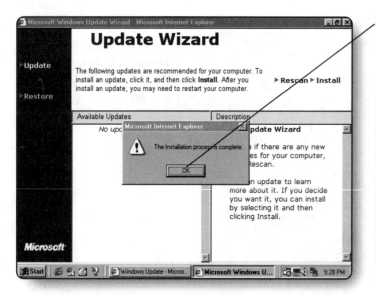

14. **Click** on **OK**. The message box will close.

TIP

If you want to uninstall an update, click on Restore on the Update Wizard Web page. A list of the updates you have installed appears. Select the update you want to remove and click on Uninstall.

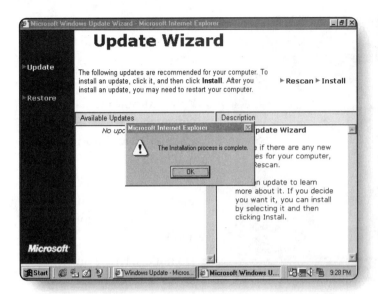

15. **Click** on the **Close button** ([X]). The Update Wizard Web page and Internet Explorer will close.

NOTE

You may need to restart your computer before any changes can take effect.

CONVERTING TO FAT32

FAT32 is an improved version of the file allocation table (FAT) file system your computer uses behind the scenes. The enhanced FAT32 file system stores files more efficiently and frees up hard disk space. Converting to FAT32 will result in applications starting up to 50 percent faster.

NOTE

Use FAT32 to format drives larger than 2GB as a single drive. Drives with storage capabilities under 512MB are not supported.

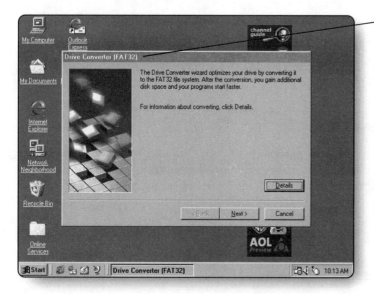

There are a couple of issues to be aware of before you run the FAT32 converter.

♦ Use Windows 98 to make a Windows Startup disk before you enable FAT32. (See Chapter 17 for information on making a Windows Startup disk.)

♦ Back up any data on your hard drive before converting it to FAT32.

♦ Do not use FAT32 on any drives that you need to access from other operating systems, including Windows 95, any version of Windows NT, and earlier versions of Windows or MS-DOS. If your computer is configured with another operating system as well as Windows 98 (dual boot), you cannot convert drive C to FAT32, even if the other operating system is installed on a different drive. However, computers that run Windows 98 can share FAT32 drives across a network.

♦ If you have antivirus software on your computer, when you reboot the system after converting the drive, your antivirus software might detect that the partition table or boot record has changed. In this case, the antivirus software might offer to repair it for you. Do not allow the antivirus software to restore the boot record or partition table. If you do, your disk and all the data on it will become inaccessible.

♦ DriveSpace does not and will not support compressing FAT32 drives. The DriveSpace utility included with Windows 98 has been modified to recognize FAT32 drives, but it will not compress them.

♦ Windows 98 does not include a utility for converting a drive back to FAT16 after it is converted to FAT32.

All that being said, you should know that converting a drive to FAT32 is a safe operation.

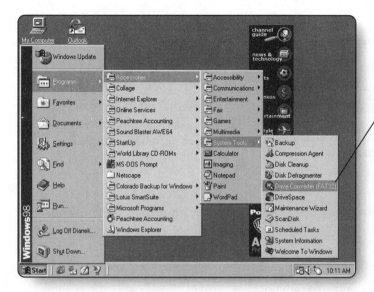

1. **Follow steps 1** through **4** in "Backing Up Your Work." The System Tools submenu will appear.

2. **Click** on **Drive Converter (FAT32)**. The Drive Converter (FAT32) Wizard will appear.

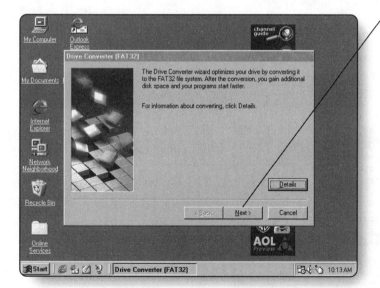

3. **Click** on **Next**. You will continue to the next screen.

4. **Click** on the **disk drive** you want to convert. It will be selected.

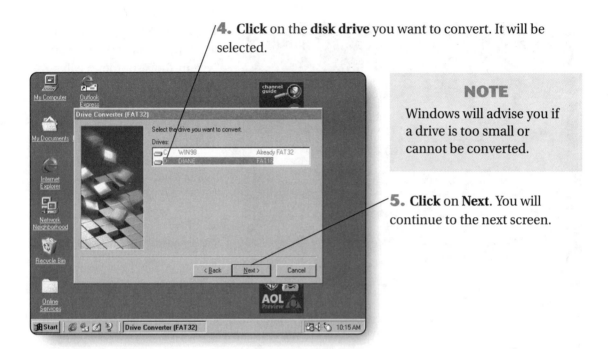

5. **Click** on **Next**. You will continue to the next screen.

If you are running a previous version of DOS or Windows, a warning box opens stating that you will not be able to access a FAT32 drive while running those systems.

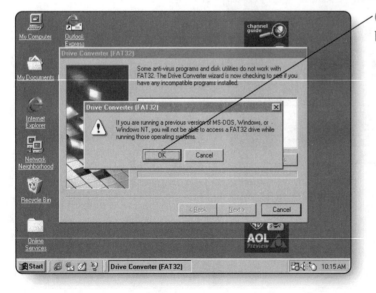

6. **Click** on **OK**. The warning box will close.

The Drive Converter Wizard will check for any antivirus programs or other utilities that do not work with FAT32. When it finishes checking, a message displays any programs found. If it does not find any conflicting programs, the Drive Converter Wizard advises you at the bottom of the dialog box that it didn't find any incompatible programs.

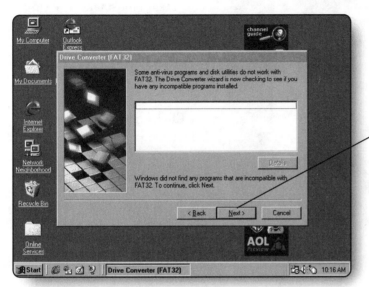

7. **Click** on **Next**. You will continue to the next screen. At this point you will be offered the opportunity to back up your hard drive before conversion. If you have not already done so, this is the time.

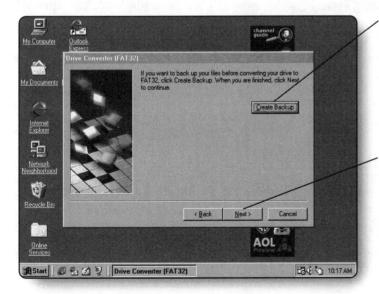

8a. **Click** on **Create Backup**. The Microsoft Backup Wizard will open. When the backup is complete, you will return to the Drive Converter Wizard.

OR

8b. **Click** on **Next**. You will continue to the next screen.

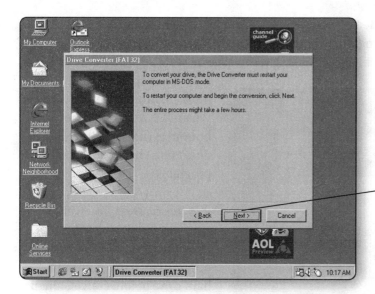

The Drive Converter Wizard is now ready to begin the conversion process. The actual conversion must take place in DOS mode, so the Drive Converter Wizard will restart your computer and begin the conversion process.

9. **Click** on **Next**. The conversion process will begin.

TIP

Do not interrupt the process once it has begun. Doing so could result in a loss of data.

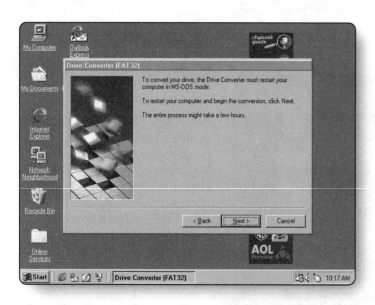

From here on, the computer takes over. It will restart in DOS mode and run ScanDisk. After that, the machine will restart. It may appear to be stopped. Leave it alone. It will eventually load Windows 98. The Drive Converter window will reappear and advise you that the conversion was successful.

10. **Click** on **OK** to acknowledge the message box. The Drive Converter Wizard will close.

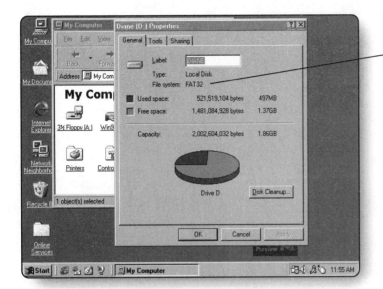

To make sure your drive did convert to FAT32, open My Computer, and right-click on the drive you converted. Click on Properties, and then on the General tab. Next to File system: FAT32 will be displayed.

12 Organizing Files and Folders

The process of organizing files has quite a history. First there was the DOS DIR command with all its switches and syntax. Later came File Manager and when Windows 95 came along, so did the Windows Explorer. Each upgrade was simpler than the previous. Windows 98 has taken this to heart again. Explorer is still here in Windows 98, but has become more powerful then ever. In this chapter, you'll learn how to:

✦ Look at Explorer

✦ Change the look of Explorer

✦ Create a new folder

✦ Move or copy a file or folder

✦ Delete and rename a file or folder

LOOKING IN THE EXPLORER WINDOW

The Windows 98 Explorer is a graphic illustration of the file and folder contents of the storage devices on or connected to your computer.

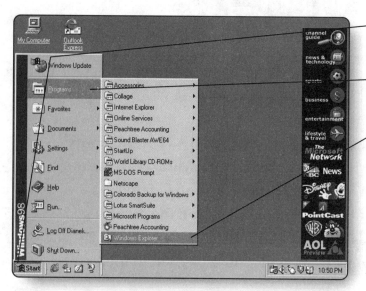

1. **Click** on the **Start button**. The Start menu will appear.

2. **Click** on **Programs**. The Programs submenu will appear.

3. **Click** on **Windows Explorer**. The Explorer window will appear.

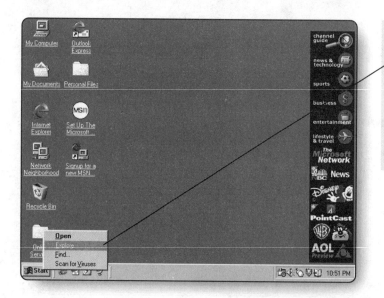

TIP

A quick way to open Explorer is to right-click on the Start button, and then click on Explore from the shortcut menu that appears.

Identifying Explorer Components

An assortment of information is displayed in the Explorer window, including the:

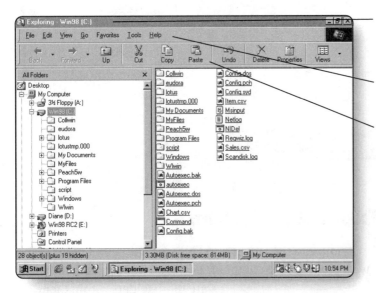

◆ **Title bar**. Contains the title of the current drive or folder being displayed.

◆ **Menu bar**. Contains Explorer's drop-down menus.

◆ **Toolbar**. Contains shortcuts to commonly-used menu choices.

NOTE

Your Explorer window may not display all the elements listed in this section. You'll learn how to change the look of the Explorer in the next section.

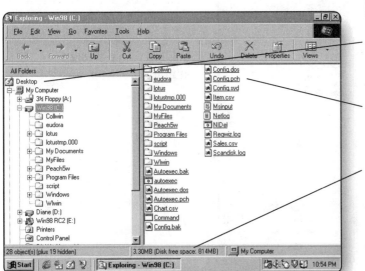

◆ **Drives and Folders section**. Displays available drives and folders on your computer.

◆ **Files and Documents section**. Displays the contents of the selected drive or folder.

◆ **Status bar**. Displays such information as the number and size of selected files.

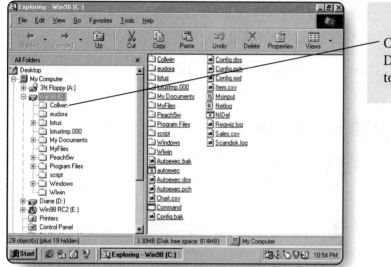

Expanding Folders

You'll notice in the Drives and Folders section that many items have a plus sign next to them. This is an indication that there are more folders within them. It's like a tree with its branches, each one expanding off the main branch.

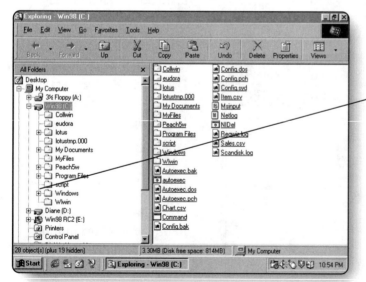

1. **Click** on a **plus sign** (+). Subfolders will appear.

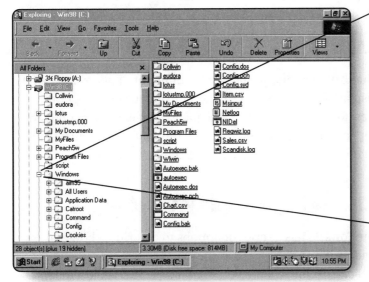

Notice that the plus sign changes to a minus sign. This indicates the folder is already expanded.

NOTE

Some subfolders may have other subfolders. Again this is indicated with a plus sign.

2. Click on the **minus sign (–)**. The subfolder will collapse and a plus sign will reappear.

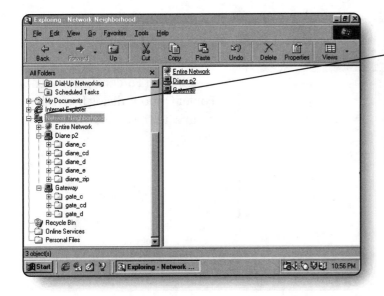

TIP

Click on the Network Neighborhood icon from the Drives and Folders section to view the contents of folders on another computer.

CHANGING THE LOOK OF EXPLORER

The Explorer window has several different toolbars that can be displayed. Toolbars make it easier to get to your programs, files, folders, and favorite Web pages. You can also modify the appearance of some toolbars and the way the contents of files and folders are displayed in the Explorer window.

Changing Display Options

Windows 98 has a series of options to determine how and what you want displayed in the Explorer window. From here, you can decide whether a file should be accessible with a single- or double-click, which type of files to display, and whether the filenames should display an extension.

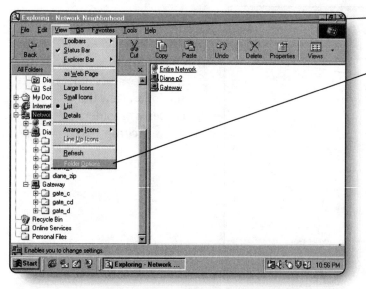

1. **Click** on **View**. The View menu will appear.

2. **Click** on **Folder Options**. The Folder Options dialog box will open with the General tab displayed.

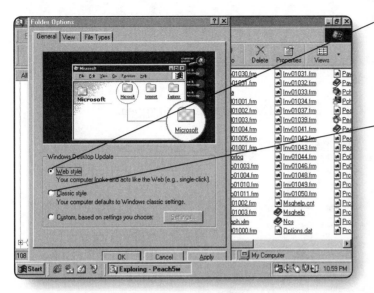

3a. **Click** on **Web style** for single-click. The option will be selected.

OR

3b. **Click** on **Classic style** for double-click. The option will be selected.

4. **Click** on the **View tab**. More display options, including showing file extensions in Explorer, will appear.

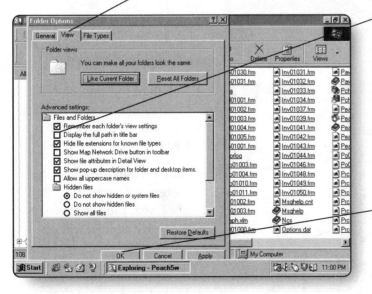

5. **Click** on any **unchecked option** to select the option. A ✔ will appear in the check box.

NOTE
Clicking on an option with a ✔ already displayed turns off the selected feature.

6. **Click** on **OK**. The Folder Options dialog box will close, and the view will change to your specifications.

Displaying Toolbars

To display or turn off the display of toolbars, look in the View menu.

1. Click on **View**. The View menu will appear.

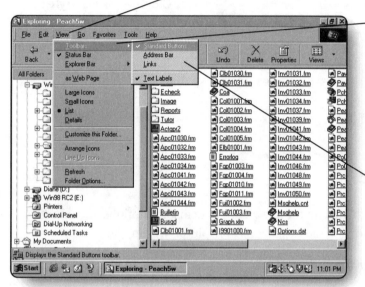

2. Click on **Toolbars**. The Toolbars submenu will appear.

TIP

A ✔ beside an item indicates the choice is active.

3. Click on any desired **toolbar**. The Toolbars submenu will close, and the toolbar will appear onscreen.

You can choose from one or several of the four types of toolbars to be displayed.

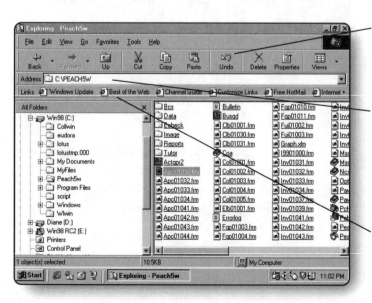

✦ **Standard Buttons**. Shows toolbar buttons such as Back, Forward, Cut, Copy, and Paste.

✦ **Address Bar**. Indicates the current folder being displayed. You can also type a Web page address without opening Internet Explorer first.

✦ **Links Bar**. Provides shortcuts to important Web sites.

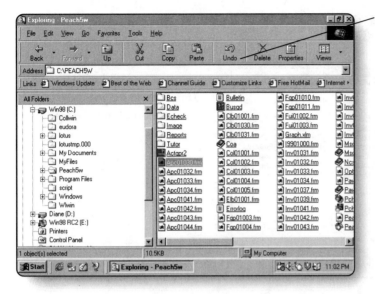

♦ **Text Labels**. Not actually a toolbar, but works in combination with the Standard Buttons toolbar to be a little more descriptive.

4. Repeat steps 1 through **3** to display any additional toolbars.

NOTE

Choosing a toolbar with a ✔ beside it will remove the ✔ and turn off that toolbar.

Changing the Way Files Are Displayed

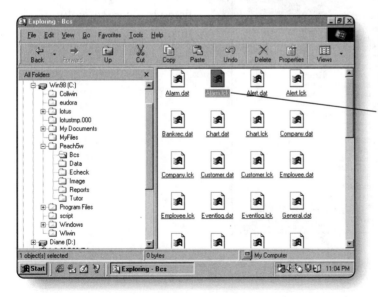

There are four different perspectives of looking at your files in the Files and Documents section:

♦ **Large Icons view**. Shows the filename and optional extension beneath a large, easy-to-see icon associated with the file. Files are listed in a horizontal multiple-column format.

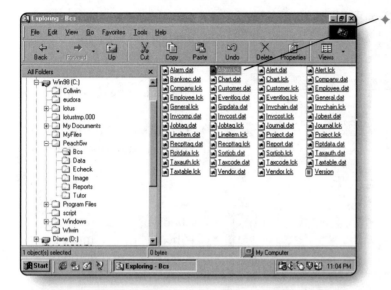

✦ **Small Icons view**. Shows the filename and optional extension beside a smaller icon associated with the file. Files are listed in a horizontal multiple-column format.

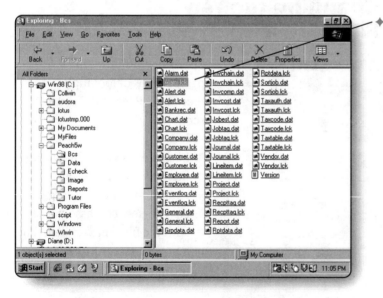

✦ **List view**. Similar to Small Icon View, but the files are listed in a vertical-column format.

♦ **Detail view**. Displays more information about the files, including the size, type, last modification date, and optionally, the attributes of the file. Files are listed in a vertical single-column format.

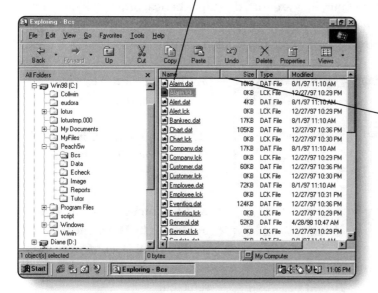

1. Click on **View**. The View menu will appear.

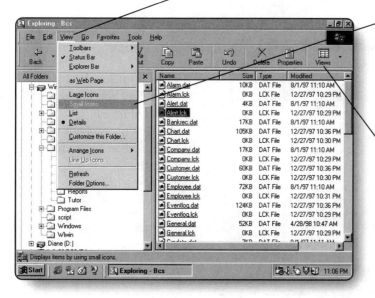

2. Click on **Large Icons**, **Small Icons**, **List,** or **Details**. The Files and Document section will change to the selected view.

Sorting Files

By default, files are sorted in alphabetical order by filename. You can also sort them by name, type, size, or date. Headings are displayed at the top of each column.

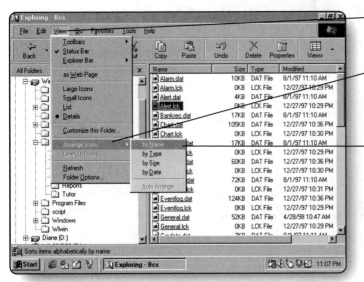

1. **Click** on **View**. The View menu will appear.

2. **Click** on **Arrange Icons**. The Arrange Icons submenu will appear.

3. **Click** on **by Name**, **by Type**, **by Size,** or **by Date**. The files in the Files and Document section will display in the order you selected.

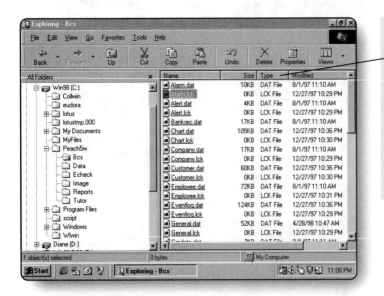

TIP

If you are in Details view, click on any heading to sort by that column in ascending order. Click on the same heading again to sort by that column in descending order.

CREATING A NEW FOLDER

Most folders are created by programs that are added to your computer. For organizational purposes, it's nice to have your own folders to separate your data. For example, most Windows 98 programs store the data files you create in a folder called *My Documents*. It might be handy to have folders in the My Documents folder to separate memos from proposals.

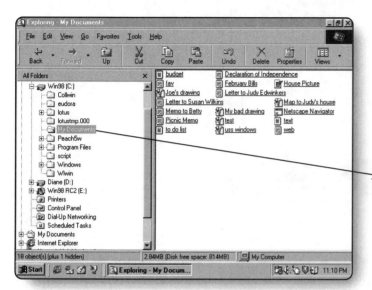

1. **Click** on the **drive** or **folder** in which you want to create a subfolder. The folder will open and its contents will appear.

2. Click on **File**. The File menu will appear.

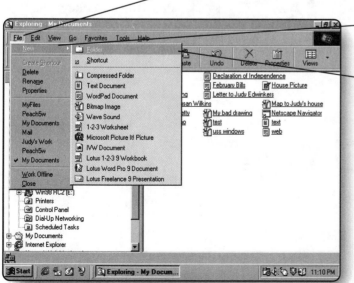

3. Click on **New**. The New submenu will appear.

4. Click on **Folder**. A new folder will appear in the Files and Documents section.

TIP

Another method to create a new folder is to right-click in the Files and Documents section and choose New, and then Folder.

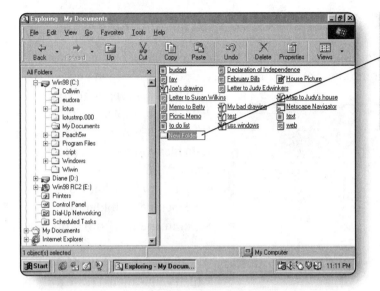

NOTE

New folders always appear at the bottom of the list of files, but will be placed in order at a later time.

5. **Type** a **name** for the new folder. The words "New Folder" will be replaced with the name you type.

6. **Press** the **Enter key**. The new folder and its name will be accepted and displayed.

MOVING OR COPYING FILES AND FOLDERS

Files or folders can be moved or copied from one location to another. For example, you can copy a file from your hard drive to a floppy disk. Or you can move a file you've been working on to a network drive. Whether you are working with a file or a folder, the steps are the same. However, if you move or copy a folder, all the contents of that folder will be moved or copied as well. In addition, if the folder contains subfolders, the directory structure will also be moved or copied to the new location.

1. **Display** the **Standard Button toolbar,** if it is not already displayed.

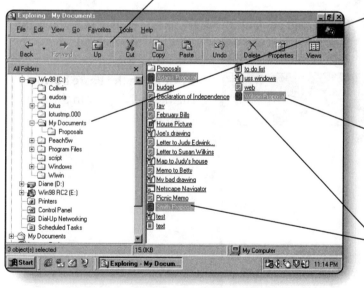

2. **Open** the **drive** and **folder** that has the file or folder you want to move or copy. The file or folder will appear on the right side of the screen.

3. **Click** on the **item** to be moved or copied. The item will be selected.

TIP

You can select multiple items to be moved or copied by holding down the Ctrl key while selecting additional items. Release the Ctrl key when you are finished selecting items.

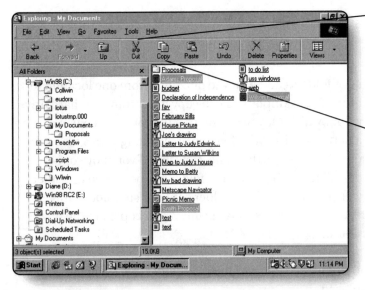

4a. **Click** on the **Cut button**, if you want to move the selected item. The item will be deleted from the original location.

OR

4b. **Click** on the **Copy button**, if you want to copy the selected item. The item will remain in its original location.

5. **Locate** and **click** on the **drive** or **folder** in which you want to place the file. The drive or folder will be selected.

6. **Click** on the **Paste button**. The file will appear in the new location.

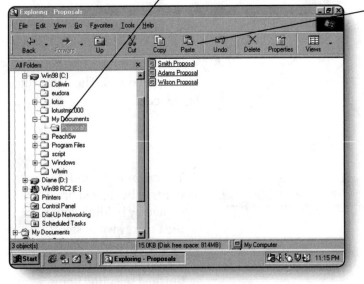

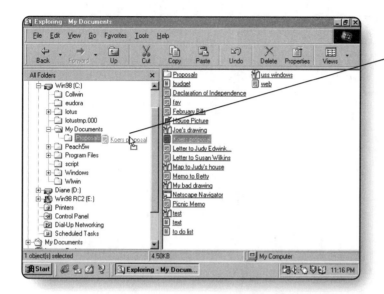

TIP

Another way to move a file
to a new folder is to drag
the selected file until it is
on top of the new folder.

DELETING FILES
AND FOLDERS

Use the Windows 98 Explorer for an easy way to delete
old files.

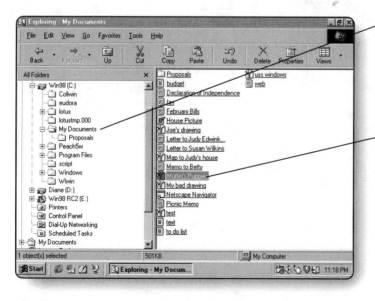

1. **Open** the **drive** and **folder**
that has the file or folder you
want to delete. The file or folder
will appear on the right side of
the screen.

2. **Position** the **mouse pointer**
over the file or folder you want
to delete. The filename will be
selected.

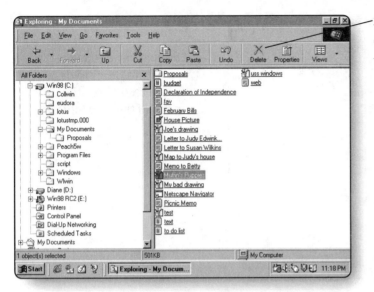

3. **Click** on the **Delete button**. A Confirm File Delete dialog box will open.

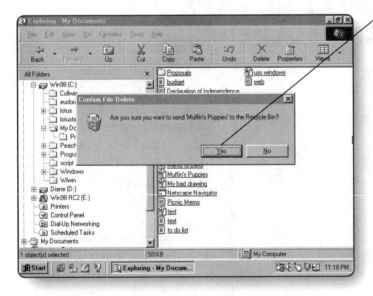

4. **Click** on **Yes**. The file will be deleted from its folder and placed in the Recycle Bin.

NOTE

If you are deleting a file from a floppy disk, it will *not* be placed in the Recycle Bin. It will be permanently deleted.

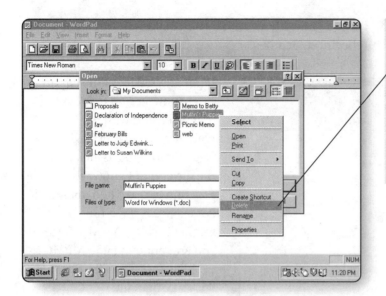

TIP

You can also delete a file from any Open or Save As dialog box in a Windows 98 program by right-clicking on the filename and choosing Delete. A confirmation message will appear.

RENAMING FILES AND FOLDERS

If you have incorrectly named a file, you can easily rename it using the Windows Explorer.

1. Open the **drive** and **folder** that has the file or folder you want to rename. The file or folder will appear on the right side of the screen.

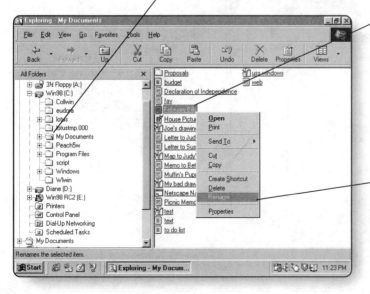

2. Position the **mouse pointer** over the file or folder you want to rename. The filename will be selected.

3. Right-click on the **file** or **folder**. A shortcut menu will appear.

4. Click on **Rename**. The filename will remain selected and a blinking insertion point will appear at the end of the filename.

5. Type the **new filename**. The old filename will be replaced with the new filename.

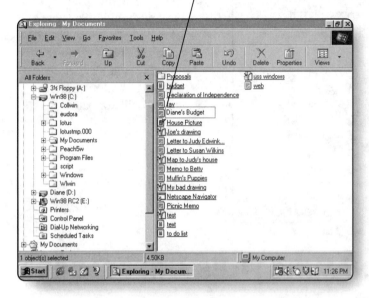

If the original filename has an extension, be sure to include that extension with the new filename. If you don't, Windows 98 could lose the association of the file and not know which program to use when opening it. For example, if the file was originally called MYMEMO and you are renaming it to MEMO TO BOB SMITH, that's fine; but if it was originally MYMEMO.DOC, you should rename it to MEMO TO BOB SMITH.DOC.

6. Press the **Enter key**. Your changes will be accepted.

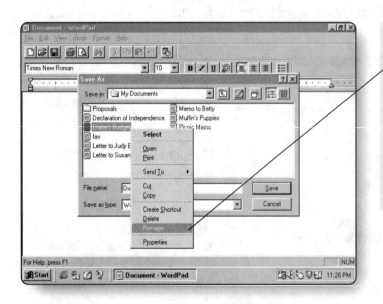

TIP

You can also rename a file from any Open or Save As dialog box in a Windows 98 program by selecting the filename, right-clicking on the file, and clicking on Rename from the shortcut menu.

13 Finding Files, Folders, and People

Programs and documents sometimes get buried quite deep in the directory structure of your hard drive. To work efficiently you should know how to find files on your computer. With the Windows 98 Explorer you can let your computer do all the searching for you, whether you're trying to locate a specific file, a group of files, or even a name from the Windows 98 Address Book. In this chapter, you'll learn how to:

✦ **Find a file or folder**

✦ **Look for a file by date**

✦ **Search for a name in the Address Book**

FINDING A FILE

Windows 98 has a powerful tool called the *Find feature* to help you find those misplaced files and folders.

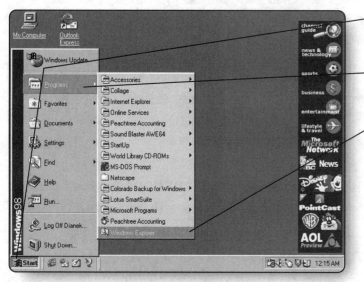

1. **Click** on the **Start button**. The Start menu will appear.

2. **Click** on **Programs**. The Programs submenu will appear.

3. **Click** on **Windows Explorer**. The Explorer window will appear.

4. **Click** on **Tools**. The Tools menu will appear.

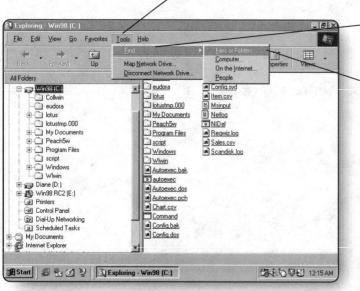

5. **Click** on **Find**. The Find submenu will appear.

6. **Click** on **Files or Folders**. The Find: All Files window will appear.

From the Name & Location tab, you can search for a file (or folder) based on the name of the file or the contents in the file. For example, you can look for a file with the word "bear" in the title or for a document with the word "bear" in its contents. If you search for the word "bear" in the body text, Windows 98 will also list any documents with "bear" in the title.

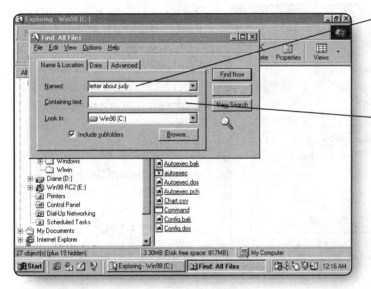

7a. **Type** any or all of the missing **filename** or **folder name** in the Named: list box.

OR

7b. **Type** the requested **word** or **phrase** in the Containing text: text box.

NOTE

If you type multiple words in the Named: list box, Windows 98 will find all files that have any of those words in the filename. If you know the exact filename, enclose it in quotation marks.

8. **Click** on the **down arrow (▼)** next to the Look in: list box, and **click** on a **drive** or **folder**.

9. **Click** on **Find Now**. The search will begin.

NOTE

If you are searching in the body of the document, the search may be quite lengthy depending on how many files are stored on the searched drive or folder.

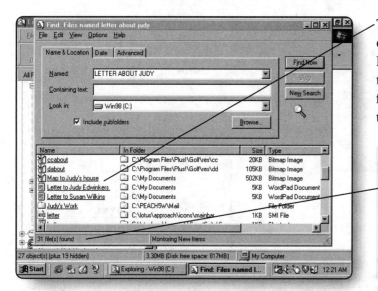

The results of the search will be displayed at the bottom of the Find: Files window. The name of the file will be listed as well as its folder location, size, type, and the date it was last modified.

NOTE

The bottom of the Find: Files window indicates the total number of files found that match the search criteria.

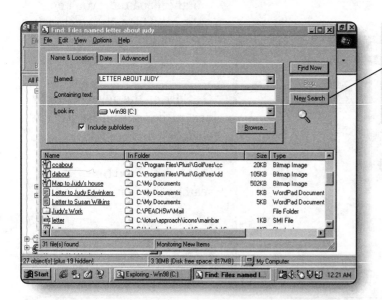

TIP

Click on New Search to remove any previous search conditions.

LOOKING FOR A FILE BY DATE

You can also find files based on the date they were created or even by the last time you modified a file. For example, you might need to find a file you worked on last week. Let Windows 98 do the work for you!

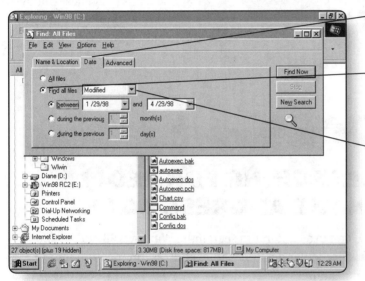

1. Click on the **Date tab**. The Date tab will move to the front.

2. Click on the **Find all files option button**. The Find all files list box will become available.

3. Click on **Modified, Created,** or **Last Accessed** from the Find all files list box.

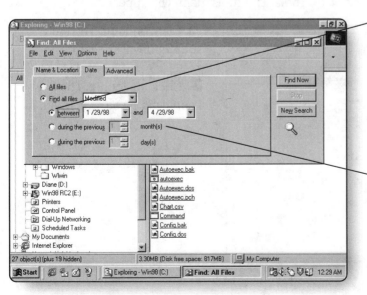

4. Click on a **time frame** to search. There are three types of time frames you can specify: Specific dates (for example, June 3rd through July 16th), during previous months, or during previous days.

5. Type a **specific amount of time** to search.

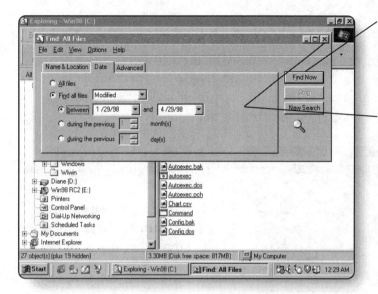

6. Click on **Find Now**. The search will begin, and the results will be displayed at the bottom of the Find: All Files window.

7. Click on the **Close button** (⊠). The Find: All Files window will close, and you will return to the Explorer window.

SEARCHING FOR PEOPLE IN THE ADDRESS BOOK

You can use Explorer to search the Windows 98 Address Book for a particular person's name, address, phone numbers, or e-mail addresses.

1. Click on **Tools**. The Tools menu will appear.

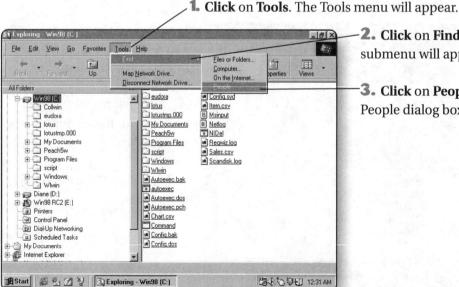

2. Click on **Find**. The Find submenu will appear.

3. Click on **People**. The Find People dialog box will open.

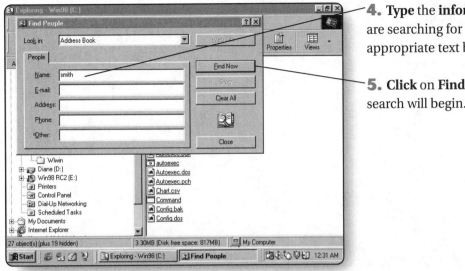

4. **Type** the **information** you are searching for in the appropriate text boxes.

5. **Click** on **Find Now**. The search will begin.

The Find People dialog box expands and any Address Book entries that match the requested criteria will be displayed at the bottom.

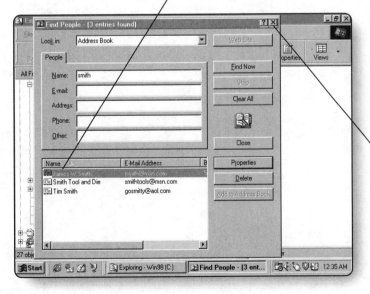

TIP

Double-click on a name to see the entire Address Book entry.

6. **Click** on the **Close button** (⊠). The Find People dialog box will close, and you will return to the Explorer window.

7. **Click** on the **Close button** (X). The Explorer program will close.

14 Discovering Multimedia

One of the most exciting reasons to use a computer today is multimedia. Multimedia is the capability of a computer application to combine with other media, such as video or sound. In this chapter, you'll learn how to:

✦ Play a music CD

✦ Adjust the volume

✦ Use the Media Player

✦ Add a media clip to a document

PLAYING A MUSIC CD

You can place your favorite music CD into the computer and listen while you work! Many computers have a feature called *AutoPlay*. As soon as you insert the CD into the CD-ROM drive, the CD Player appears and the music begins playing. If your computer does not have AutoPlay, you can start the CD Player yourself.

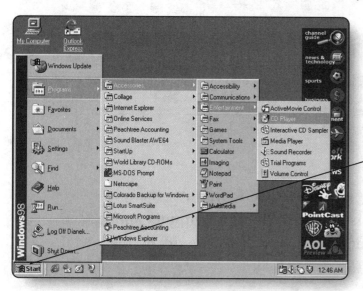

1. **Click** on the **Start button**. The Start menu will appear.

2. **Click** on **Programs**. The Programs submenu will appear.

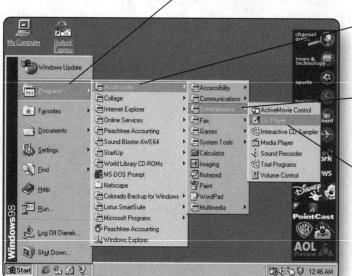

3. **Click** on **Accessories**. The Accessories submenu will appear.

4. **Click** on **Entertainment**. The Entertainment submenu will appear.

5. **Click** on **CD Player**. The CD Player window will appear.

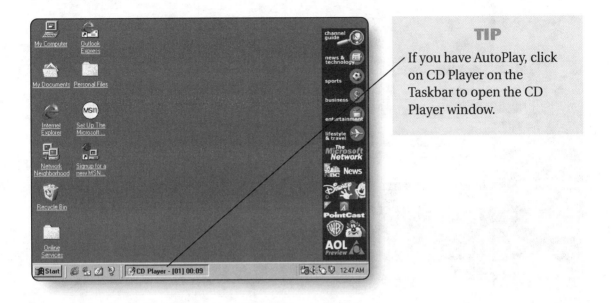

TIP

If you have AutoPlay, click on CD Player on the Taskbar to open the CD Player window.

The CD Player window has many of the same buttons that are on a standard CD player.

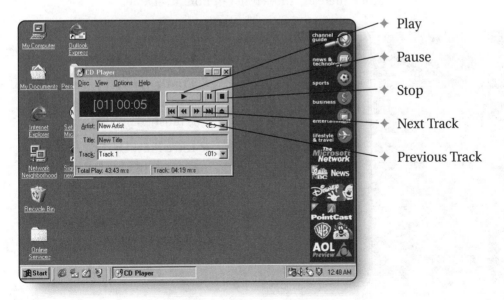

◆ Play

◆ Pause

◆ Stop

◆ Next Track

◆ Previous Track

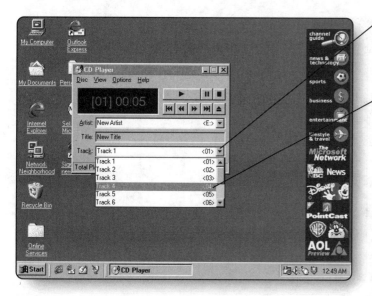

6. **Click** on the **down arrow (▼)** next to the Track: list box. A list of available tracks will appear.

7. **Click** on the **track** you want to play. The song will start playing.

8. **Click** on **Options**. The Options menu will appear.

In addition to the standard play of the CD tracks in numerical order, there are three other options available.

✦ **Random Order**. The tracks will play in a random order.

✦ **Continuous Play**. The CD will start over when the last track is finished playing.

✦ **Intro Play**. The first 10 seconds of each track will play.

9. **Click** on any desired **options**. A ✔ will appear beside each selected item.

TIP

Repeat steps 8 and 9 to deselect any of the options.

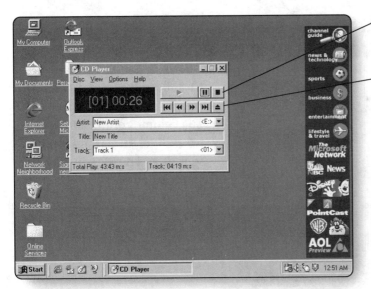

10. **Click** on **Stop**. The CD player will stop.

11. **Click** on **Eject**. The CD will be ejected from the CD-ROM drive.

12. **Click** on the **Close button** (☒). The CD Player will close.

TIP

You can also play a CD by opening My Computer, and then right-clicking on the CD drive and choosing Play.

USING THE VOLUME CONTROL

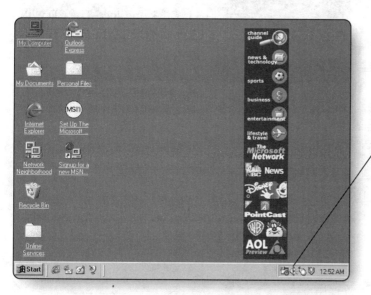

It's almost like having a remote control right at your fingertips! The volume control allows you to set different settings for the sounds and music you play on your computer.

1. **Click** on the **speaker icon** in the System Tray. The Volume slider will appear.

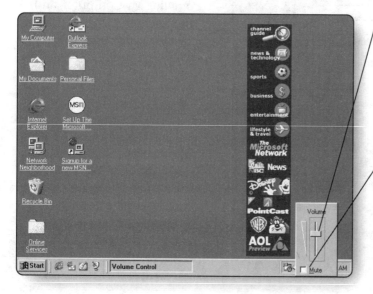

2. **Click** and **drag** the **Volume slider** up or down with the mouse to control the overall volume level.

TIP

Click on Mute to mute all speaker volume.

3. **Click anywhere** on the **desktop**. The Volume slider will close.

4. **Double-click** on the **speaker** in the System Tray. The Volume Control window will appear.

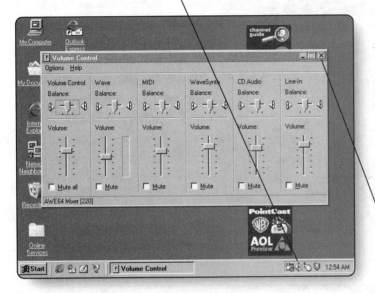

The Volume Control window allows you to balance and adjust other mixer properties as well as the volume. The options available in the Volume Control window will vary with different sound cards installed.

5. **Adjust** any desired **settings**.

6. **Click** on the **Close button** ([×]). The Volume Control window will close.

USING THE MEDIA PLAYER

Windows 98 and the Media Player can make beautiful music together. The Media Player can play several types of sound or video files.

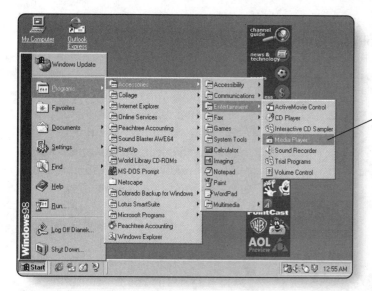

1. **Follow steps 1** through **4** in "Playing a Music CD." The Entertainment submenu will appear.

2. **Click** on **Media Player**. The Media Player window will appear.

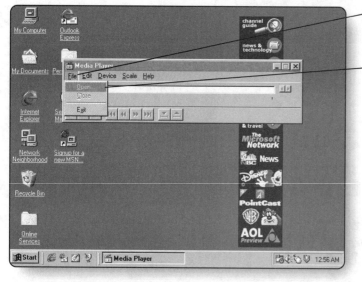

3. **Click** on **File**. The File menu will appear.

4. **Click** on **Open**. The Open dialog box will open.

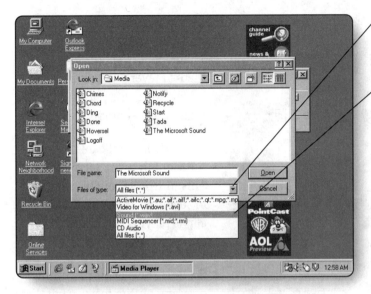

5. Click on the **down arrow (▼)** next to the Files of type: list box. A list of file formats will appear.

6. Click on the **file format** for which you are looking.

Some of the file formats that the Media Player can work with include:

✦ **WAV**. Windows Audio Visual. A file format made of digitally-recorded sounds. The sounds are stored as waveforms.

✦ **MIDI**. Musical Instrument Digital Interface. A standard format used for creating, recording, and playing back music. With MIDI, computers, synthesizers, and other equipment can communicate with each other.

✦ **MPEG**. Moving Pictures Expert Group. A standard format for audio and video compression.

✦ **AVI**. Audio Video Interleaved. A multimedia format for sound and moving pictures.

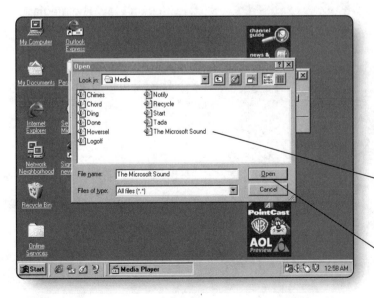

7. Locate and **click** on the **sound** or **video file** you want to play.

8. Click on **Open**. The media file will open.

The media filename appears at the top of the Media Player.

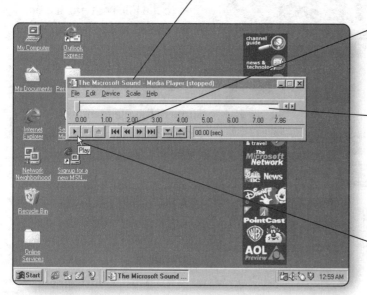

There are lots of buttons on the Media Player window. It's very much like a tape player you might have at home.

The slide bar indicates the total time length of the media clip. This time is generally measured in seconds. As the multimedia clip is playing, the slide bar moves to indicate its progress.

9. Position the **mouse pointer** over any button to see what that particular button does.

NOTE

If the clip is a video file, a video window will appear.

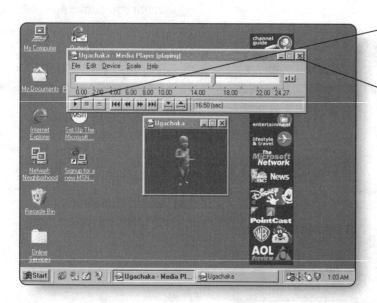

10. Click on **Play**. The media clip will start to play.

11. Click on the **Close button** (×). The Media Player will close.

ADDING A MEDIA CLIP TO A DOCUMENT

Today's applications, such as Word, WordPerfect, Excel, Lotus 1-2-3 and many others, have the capability to embed media files within documents. Adding sound or video to a file sent electronically can add additional pizzazz. The only limitation is that the person receiving the file must have multimedia capabilities (speakers and a sound card).

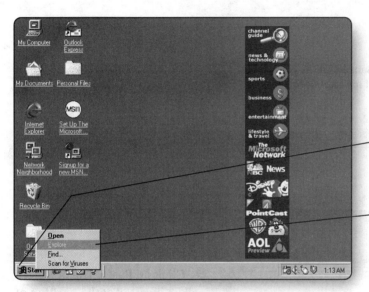

1. Right-click on the **Start button**. The Start shortcut menu will appear.

2. Click on **Explore**. The Explorer window will appear.

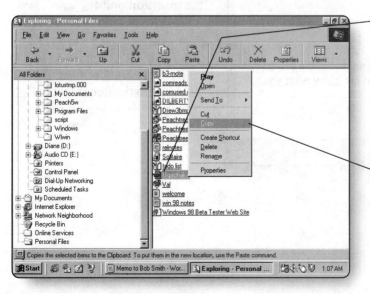

3. Click on the **media file** you want to place in the document. It will be selected.

4. Right-click on the **media file**. The Explorer shortcut menu will appear.

5. Click on **Copy**. The media file will be copied to the Windows Clipboard.

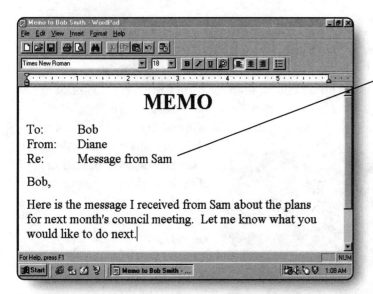

6. **Open** the **program** in which you want to place the media file.

7. **Open** the **document** or **create** any **text** you want to appear in the document.

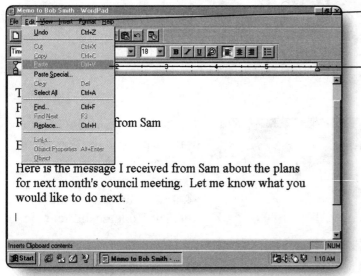

8. **Click** on **Edit**. The Edit menu will appear.

9. **Click** on **Paste**. The object will be inserted at the position of the insertion point.

NOTE

The appearance of the object in the document will vary between applications.

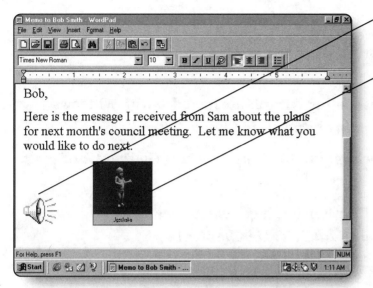

A sound clip inserted into a document.

A video clip inserted into a document.

TIP

Double-click on a media clip to play it.

PART III REVIEW QUESTIONS

1. How many Troubleshooting Wizards are included with Windows 98? *See "Troubleshooting Wizards" in Chapter 10*

2. Why should you backup your files? *See "Backing Up Your Work" in Chapter 11*

3. What happens to a file when it is fragmented? *See "Defragmenting Your Hard Drive" in Chapter 11*

4. What kind of a disk should you create before you run the FAT32 converter? *See "Converting to FAT32" in Chapter 11*

5. How can you tell if your drive is FAT32? *See "Converting to FAT32"in Chapter 11*

6. What program is a graphic illustration of the files and folder contents of your computer? *See "Looking in the Explorer Window" in Chapter 12*

7. Where do you go to make your folders and icons accessible with a single-click instead of a double-click? *See "Changing Display Options" in Chapter 12*

8. What type of information is displayed when you show your files in Detail view? *See "Changing the Way Files Are Displayed" in Chapter 12*

9. When a file is deleted, where is it placed? *See "Deleting Files and Folders" in Chapter 12*

10. What does "intro play" do in the CD Player? *See "Playing a Music CD" in Chapter 14*

PART IV

Customizing Windows 98

15 Customizing the Desktop

As you've noticed, there are lots of different items on the Windows 98 desktop. In Chapter 2, you took a brief look at many of the desktop items, such as Network Neighborhood, My Computer, the Taskbar, and the System Tray. You'll find you will use the right mouse button quite a bit when working on the Windows 98 desktop. In this chapter, you'll learn how to:

✦ **Create new desktop folders**

✦ **Move and delete icons**

✦ **Work with the Recycle Bin**

✦ **Create a shortcut**

✦ **Rename an icon**

✦ **Edit the Start menu**

✦ **Customize the Taskbar**

CREATING A NEW FOLDER

Occasionally, you might want a folder to organize some of the shortcut icons that appear on the desktop.

1. **Position** the **mouse pointer** anywhere over a blank area of the desktop.

2. **Click** on the **right mouse button**. A shortcut menu will appear.

3. **Click** on **New**. The New submenu will appear.

4. **Click** on **Folder**. A new folder will appear on the desktop ready to be named.

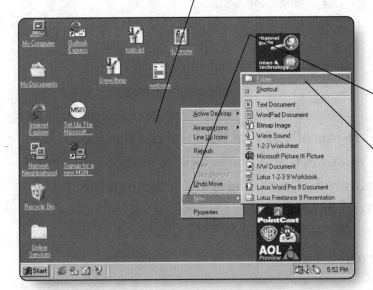

5. **Type** a **name** for the new folder. The words "New Folder" will be replaced with the text you type.

6. **Press** the **Enter key**. The folder will be ready to use.

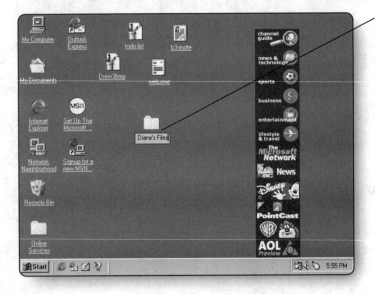

MOVING AND DELETING ICONS

Icons appear all over the desktop—some you want and some you don't. Icons can be moved or deleted with a click of the mouse.

Moving an Icon

If you want to move an icon to a different location, a feature called *Auto Arrange* must be turned off. If Auto Arrange is activated, you can move an icon but it will pop right back into its previous location.

1. Position the **mouse pointer** anywhere over a blank area of the desktop.

2. Click on the **right mouse button**. A shortcut menu will appear.

3. Click on **Arrange Icons**. The Arrange Icons submenu will appear.

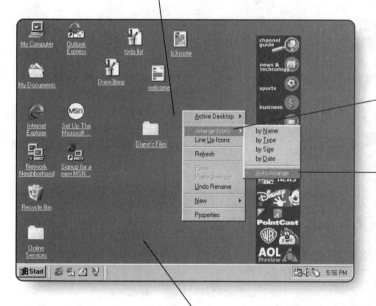

4a. Click on **Auto Arrange**, if there is a ✔ already next to it. The feature will be deactivated and the shortcut menu will close.

OR

4b. Click anywhere on the **desktop**, if no ✔ appears next to Auto Arrange. The shortcut menu will close with no changes made.

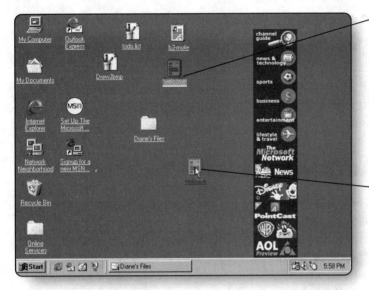

5. **Position** the **mouse pointer** over the icon to be moved. The icon will be selected.

6. **Press** and **hold** the **mouse button** as you move the mouse. The icon will move with the mouse.

7. **Release** the **mouse button**. The icon will remain in the new location.

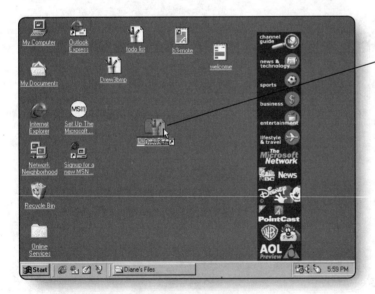

Deleting an Icon

The only icons you cannot delete on the desktop are My Computer, Network Neighborhood, and Recycle Bin.

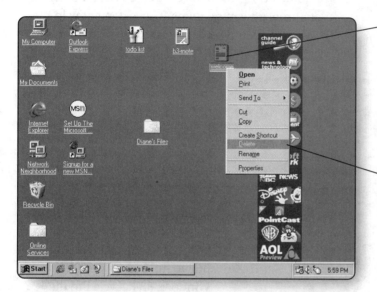

1. **Position** the **mouse pointer** over the icon to be deleted. The icon will be selected.

2. **Click** on the **right mouse button**. A shortcut menu will appear.

3. **Click** on **Delete**. The Confirm File Delete dialog box will open.

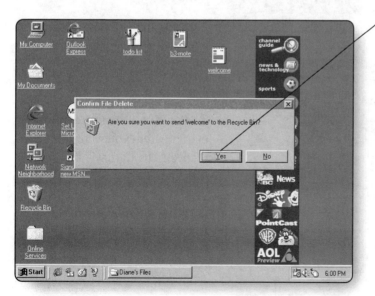

4. **Click** on **Yes**. The icon will be deleted and placed in the Recycle Bin.

TIP

An optional method of deleting files or icons is to drag them directly to the Recycle Bin.

NOTE

When the Recycle Bin is empty, the wastebasket icon looks empty. When the Recycle Bin has items in it, pieces of paper stick out the top of the wastebasket.

WORKING WITH THE RECYCLE BIN

At home or work you have a wastebasket into which you throw unwanted items. Those items stay in the wastebasket until someone actually takes them out. It's the same with the Windows 98 Recycle Bin. It's an area to temporarily hold unwanted items.

Recovering an Item from the Recycle Bin

At home or work, if you want to recover an item from the wastebasket you can reach in and pull it out. You work with the Windows 98 Recycle Bin the same way.

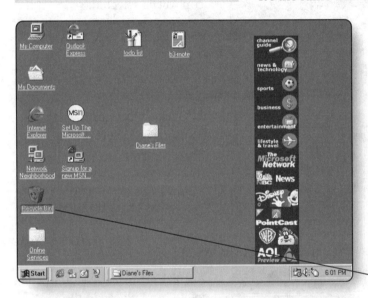

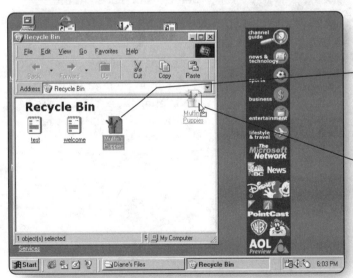

1. **Click** on the **Recycle Bin icon**. The Recycle Bin window will appear, displaying the contents of the Recycle Bin.

2. **Position** the **mouse pointer** over the item you want to recover. The item will be selected.

3. **Drag** the **item** out of the Recycle Bin window and on to the desktop.

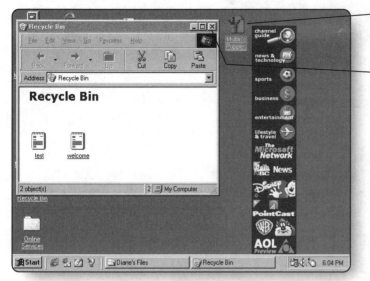

4. **Release** the **mouse button**. The item will be recovered.

5. **Click** on the **Close button** (☒). The Recycle Bin window will close.

Emptying the Recycle Bin

Items stored in the Recycle Bin are using disk space on your computer. It's a good idea to periodically empty the Recycle Bin just like you would periodically empty your wastebasket at home. Be aware though that once the Recycle Bin has been emptied, the items that were in it are permanently deleted.

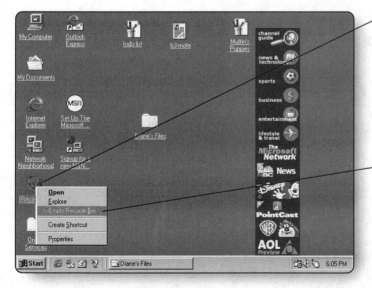

1. **Position** the **mouse pointer** over the Recycle Bin. The Recycle Bin icon will be selected.

2. **Click** on the **right mouse button** on top of the icon. A shortcut menu will appear.

3. **Click** on **Empty Recycle Bin**. A confirmation message will open.

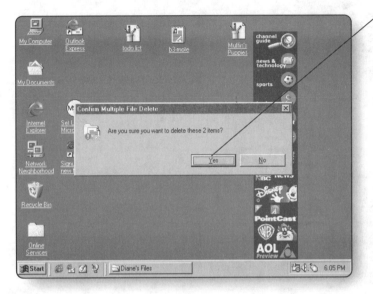

4. **Click** on **Yes** to confirm the deletion. The Recycle Bin will now be empty.

CREATING A SHORTCUT

It can be an annoyance to dig through the profusion of selections on the Start menu just to get to your favorite program. You can create a shortcut to a program or for a document that you use frequently. When you click on a shortcut for a document, Windows 98 will open the creating program and that specific file for you.

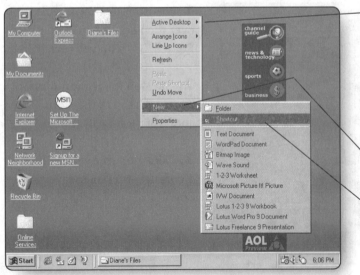

1. **Position** the **mouse pointer** over a blank area of the Windows 98 desktop.

2. **Click** on the **right mouse button**. A shortcut menu will appear.

3. **Click** on **New**. The New submenu will appear.

4. **Click** on **Shortcut**. The Create Shortcut dialog box will open.

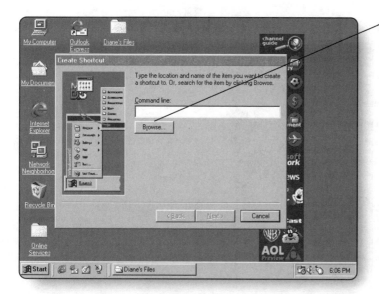

5. **Click** on **Browse**. The Browse dialog box will open.

6. **Locate** the **folder** that has the program or document to which you want to create a shortcut. A list of all available programs in that folder will appear.

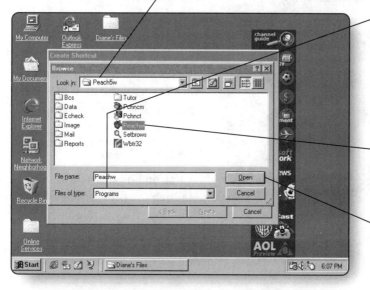

If you are looking for a document and not a program, change the Files of type: list box to All Files instead of Programs. You will then see documents as well as programs.

7. **Click** on the **desired program** or **document**. The item will be selected.

8. **Click** on **Open**. The Browse dialog box will close, and the program or document name (including the location) will appear in the Create Shortcut dialog box.

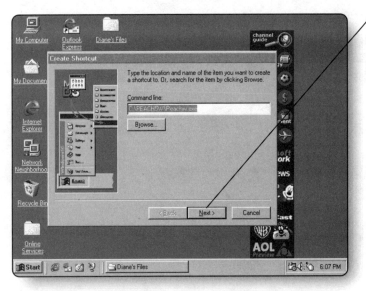

9. **Click** on **Next**. The Select a Title for the Program dialog box will open.

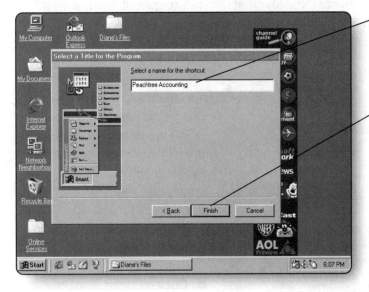

10. **Type** a **new name** for the icon, if desired. This only represents what you see on the desktop, not the actual filename.

11. **Click** on **Finish**. The Select a Title for the Program dialog box will close, and the new shortcut will appear on your desktop.

TIP

Click on any shortcut to launch the program and/or document associated with it.

Changing an Icon

TIP

Shortcuts can be identified by a small arrow in the lower left corner of the shortcut icon.

Shortcuts that you create have icons associated with them. If you've created a shortcut to a document, the icon used is the one associated with the document's program icon. You can select from other icons.

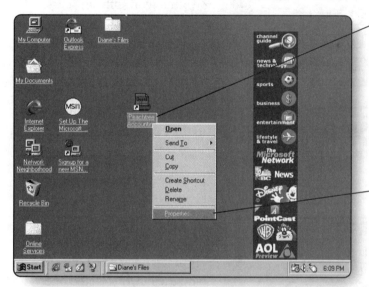

1. Position the **mouse pointer** over the icon you want to change. The icon will be selected.

2. Click on the **right mouse button**. A shortcut menu will appear.

3. Click on **Properties**. The Properties dialog box will open.

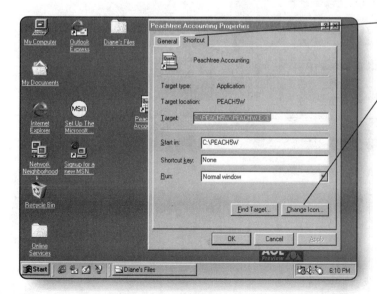

4. Click on the **Shortcut tab**, if necessary. The Shortcut tab will move to the front.

5. Click on **Change Icon**. The Change Icon dialog box will open.

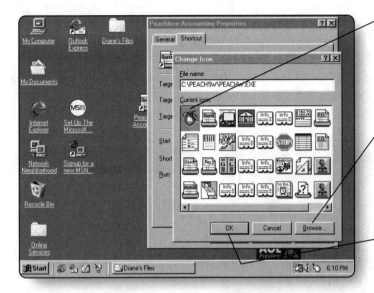

6. Click on the **icon** you want to use. The icon will be selected.

7. Click on **OK**. You will return to the Properties dialog box.

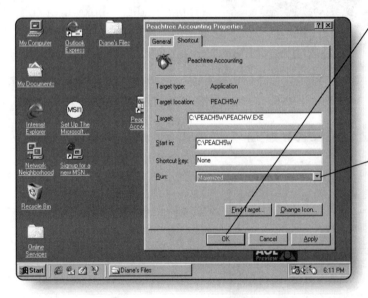

8. Click on **OK**. The Properties dialog box will close, and the current icon will be replaced with the newly selected one.

RENAMING AN ICON

You can rename any icon on your desktop except the Recycle Bin and the Set Up The Microsoft Network icons.

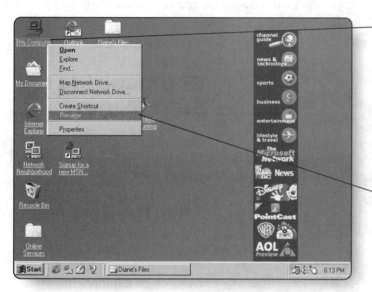

1. **Position** the **mouse pointer** over the icon you want to rename. The icon will be selected.

2. **Click** on the **right mouse button**. A shortcut menu will appear.

3. **Click** on **Rename**. The current icon name will be selected.

4. **Type** a **new name** for the icon. The current name will be replaced with the new name.

5. **Press** the **Enter key** to accept the change.

EDITING THE START MENU

If you look in Windows Explorer, in the Windows folder you will see another folder called *Start Menu*. The items you see when you click on the Start button are stored in this folder. You can control which items are accessible from the Start menu and in which order they are displayed.

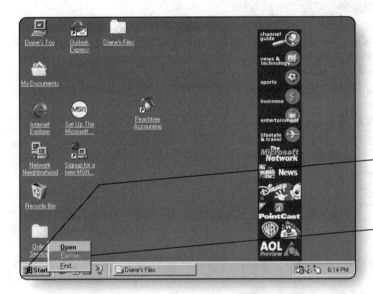

Reorganizing the Start Menu

You have the capability to easily reorganize the Start menu in Windows 98.

1. Right-click on the **Start button**. A shortcut menu will appear.

2. Click on **Explore**. The Explorer window will open at the Start Menu folder.

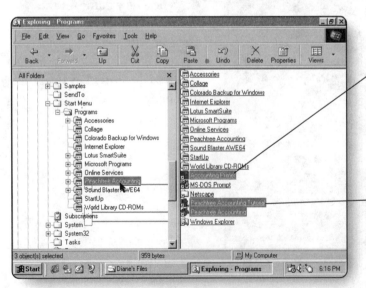

3. Navigate to the **shortcut** or **folder** you want to move.

4. Press and **hold** the **mouse button** on the item to be moved. The selected item will be highlighted.

TIP

Hold down the Ctrl key to select multiple items to move at the same time, or hold down the Shift key to select a consecutive list of items.

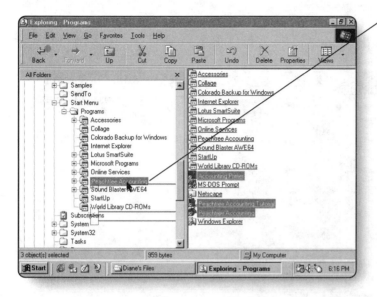

5. **Drag** the **item** to the new folder or location.

6. **Release** the **mouse button**. The selected item will drop into the new location.

7. **Click** on the **Close button** ([X]). Windows Explorer will close.

Adding an Item to the Start Menu

You can add a program shortcut or frequently-used document to the Start menu. There are several ways to accomplish this, but you'll use the easiest method.

1. **Click** on the **Start button**. The Start menu will appear.

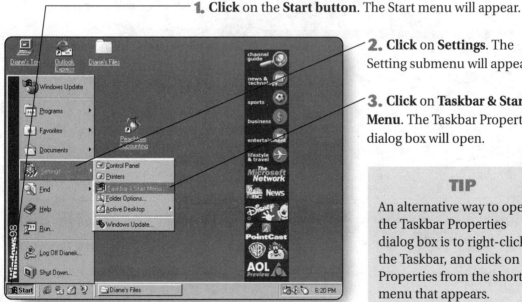

2. **Click** on **Settings**. The Setting submenu will appear.

3. **Click** on **Taskbar & Start Menu**. The Taskbar Properties dialog box will open.

TIP

An alternative way to open the Taskbar Properties dialog box is to right-click on the Taskbar, and click on Properties from the shortcut menu that appears.

4. **Click** on the **Start Menu Programs tab**. The tab will move to the front.

5. **Click** on **Add**. The Create Shortcut dialog box will open.

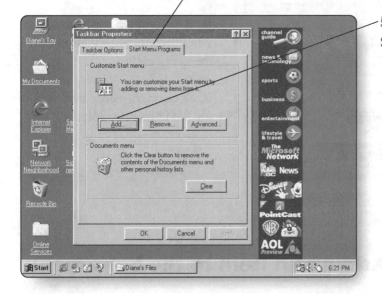

6. **Click** on **Browse**. The Browse dialog box will open.

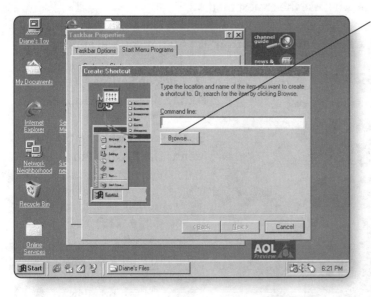

7. Locate the **folder** that has the program or document to which you want to create a shortcut. A list of all available programs in that folder will appear.

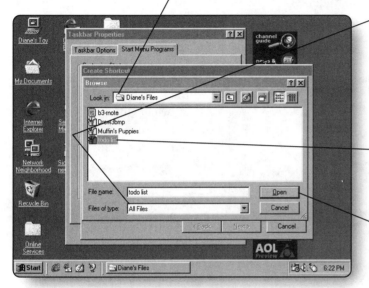

If you are looking for a document and not a program, change the Files of type: list box to All Files instead of Programs. You will then see documents as well as programs.

8. Click on the **desired program** or **document**. The item will be selected.

9. Click on **Open**. The Browse dialog box will close and the program or document name (including the location) will appear in the Create Shortcut dialog box.

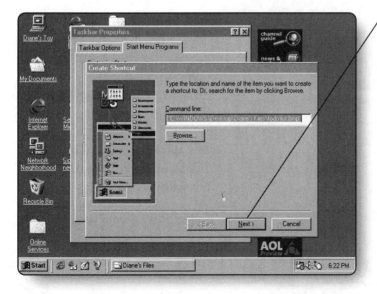

10. Click on **Next**. The Select Program Folder dialog box will open.

11. Click on the **folder** in which you want the shortcut to appear. The folder will be selected. If you want the item to be stored on the first level of the Start menu, click on the Start Menu folder.

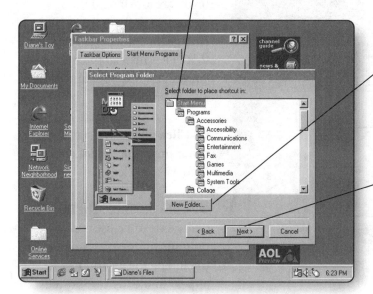

TIP

You can also create a new folder to store the shortcut in by clicking on the New Folder button and typing a name for the new folder.

12. Click on **Next**. The Select a Title for the Program dialog box will open.

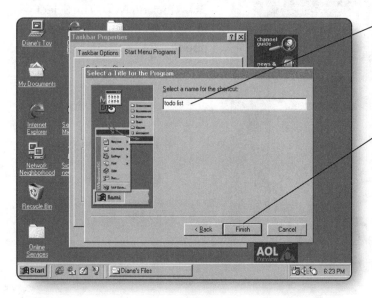

13. Type a **new name** for the icon, if desired. This will represent what you see on the Start menu, not the actual filename.

14. Click on **Finish**. The Select a Title for the Program dialog box will close.

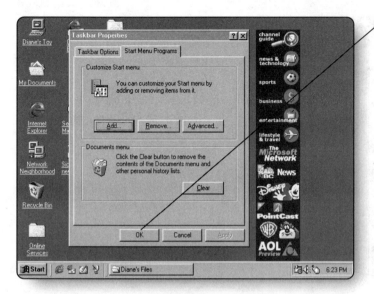

15. Click on **OK**. The Taskbar Properties dialog box will close, and the new item will be displayed on the Start menu.

Removing an Item from the Start Menu

When you delete an item from the Start menu, you are not deleting a program or document itself, only the shortcut that points to that particular program or document. The shortcut is then placed in the Recycle Bin.

1. Follow steps 1 through **4** in "Adding an Item to the Start Menu." The Start Menu Programs tab will move to the front of the Taskbar Properties dialog box.

2. Click on **Remove**. The Remove Shortcuts/Folders dialog box will open with a list of all folders and documents on the Start menu displayed.

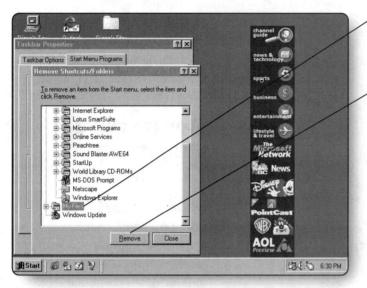

3. Click on the **folder** or **shortcut** you want to delete. The item will be selected.

4. Click on **Remove**. A confirmation box may appear.

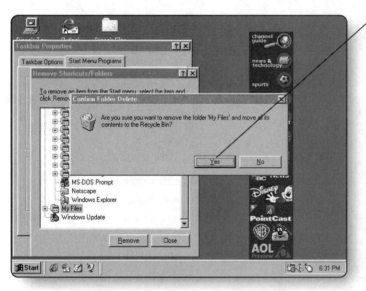

5. Click on **Yes** to confirm the deletion.

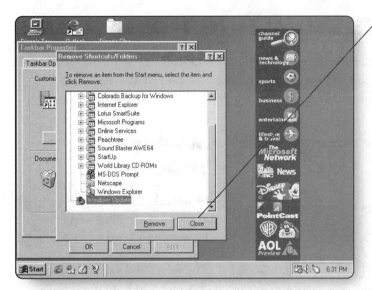

6. Click on **Close**. The Remove Shortcuts/Folders dialog box will close.

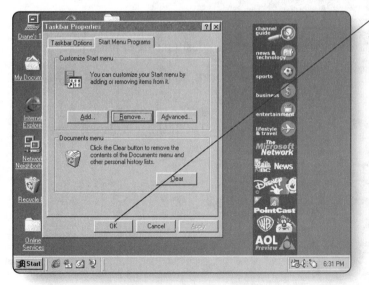

7. Click on **OK**. The Taskbar Properties dialog box will close.

TIP

Another way to remove an item from the Start menu is to drag the undesired item on to the Windows 98 desktop, and then drag the item from the desktop to the Recycle Bin.

CUSTOMIZING THE TASKBAR

You can control the actions of the Taskbar. You can decide when and where the Taskbar is displayed or even add additional toolbars to the Taskbar.

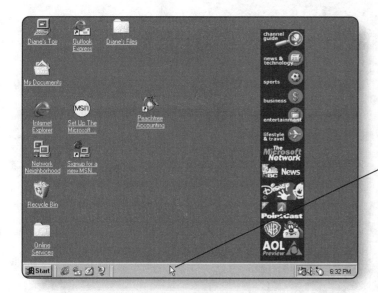

Moving the Taskbar

By default, the Taskbar is located at the bottom of the screen. However, you can move it to any side of your screen.

1. **Press** and **hold** the **mouse button** on a blank area of the Taskbar.

2. **Drag** the **Taskbar** to the desired side of the screen.

3. **Release** the **mouse button**.

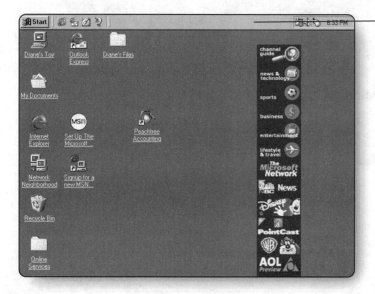

The Taskbar is displayed at the new location.

Changing Taskbar Options

You can change the display of the Taskbar so it will remain hidden until you call for it.

1. **Follow steps 1** through **3** in "Adding an Item to the Start Menu." The Taskbar Properties dialog box will open.

The Taskbar display options include:

✦ **Always on top**. Guarantees that the Taskbar is always visible, even when running a program in a maximized window.

✦ **Auto hide**. Allows the Taskbar to be hidden until you point to the location where the Taskbar usually resides, and then the Taskbar will reappear.

✦ **Show small icons in Start menu**. Reduces the size of the menu items on the Start menu.

✦ **Show clock**. Controls whether the clock displays in the System Tray of the Taskbar.

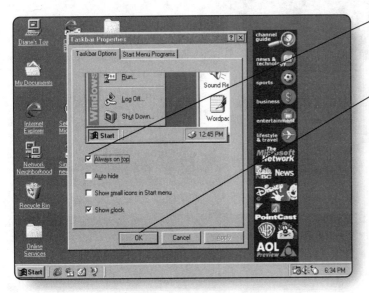

2. **Click** on the desired **options**. A ✔ will appear by each selected choice.

3. **Click** on **OK**. The dialog box will close, and the new options will be applied.

Adding a Toolbar to the Taskbar

The Taskbar already includes the Quick Launch bar, but there are several others available. You can have as many toolbars displayed as you want.

Three of the toolbars provided with Windows 98 include:

✦ **Address**. Displays a toolbar into which you can type Web addresses.

✦ **Links**. Displays a list of favorite Web site links.

✦ **Desktop**. Lets you select a desktop item even when another window is maximized.

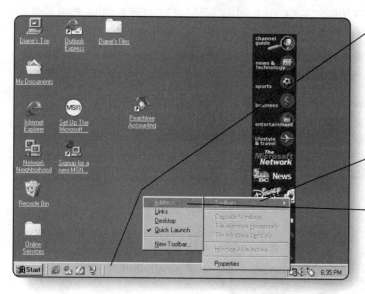

1. **Position** the **mouse pointer** over a blank area on the Taskbar.

2. **Click** on the **right mouse button**. A shortcut menu will appear.

3. **Click** on **Toolbars**. The Toolbars submenu will appear.

4. **Click** on a **toolbar**. The selected toolbar will appear on the Taskbar.

5. **Repeat steps 1** through **4** to remove a toolbar.

16 Tinkering with the Control Panel

How can I make my mouse less sensitive? Where do I set the current date? The answers to these questions and other issues about the response of your computer lie in the Control Panel. In this chapter, you'll learn how to:

✦ Change the current date and time

✦ Change the way the mouse works

✦ Add new hardware and software

✦ Create a Windows 98 startup disk

✦ Set up and change passwords

✦ Set up multiple users

✦ Change accessibility options

OPENING THE CONTROL PANEL

The Control Panel can be accessed from the Start menu or from the My Computer icon.

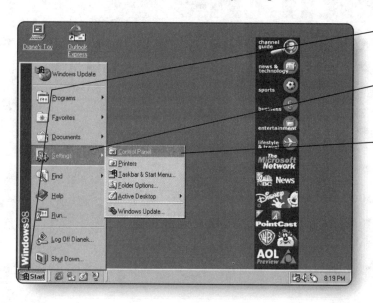

1. Click on the **Start button**. The Start menu will appear.

2. Click on **Settings**. The Settings submenu will appear.

3. Click on **Control Panel**. The Control Panel window will appear.

CHANGING THE CURRENT DATE AND TIME

Having the correct date and time is quite important, especially when you need to insert the current date into a document on which you are working.

1. Click on **Date/Time**. The Date/Time Properties dialog box will open.

From here you have four options that you can set:

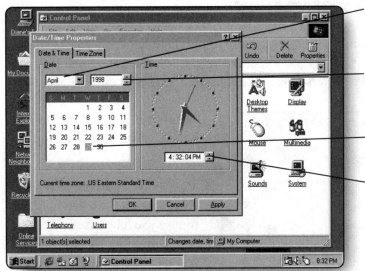

✦ **The current month**. Click on the down arrow (▼) to choose the current month.

✦ **The current year**. Click on the up and down arrows (◆) to select the current year.

✦ **The current day**. Click on the current day of the month.

✦ **The current time**. Click in the portion of the time you want to change, and then click on the up and down arrows (◆).

2. Make any desired **changes** to the date or time.

NOTE

Be sure you make adjustments according to your time zone. Windows 98 knows when time changes, such as Daylight Savings Time, occur and will adjust the time accordingly. Click on the Time Zone tab to select your zone.

3. Click on **OK**. The Date/Time Properties dialog box will close.

TIP

A quick way to access the Date/Time Properties dialog box is to double-click on the current time on the System Tray.

CHANGING MOUSE RESPONSE

You can make the mouse respond better to you. You can also temper the motion of the mouse, select different pointers, or even reverse the mouse buttons.

1. **Click** on **Mouse**. The Mouse Properties dialog box will open.

The choices displayed in the Mouse Properties dialog box vary depending on the brand of mouse you have installed on your computer. The selections you see displayed in this section are for the Microsoft IntelliPoint mouse.

Changing Basic Mouse Responses

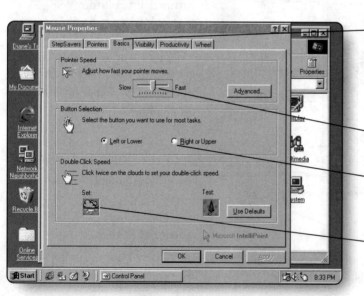

1. **Click** on the **Basics (or General) tab**. The tab will move to the front.

From here you can:

✦ Adjust how fast the mouse moves onscreen.

✦ Choose which button you want to be the main mouse button.

✦ Select how fast you must click the mouse to make a double-click action work.

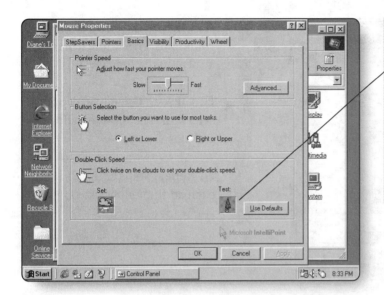

Test the double-click speed by double-clicking in the test area. If you can easily make the umbrella (or sometimes a jack-in-the-box) pop up or down, then you have set the double-click speed correctly.

Changing Mouse Pointers

Instead of the traditional hourglass or arrowhead on the mouse pointer, how about an apple or a hand? You can choose from a wide variety of optional pointers.

1. Click on the **Pointers tab**. The Pointers tab will move to the front.

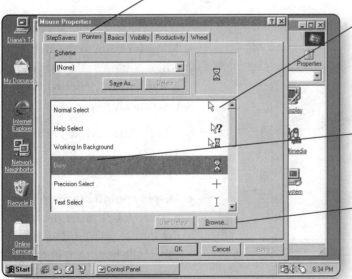

The current selection of mouse pointers for the various tasks of the computer are displayed. There are many others from which you can choose.

2. Click on the **pointer** you want to change. The pointer will be selected.

3. Click on **Browse**. The Browse dialog box will open and display a selection of mouse pointers.

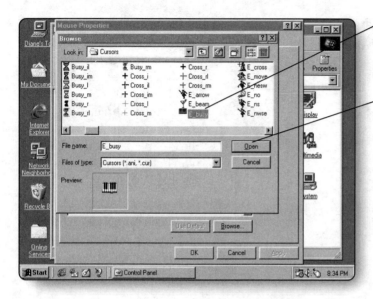

4. **Click** on the **pointer** you want to use. A sample will appear in the Preview: box.

5. **Click** on **Open** to accept the selection. The Browse dialog box will close.

6. **Repeat steps 2** through **5** for each additional mouse pointer you want to change.

Changing Mouse Visibility

Changing the visibility of the mouse pointer can be very helpful, especially when using a laptop computer. Sometimes the mouse appears to get "lost."

1. **Click** on the **Visibility tab**. The Visibility tab will move to the front.

From here you can:

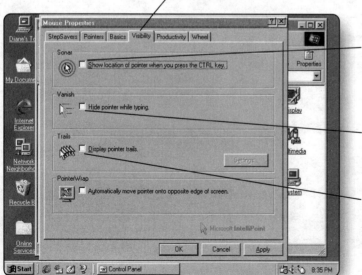

+ **Show location of pointer when you press the Ctrl key.** A series of gray circles help you quickly locate the mouse.

+ **Hide pointer while typing**. The pointer reappears when you move the mouse.

+ **Display pointer trails**. Shows a comet-like trail as you move the mouse pointer. This one is especially handy on notebook computers.

✦ **Automatically move pointer on to opposite edge of the screen**. When you move the mouse pointer past the edge of a screen, it automatically reappears on the opposite side of the screen.

2. Click in the **check box** next to any desired choice. A ✔ will appear in the box.

3. Click on **OK** when you have completed making mouse pointer changes. The new options will be applied, and the Mouse Properties dialog box will close.

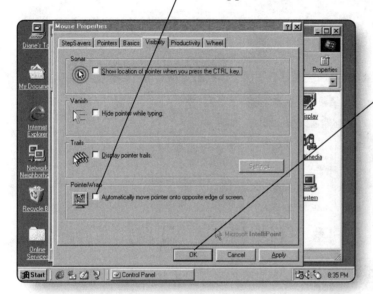

ADDING AND REMOVING PROGRAMS

When it comes time to install or uninstall software on your computer, the Add/Remove Programs icon makes the process simple. This is also the place to go when you need to add additional Windows 98 components, such as Accessibility Options, or additional System tools, such as Microsoft Backup.

1. Click on **Add/Remove Programs**. The Add/Remove Programs Properties dialog box will open.

Installing a New Program

When installing a new software program, follow the manufacturer's instructions or the following steps.

1. Click on the **Install/Uninstall tab**. The Install/Uninstall tab will move to the front.

2. Click on **Install**. The Install Wizard will start.

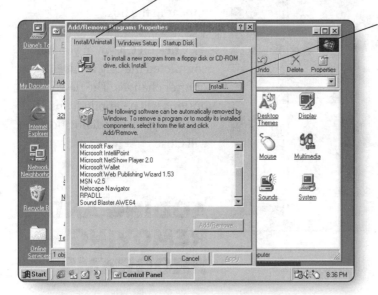

3. Insert the software installation **disk** or **CD**.

4. Click on **Next**. You will continue to the next screen.

Windows 98 searches the floppy disk drive first; then, if it doesn't find any type of installation or setup program, it searches the CD-ROM drive. The suggested setup program Windows 98 comes up with is usually the right one to install.

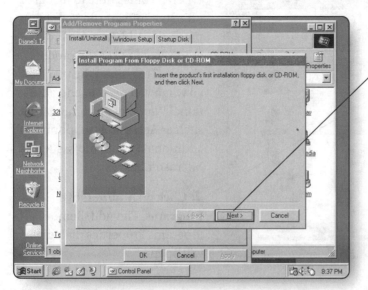

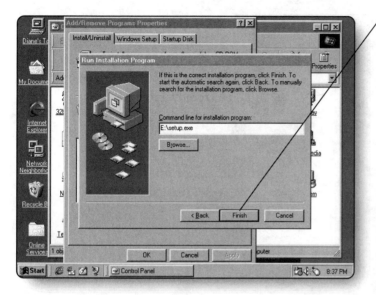

5. **Click** on **Finish**. The installation will begin. You may need to answer individual questions from the software manufacturer.

Uninstalling a Program

If you have a program you no longer want on your computer, you usually can use the Windows 98 uninstaller to remove the program. This is usually the cleanest way to remove a program, because Windows 98 will not only delete the program files, but also clean the Windows 98 Registry of any markers related to that program. Also, any extra files frequently stored in the Windows directory, such as .dll or .ini files, will safely be removed. Not all programs will be available to uninstall using this method.

NOTE

The Windows 98 Registry is an encoded central file that Windows uses to store information about the hardware, software, and preferences on your computer.

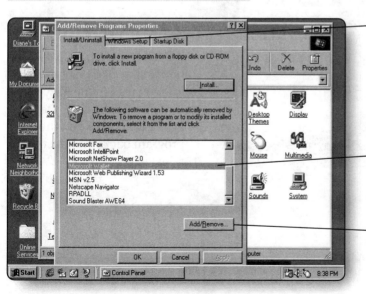

1. **Click** on the **Install/Uninstall tab**. The Install/Uninstall tab will move to the front, and a list of programs that can be automatically removed by Windows will be displayed.

2. **Click** on the **program** you want to uninstall. The selected item will be highlighted.

3. **Click** on **Add/Remove**. The Confirm File Deletion dialog box will open.

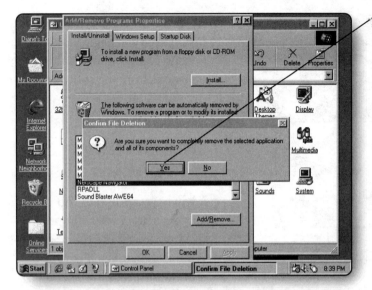

4. **Click** on **Yes**. The Remove Programs From Your Computer dialog box will open, and Windows 98 will begin the removal process.

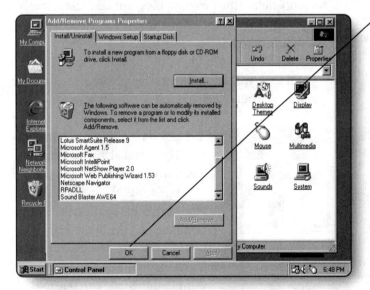

5. **Click** on **OK** when the uninstall process is completed. The Add/Remove Programs Properties dialog box will close.

NOTE

When a program is uninstalled and deleted, it is not placed in the Recycle Bin. There is no undo step available. If you want the program back, you must reinstall it.

Creating a Windows 98 Startup Disk

An absolute *must have* item is a Windows 98 emergency startup disk. If your system refuses to boot up, this disk stores the most critical files needed to get you back up and running again. When you install Windows 98, you are advised to create a startup disk at that time. If you didn't, you should do it now. You will need one disk for this process.

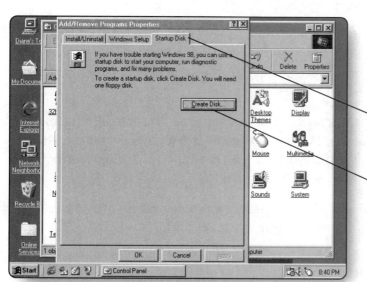

1. **Click** on the **Startup Disk tab**. The Startup Disk tab will move to the front.

2. **Click** on **Create Disk**. The files to be copied will be prepared.

3. **Insert** the **disk** that will hold the startup files. Any existing files on this disk will be deleted.

NOTE

You may be prompted to insert the Windows 98 CD-ROM.

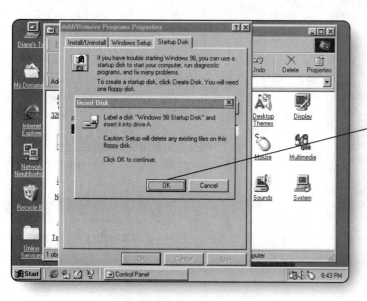

4. **Click** on **OK**. Windows will prepare the startup disk.

If you need to use the emergency startup disk, place the disk in the disk drive before you turn the power on to your computer. Windows 98 will recognize it as a startup disk and take over from there.

Adding Windows Program Components

Some items that are discussed in this book are not installed during a default installation of Windows 98. If you want these additional features, you must add them with the Windows Setup program.

Some of the commonly used items not installed by default include the games (see Chapter 9), the Microsoft Backup program (see Chapter 10), the Accessibility options, and the Desktop Themes.

1. **Click** on the **Windows Setup tab**. The tab will move to the front, and Windows 98 will search for the components already installed on your PC. A list of Windows 98 components categories will be displayed.

Windows 98 uses the following designations to indicate if any, all, or none of a category is already installed:

✦ Items with no ✔ in the check box indicates none of that category is installed.

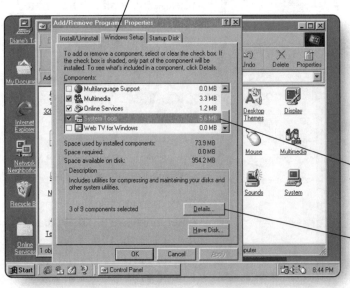

✦ Items with a ✔ in a gray check box indicates only part of the category is installed.

✦ Items with a ✔ in a white check box indicates that the entire category is already installed.

2. **Click** on the **category** you want to install. The category will be selected.

3. **Click** on **Details**. The dialog box for that category will open.

4. Click on as many **components** of that category that you want to install. A ✔ will appear in the check box.

Some components require additional choices to operate correctly. Windows 98 Setup will advise you of this with a Setup dialog box.

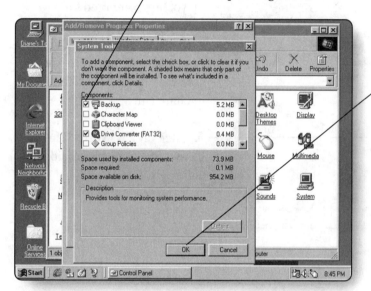

5. Click on **Yes** to add the additional components. The Setup dialog box will close.

6. Click on **OK**. The category dialog box will close.

TIP

To remove a Windows 98 component, remove the ✔ from the items you want to uninstall and continue with step 7.

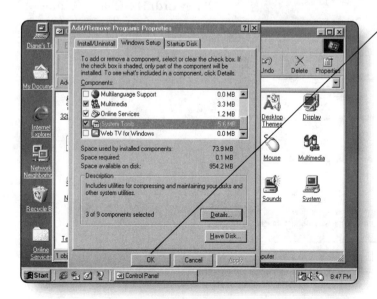

7. Click on **OK** when you have completed your selections. The Add/Remove Programs Properties dialog box will close, and the individual components will be installed or removed. You may be prompted to insert your Windows 98 Setup disks or CD-ROM.

NOTE

You may be prompted to restart Windows.

CHANGING YOUR WINDOWS PASSWORD

If you are connected to a network, when Windows starts up you are prompted for a password. This setting is stored in the Password area of the Control Panel. You must know your current password in order to change it.

1. Click on **Passwords**. The Passwords Properties dialog box will open.

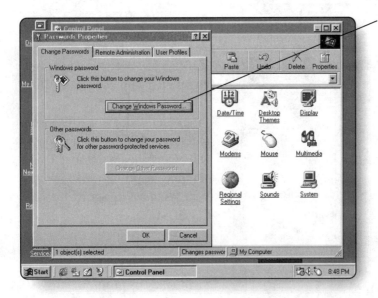

2. Click on **Change Windows Password**. The Change Windows Password dialog box will open.

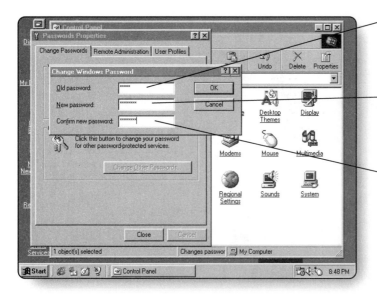

3. Type your **old password** in the Old password: text box. A series of asterisks will appear.

4. Type your **new password** in the New password: text box. A series of asterisks will appear.

5. Type your **new password** in the Confirm new password: text box. A series of asterisks will appear.

TIP

To remove your password completely, enter the existing password in the Old password: text box and leave both of the new password text boxes blank.

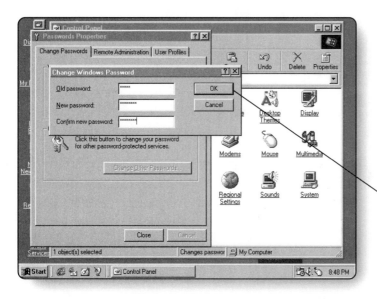

NOTE

You are asked to type your new password twice to make sure you didn't make a typing error because you cannot see what you are typing.

6. Click on **OK**. The Change Windows Password dialog box will close, and you will be advised that the password has changed.

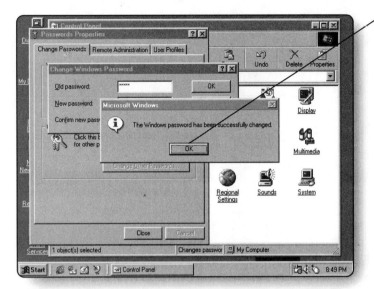

7. Click on **OK**. The acknowledgement message will close, and your new password will take effect the next time you start Windows 98.

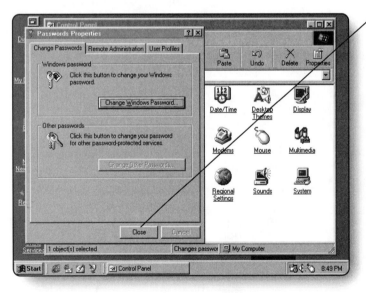

8. Click on **Close**. The Passwords Properties dialog box will close.

SETTING UP MULTIPLE USERS

Windows 98 allows you to set up your computer to be used by more than one person. Each user can have his own set of preferences, such as wallpaper, backgrounds, screen savers, and icons. The settings used by Windows 98 are determined by which user is logged on.

1. Click on **Users**. The User Settings dialog box will open.

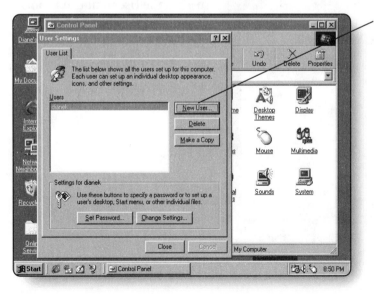

2. Click on **New User**. The Add User dialog box will open.

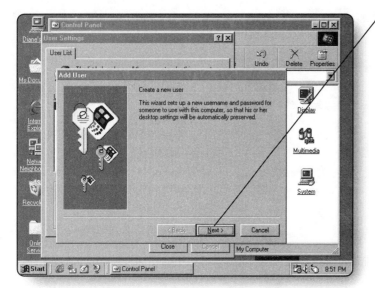

3. Click on **Next**. You will continue to the next screen.

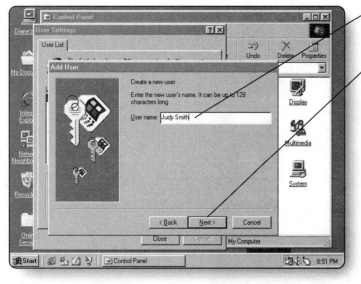

4. Enter a **name** for the new user in the User name: text box.

5. Click on **Next**. The Enter New Password dialog box will open.

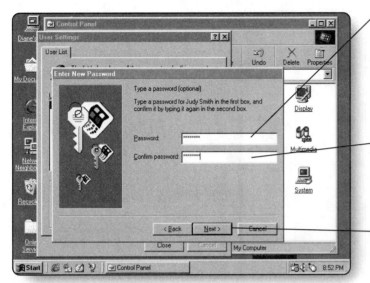

6. **Type** a **password** to use when logging on to Windows, if desired. A series of asterisks will appear. You can leave this text box blank if the new user doesn't want to use a password.

7. **Type** the **new password** in the Confirm password: text box to confirm your typing. A series of asterisks will appear.

8. **Click** on **Next**. The Personalized Items Settings dialog box will open.

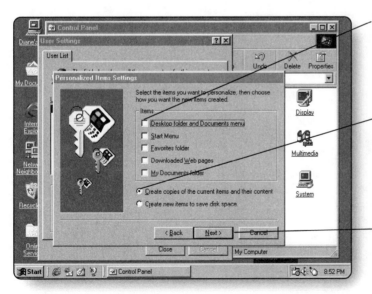

9. **Click** on each **item** you want to personalize. A ✔ will appear in the check box for each selected item.

10. **Click** on **Create copies of the current items and their content**. The current user's settings will be duplicated for the new user.

11. **Click** on **Next**. The Ready to Finish dialog box will open.

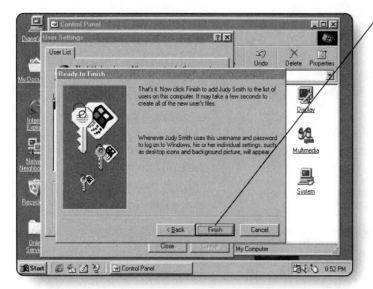

12. **Click** on **Finish**. Windows will create personalized settings folders for the new user.

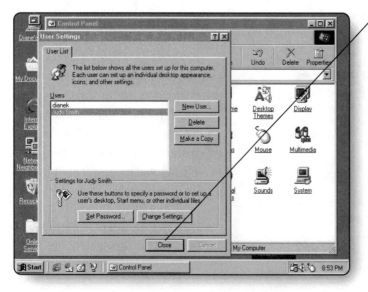

13. **Click** on **Close**. The User Settings dialog box will close. You may be prompted to restart Windows.

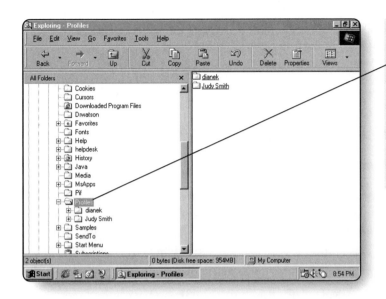

CHANGING ACCESSIBILITY OPTIONS

Windows 98 offers many enhancements designed to make using a PC easier for people with physical limitations. Accessibility features include enhancements for easier keyboard and mouse input as well as features for users who are visually or hearing impaired.

1. **Click** on **Accessibility Options**. The Accessibility Properties dialog box will open.

Changing Keyboard Options

Keyboard options include enhancements for easier keyboard use.

1. Click on the **Keyboard tab,** if necessary. The Keyboard tab will move to the front.

There are three main options available on the Keyboard tab:

✦ **StickyKeys**. Turn this feature on if you want to be able to press the Ctrl, Alt, or Shift key and have it remain operative until the next key other than Ctrl, Alt, or Shift is pressed. This feature is very useful for someone who has difficulty pressing two keys at the same time.

✦ **FilterKeys**. Turn this feature on if you have a tendency to hold a key down too long and you find it repeats itself. Windows will ignore brief or repeated keystrokes with this feature activated.

✦ **ToggleKeys**. Turn this feature on to hear a light noise when you press the Caps Lock, Num Lock, or Scroll Lock key. When you press one of these keys you will hear a low clicking noise.

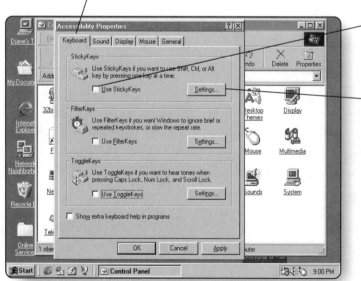

2. Click on the **features** you want to use. A ✔ will appear next to activated features.

3. Click on **Settings** for each feature you activate, if desired. The Settings dialog box will open.

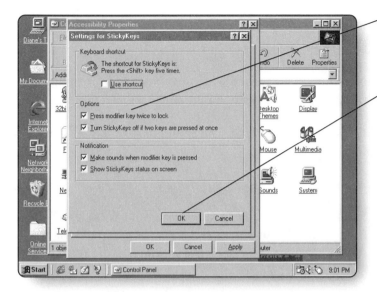

4. Click on any additional **options** you want for the selected keyboard option.

5. Click on **OK**. The Settings dialog box will close.

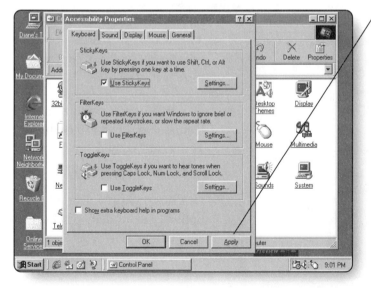

6. Click on **Apply**. The keyboard options will immediately be applied.

TIP

See "Using MouseKeys" later in this chapter for information on an additional feature to aid those with hand impairments.

Setting Options for the Hearing Impaired

These options can assist the hearing impaired by turning normal sounds from the computer into visible reminders.

1. Click on the **Sound tab**. The Sound tab will move to the front.

Two options appear here:

✦ **SoundSentry**. Use this feature if you want Windows 98 to flash a part of your screen each time the computer plays a sound. The part of the screen is specified in the Settings for SoundSentry dialog box.

✦ **ShowSounds**. Use this feature to instruct programs that usually relay information only by sound to also provide the information by displaying icons or text captions.

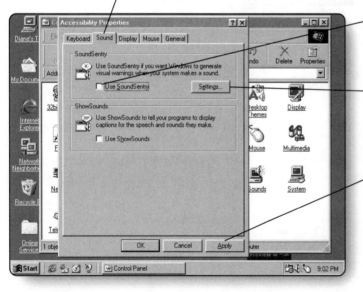

2. Click on the **features** you want to use. A ✔ will appear next to activated features.

3. Click on **Settings** for each feature you activate, if desired. The Settings dialog box for the selected feature will open.

4. Click on **Apply**. The sound options will immediately be applied.

Setting Options for the Visually Impaired

The Display option has a feature for those with limited vision. For better visibility, it can instruct a program to use a specified color scheme instead of the one indicated by a specific program.

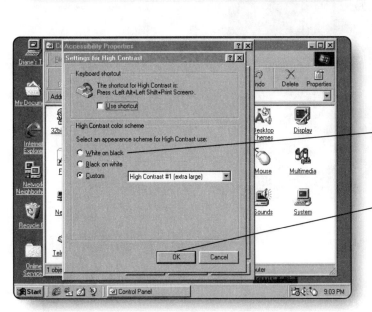

1. Click on the **Display tab**. The Display tab will move to the front.

2. Click on the **Use High Contrast check box**. A ✔ will appear in the check box.

3. Click on **Settings**. The Settings for High Contrast dialog box will open.

There are several High Contrast color schemes available. Options include white on black, black on white, or custom.

4. Click on the **color scheme** you want to use. The option will be selected.

5. Click on **OK**. The Settings for High Contrast dialog box will close.

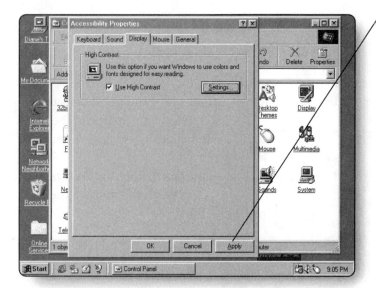

6. Click on **Apply**. The display options will immediately be applied.

This figure shows a screen with High Contrast #1, extra large fonts selected.

Using MouseKeys

MouseKeys are very useful for someone who has difficulty handling a mouse. By using MouseKeys you can control the mouse pointer by using the numeric keypad of the keyboard.

1. Click on the **Mouse tab**. The Mouse tab will move to the front.

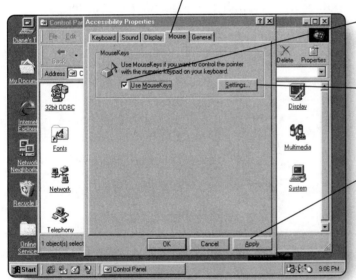

2. Click on the **Use MouseKeys check box**. A ✔ will appear in the check box.

Clicking on the Settings button allows you to determine how fast is fast when you are using the MouseKeys.

3. Click on **Apply**. The MouseKeys options will immediately be applied.

Setting General Accessibility Options

The General options are for the overall properties and actions of the accessibility features.

1. Click on the **General tab**. The General tab will move to the front.

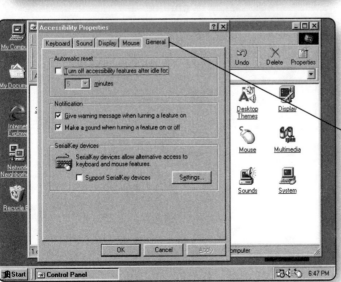

Several general options are available that can affect the operations of the accessibility features:

✦ **Automatic reset**. Turns off the accessibility features if your computer has been idle for a specified period of time.

✦ **Notification**. Notifies you when you have activated accessibility features via shortcut keys.

✦ **SerialKey devices**. Indicates whether Windows 98 can support an alternative input device (called an *augmentative communication device*). This feature is for those who are unable to use a standard mouse or keyboard. This feature is not affected by the Automatic Reset.

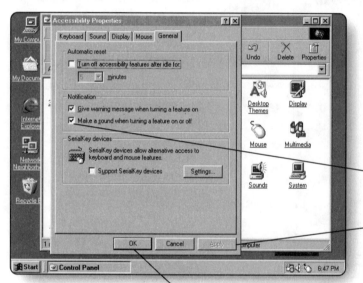

2. Click on any desired **options**.

3. Click on **Apply**. The general options will immediately be applied.

4. Click on **OK**. The Accessibility Properties dialog box will close.

17 Having Fun with the Control Panel

In the previous chapter, you learned how to use some of the system support items that the Control Panel offers. Now, how about learning to use the Control Panel to maximize the fun you can have with your computer? Do you want something nicer to look at than the standard Windows 98 desktop? How about changing the sound you hear every time a message appears? In this chapter, you'll learn how to:

✦ Change sounds

✦ Switch your desktop from the Standard Desktop to the Active Desktop

✦ Add special effects to your desktop

✦ Use the Desktop Themes

✦ Install fonts

CHANGING SOUNDS

Every time you take a step in Windows 98, you may hear a sound. It could sound like a ding or a chord, or even a drum roll or an owl. These sounds are established through the Windows 98 Control Panel.

1. **Open** the **Control Panel**.

2. **Click** on **Sounds**. The Sounds Properties dialog box will open. A list of Windows events, such as closing a program or the appearance of a warning message, will be displayed in the dialog box. Events that have a sound already assigned will display a speaker next to the event name.

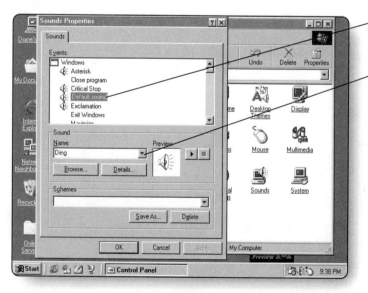

3. **Click** on an **event**. The event will be selected.

4. **Click** on the **down arrow (▾)** next to the Name: list box. A list of available sounds will appear.

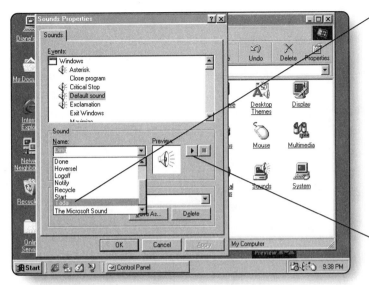

5. Click on the **sound name** you want to associate with the event. The sound name will appear in the Name: list box.

TIP

If you do not want a sound associated with an event, click on [None] from the Name: list box.

6. Click on the **Play button** to preview the sound. You will hear the sound.

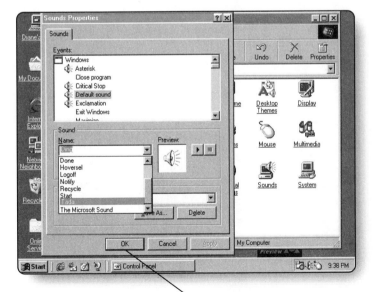

NOTE

If you installed any of the Desktop Themes with Windows 98, you can choose a sound from each Desktop Theme's sound collection. Click on the Browse button, navigate to the C:\Program Files\Plus!\Themes folder, and choose a sound from the list.

7. Repeat steps 3 through **6** for each event you want to change.

8. Click on **OK**. The Sounds Properties dialog box will close.

ENHANCING YOUR DISPLAY

Windows 98 offers several major options to the way you view your desktop. With only a couple of mouse clicks, you can set your eyes on the world—via the Internet. This feature is called *Active Desktop*. Active Desktop is only one of the many changes you can make to your display.

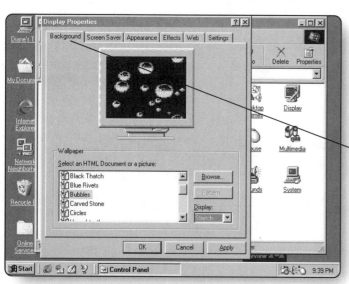

1. Click on **Display** in the Control Panel window. The Display Properties dialog box will open.

Changing Backgrounds

Any .bmp or .html document can be displayed as your wallpaper for your Windows desktop! If you turn on the Active Desktop feature, you can also use .jpeg or .gif images.

1. Click on the **Background tab** (if necessary). The Background tab will move to the front.

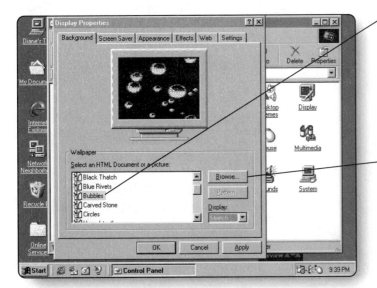

2a. **Click** on a **wallpaper** from the selections provided. A sample of the wallpaper will appear in the Preview screen. Skip to step 6.

OR

2b. **Click** on the **Browse button**, if you do not find a wallpaper you like in the selections provided. The Browse dialog box will open.

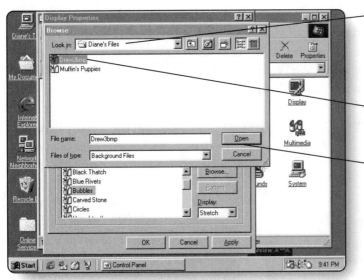

3. **Navigate** to the **folder** that contains the image you want to display as your desktop wallpaper.

4. **Click** on the desired **image**. The filename will be selected.

5. **Click** on **Open**. The Browse dialog box will close.

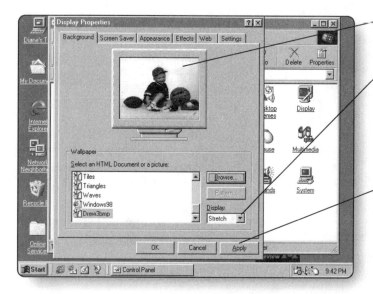

A sample appears in the preview screen.

6. Click on the **down arrow (▼)** next to the Display: list box. You can choose to center, tile, or stretch the wallpaper across your screen.

7. Click on **Apply**. Your new background selection will be applied.

Selecting a Screen Saver

Screen savers display moving images that appear on your screen when the computer is idle for a specified period of time. You can choose from the abundance of screen savers included with Windows 98 or you can purchase many different themes from third-party software manufacturers.

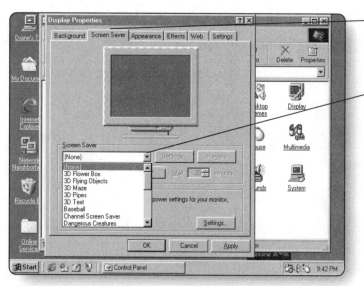

1. Click on the **Screen Saver tab**. The Screen Saver tab will move to the front.

2. Click on the **down arrow (▼)** of the Screen Saver list box. A list of available choices will appear.

NOTE

If you install the Desktop Themes, you will have additional choices listed.

3. **Click** on the **screen saver** you want to use. Your selection will appear in the Screen Saver list box.

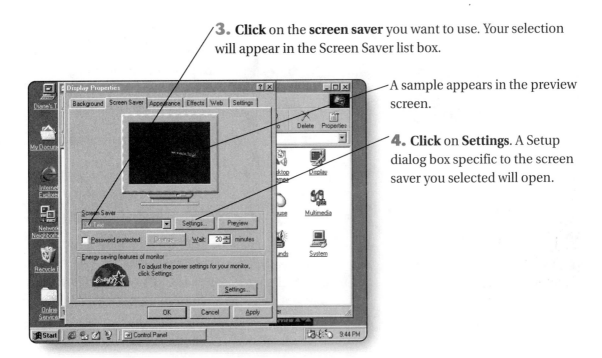

A sample appears in the preview screen.

4. **Click** on **Settings**. A Setup dialog box specific to the screen saver you selected will open.

In this dialog box, you can set various options, such as size, color, and speed. The available options vary with different screen savers.

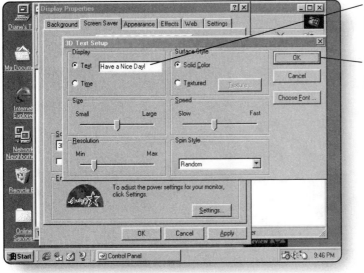

5. **Change** any desired **option** in the Setup dialog box.

6. **Click** on **OK**. The Setup dialog box will close.

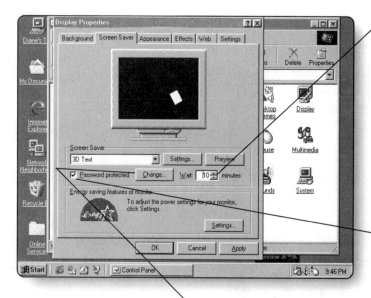

7. Click on the **up** or **down arrow** (◆) next to the Wait: spin box to set the amount of time before the screen saver starts. An average time is 10 minutes.

Optionally, you can set a password to lock your screen when the screen saver is activated. This can keep prying eyes away while you are otherwise occupied.

8. Click on the **Password protected check box**. A ✔ will appear and the Change button will become available.

9. Click on **Change**. The Change Password dialog box will open.

10. Type the **new password** in both text boxes. A series of asterisks will be displayed.

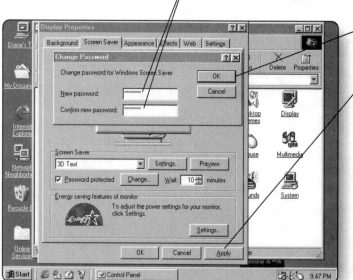

11. Click on **OK**. The Change Password dialog box will close.

12. Click on **Apply**. Your new screen saver selection will be applied.

Changing the Colors of Your Windows

You can adjust the appearance of your screen by changing the colors that are displayed in any Windows 98 program. Windows 98 includes some nice (and some not so nice) color combinations from which you can choose. Color schemes affect everything from the color of a window title bar to the text displayed in a menu.

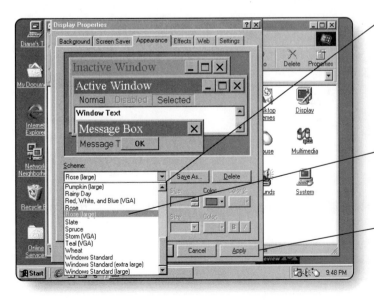

1. **Click** on the **Appearance tab**. The Appearance tab will move to the front.

2. **Click** on the **down arrow (▼)** next to the Scheme: list box. A selection of color schemes will appear.

3. **Press** the **up** or **down arrow keys** on your keyboard or **use** the **scroll bar** to preview the different color schemes. Each choice will appear in the preview box.

4. **Click** on the **color scheme** you want to use. It will appear in the Scheme: list box.

5. **Click** on **Apply**. The new color settings will be applied.

Adding Special Effects to Your Desktop

Special effects can be added to your desktop by changing or enlarging some of the icons for the desktop items or by adding other visual effects.

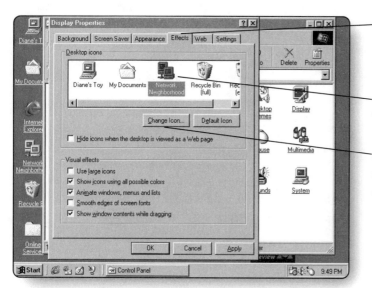

1. Click on the **Effects tab**. The Effects tab will move to the front.

2. Select an **icon** to be changed. The icon will be selected.

3. Click on **Change Icon**. The Change Icon dialog box will open.

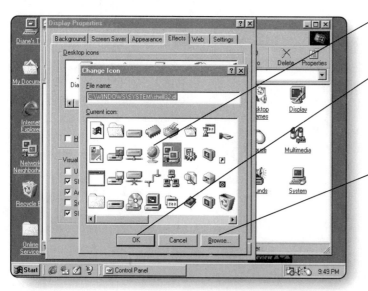

4. Click on **one** of the **available icons**. It will be selected.

5. Click on **OK**. The Change Icon dialog box will close.

NOTE

If you purchased other icon software, click on the Browse button to navigate to the folder that contains the other icons.

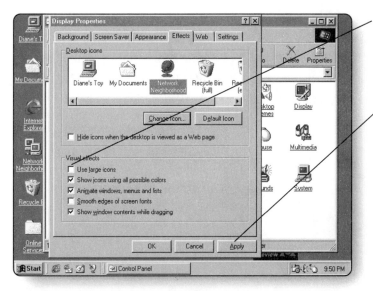

6. **Click** on any other **visual effect** you want to use. A ✔ will appear in the check box for any active effect.

7. **Click** on **Apply**. The new settings will be applied.

Integrating Your Desktop with the Web

Active Desktop makes your desktop come alive with content, such as continuous stock information, sports scores, or weather updates. Icons on an Active Desktop function like a Web page in that they only need a single click to be activated.

1. **Click** on the **Web tab**. The Web tab will move to the front.

2. **Click** on the **View my Active Desktop as a web page check box**. A ✔ will appear in the box and the dialog box will display selections appropriate to the Active Desktop.

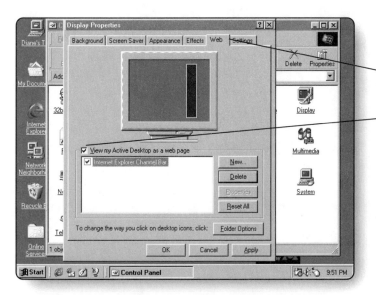

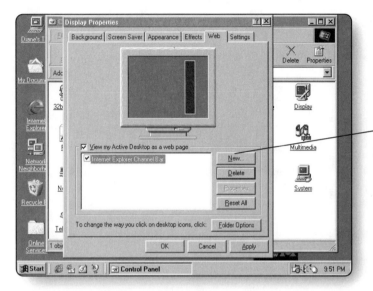

You can add other active items to your desktop, such as stock tickers or weather maps. The best place to start is the Microsoft Active Desktop gallery.

3. **Click** on **New**. The New Active Desktop Item dialog box will open, asking if you want to visit the gallery.

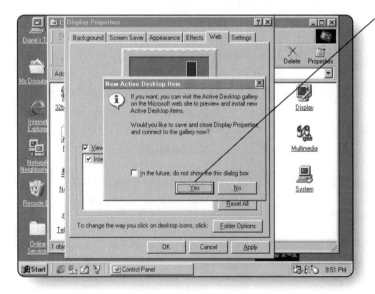

4. **Click** on **Yes**. Your Web browser will launch. If you are not already connected to the Internet, you must connect now.

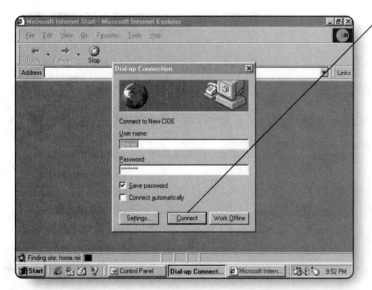

5. **Click** on **Connect**. Your Internet Service Provider (ISP) will connect you to the Internet. You will be automatically taken to the Microsoft Active Desktop Gallery Web page.

NOTE

One or more security warning messages may appear. If so, click on Yes.

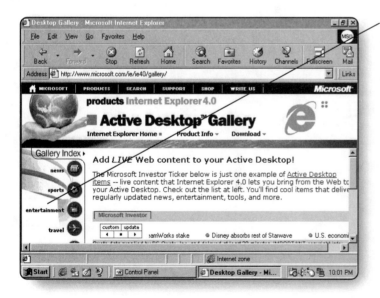

6. **Click** on the **category** to which you want to subscribe. A list of items under that category will appear.

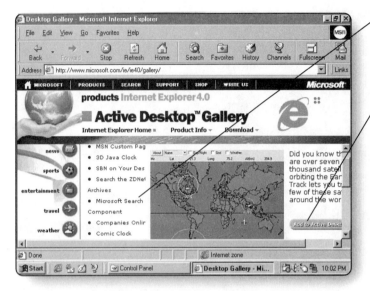

7. Click on the **item** you want to add to your desktop. The Web page for that gallery item will appear.

8. Click on **Add to Active Desktop**. A Security Alert message box will appear.

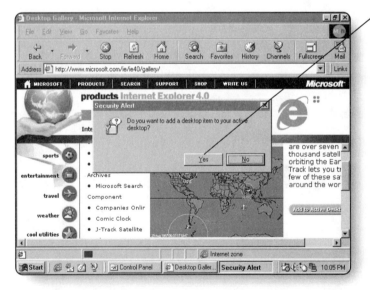

9. Click on **Yes**. A message will appear asking you to confirm your subscription.

10. **Click** on **OK**. The Active Desktop Gallery item will be downloaded to your computer.

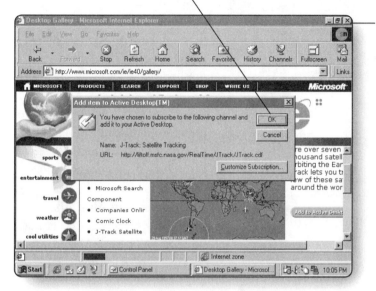

11. **Click** on the **Close button** (X). The Web browser window will close.

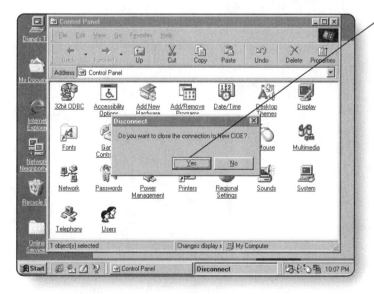

12. **Click** on **Yes** if you want to close your Internet connection.

NOTE

If you are subscribing to a channel with frequent updates, such as stock market items, you may want to keep your Internet connection open.

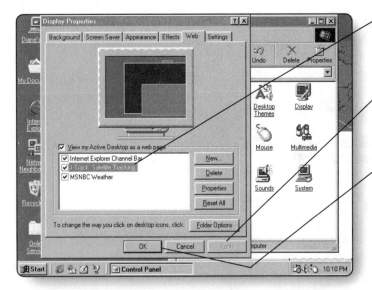

The item you subscribed to appears in the Display Properties dialog box.

13. Click on **Apply**. The Active Desktop selections will be applied.

14. Click on **OK** when you have completed making changes to your display. The Display Properties dialog box will close.

15. Click on the **Minimize button** ([_]). The Control Panel window will be minimized, and you will return to the desktop.

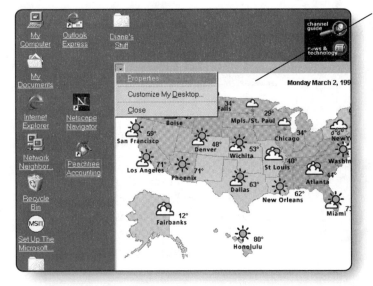

In this example, the MSNBC Weather Map has been added to the Active Desktop.

As you position your mouse pointer on top of an Active Desktop item, a small gray bar will appear. From the bar you can edit the properties of the Active Desktop item or close it.

NOTE

If the downloaded item from the Active Desktop Gallery does not automatically appear on the desktop, right-click on a blank space of your desktop and click on Refresh from the shortcut menu that appears.

USING DESKTOP THEMES

In the previous chapter, you learned how to install additional Windows 98 components. One of those possibilities was the Desktop Themes component. If you have the disk space available (it takes about 17MB for all of it), I recommend it!

There are some really cool themes available—themes like Jungle, Tropical Fish, Leonardo da Vinci, Science, Travel, Sports, or The 60s, just to name a few. These themes include background wallpapers, sounds, screen savers, icons, and other Windows items.

1. Click on **Control Panel** on the Taskbar.

2. Click on **Desktop Themes**. The Desktop Themes window will appear.

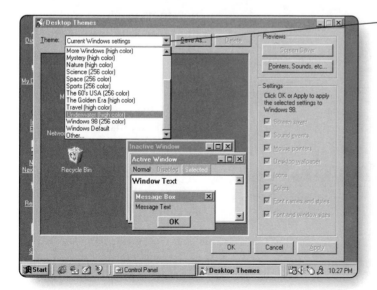

3. Click on the **down arrow (▼)** next to the Theme: list box. A list of available themes will appear.

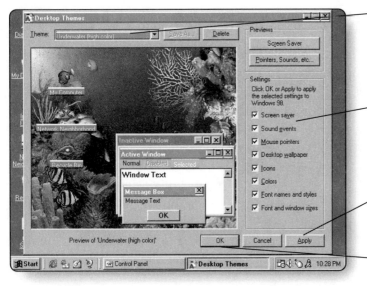

4. **Click** on your favorite **theme**. The theme will appear in the Theme: list box, and you will see it in the Preview box.

5. **Click** on the **check boxes** you want in the Settings area. You can include or exclude any combinations you want.

6. **Click** on **Apply**. The desktop theme will be applied.

7. **Click** on **OK**. The Desktop Themes window will close.

INSTALLING FONTS

If you're a "font-a-holic" like I am, too many fonts is still not enough! You can purchase inexpensive software with tons of new fonts to add to your system. The fonts are easy to install with Windows 98!

1. **Click** on **Fonts**. The Fonts window will appear and a list of your currently installed fonts will be displayed.

2. **Click** on **File**. The File menu will appear.

3. **Click** on **Install New Font**. The Add Fonts dialog box will open.

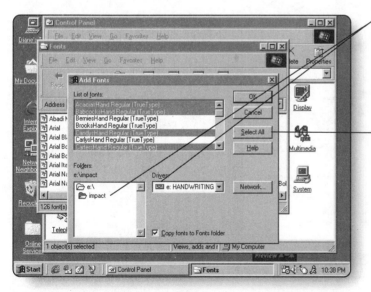

4. **Locate** the **drive** and **folder** that holds the fonts to be installed. A list of possible fonts will appear in the List of fonts: list box.

5a. **Click** on **Select All** to install all the available fonts. All of the font names will be selected.

OR

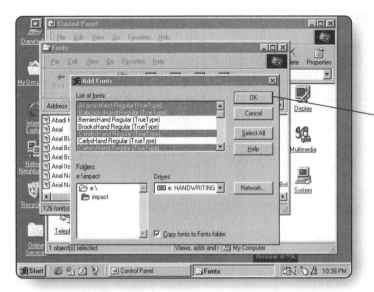

5b. **Hold down** the **Ctrl key** and **click** on each **font name** you want to install. The fonts you choose will be selected.

6. **Click** on **OK**. The font(s) will be added to your system.

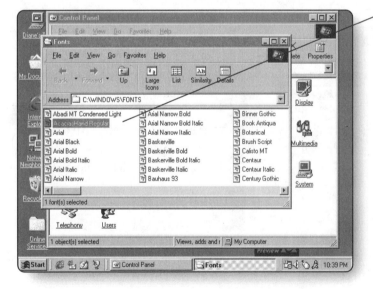

The new font names appear in the Fonts window.

7. **Click** on the **Close button** (⊠). The Fonts window will close.

8. **Click** on the **Close button** (⊠). The Control Panel will close.

NOTE

Many productivity software packages install their own fonts when the software is installed.

18 Working with Printers

Printing is still the most common way to distribute information to others. When you work with a Windows-based program, all the printing is controlled by Windows, not by the individual software program. This has the advantage of consistency and the ability to resolve all printing issues in one central area. In this chapter, you'll learn how to:

✦ Install a new printer

✦ Discover properties of a printer

✦ Share a printer

✦ Connect to a network printer

✦ Make a printer the default printer

✦ Create a printer shortcut

INSTALLING A NEW PRINTER

Most of the time, when you hook up a printer to your computer, the Windows 98 Plug & Play feature will detect the new printer and automatically install the necessary printer settings. Occasionally, however, you must manually tell the computer what kind of printer you're using. Windows 98 includes the Add Printer Wizard to assist you in installing a new printer.

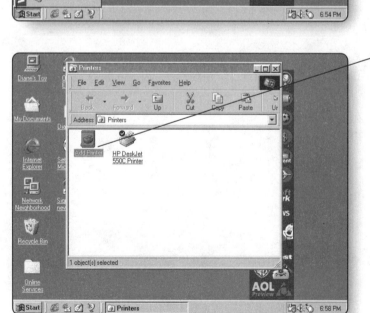

1. **Click** on the **Start button**. The Start menu will appear.

2. **Click** on **Settings**. The Settings submenu will appear.

3. **Click** on **Printers**. The Printers window will appear.

4. **Click** on **Add Printer**. The Add Printer Wizard will open.

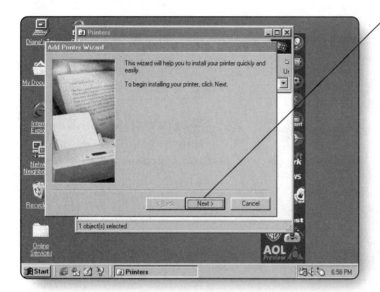

5. **Click** on **Next**. You will proceed to the next screen.

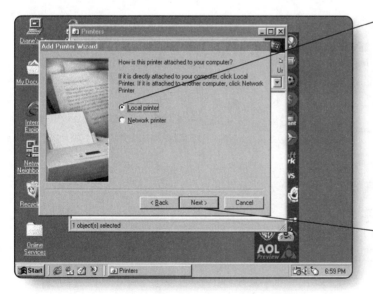

6. **Click** on **Local printer**. The option will be selected.

NOTE

Hooking up to a network printer is discussed in "Connecting to a Network Printer" later in this chapter.

7. **Click** on **Next**. You will proceed to the next screen.

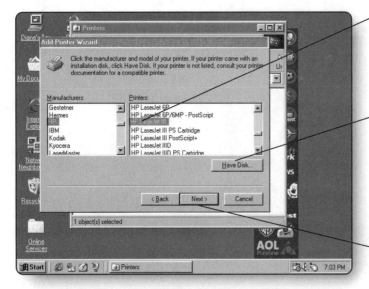

8a. **Click** on the **manufacturer** and **model** of your printer. They will be selected.

OR

8b. **Click** on **Have Disk** if your printer is not listed and you have the installation disk that came with the printer. The Install from Disk dialog box will open. Follow the prompts in this dialog box.

9. **Click** on **Next**. You will proceed to the next screen.

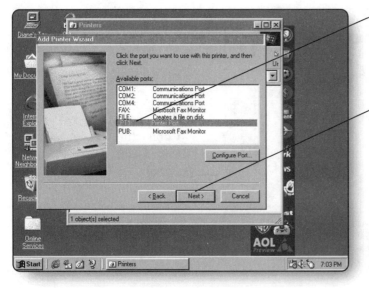

10. **Click** on **LPT1** or whatever printer port to which you attached the printer cable. It will be selected.

11. **Click** on **Next**. You will proceed to the next screen.

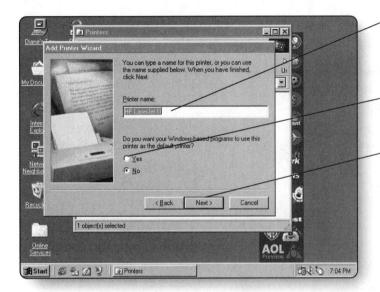

12. **Type** a **descriptive name** for the printer, if desired, in the Printer name: text box.

13. **Click** on **Yes**, if this printer is your main printer.

14. **Click** on **Next**. You will proceed to the next screen.

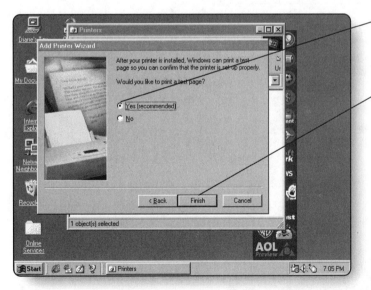

15. **Click** on **Yes** if you want to print a test page to check the connections to your printer.

16. **Click** on **Finish**. The Add Printer Wizard will close and the necessary files will be copied to your computer. You might be prompted to insert the Windows 98 CD-ROM or another specified disk.

If you elected to print a test page, a dialog box opens, asking you if the test page printed correctly.

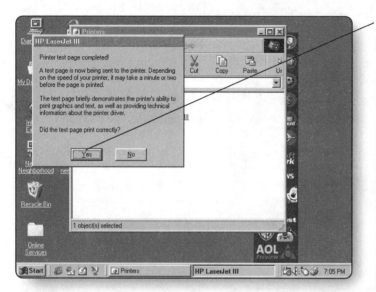

17. Click on **Yes** if the page printed correctly.

NOTE

If the test page did not print correctly and you answer no to the previous question, Windows 98 will start the Windows 98 Print Trouble-shooter (see Chapter 10). Answer the questions in the Print Troubleshooter to determine the printing problem.

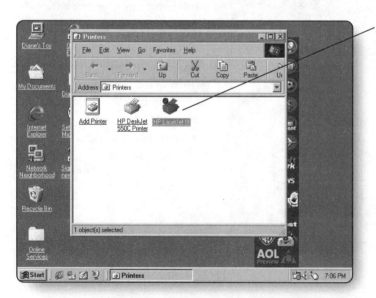

An icon representing the new printer appears in the Printers window.

DISCOVERING PRINTER PROPERTIES

Printers have options that determine what the default settings for a specific printer should be. These options are called *properties*.

1. **Right-click** on the **printer** you want to modify. A shortcut menu will appear.

2. **Click** on **Properties**. A Properties dialog box specific to your printer will open.

The Properties dialog box varies depending on the type of printer you selected. Some printers have more choices available than others.

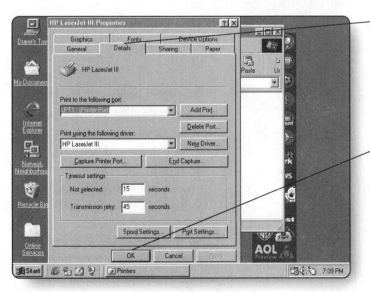

3. **Click** on the **Details tab**. The Details tab will move to the front. From here you can change the printer port, edit timeout settings, and select various other options.

4. **Click** on **OK** when you have finished making any property changes. The Properties dialog box will close.

Sharing a Printer

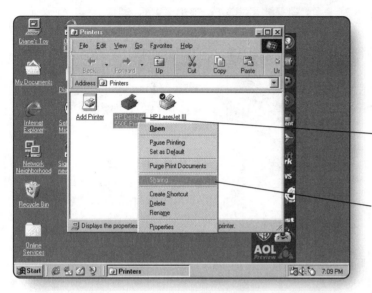

If you want to share your printer with others on your network, you must first tell the printer it has permission to be used by others.

1. Right-click on the **printer** that you want to share. A shortcut menu will appear.

2. Click on **Sharing**. The Printer Properties dialog box will open with the Sharing tab on top.

3. Click on **Shared As**. The option will be selected and the Shared As choices will become available.

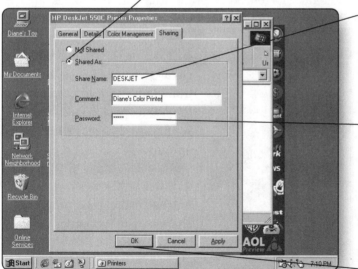

4. Type a **name** for the printer in the Share Name: text box. This is the name others will use to recognize that this is your printer.

5. Type a **password**, if desired. A series of asterisks will appear in the Passwords: text box. If you enter a password here, anyone attempting to print to your printer must enter the password for the print job to begin.

6. Click on **OK**. The Printer Properties dialog box will close.

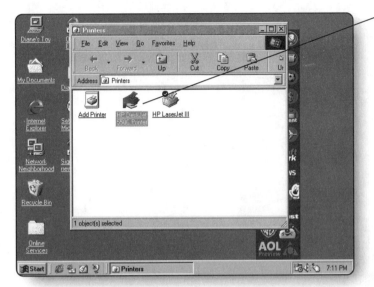

A shared printer is represented with a small hand under it.

CONNECTING TO A NETWORK PRINTER

If you want to print to a printer across a network, two conditions must exist. The printer must be a shared printer and you must have that printer set up in your list of printers.

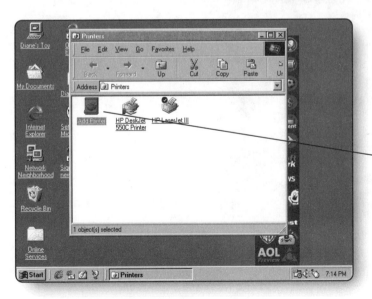

1. Click on **Add Printer**. The Add Printer Wizard will open.

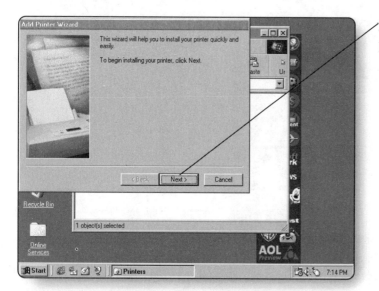

2. **Click** on **Next**. You will proceed to the next screen.

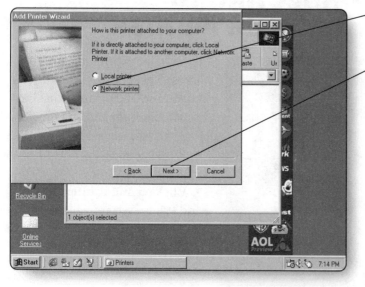

3. **Click** on **Network printer**. The option will be selected.

4. **Click** on **Next**. You will proceed to the next screen.

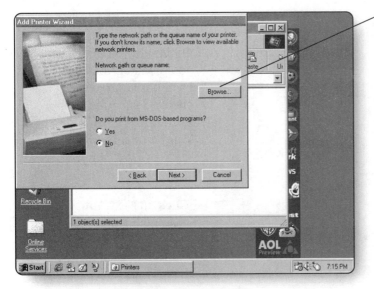

5. **Click** on **Browse**. The Browse for Printer dialog box will open with your Network Neighborhood connection displayed.

6. **Click** on the **+ (plus sign)** next to the computer that has the printer to which you want to connect. A list of available printers will appear.

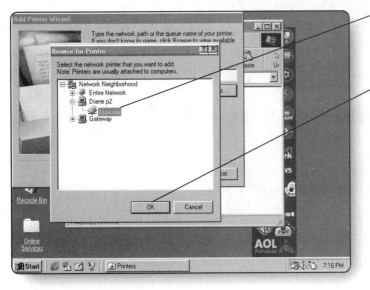

7. **Click** on the **printer** you want to use. The printer will be selected.

8. **Click** on **OK**. The Browse for Printer dialog box will close, and the network path will appear in the Add Printer Wizard dialog box.

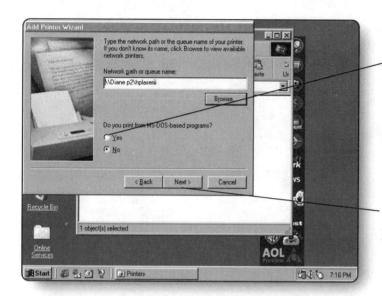

Optionally, click on Yes if you plan to print from DOS-based programs, such as Peachtree Accounting for DOS or WordPerfect for DOS.

9. **Click** on **Next**. You will proceed to the next screen.

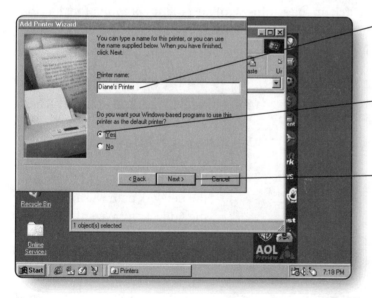

10. **Type** a descriptive **name** for this printer or leave the one Windows suggests.

11. **Click** on **Yes** if this printer is to be your main printer. The option will be selected.

12. **Click** on **Next**. You will proceed to the next screen.

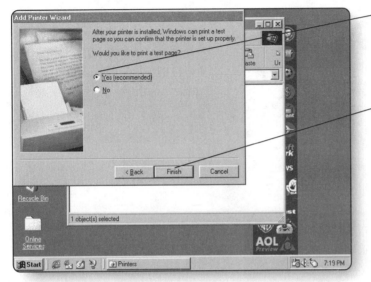

13. Click on **Yes** if you want Windows to print a test page to check the connections to your printer.

14. Click on **Finish**. The Add Printer Wizard will close, and the necessary files will be copied to your computer. You may be prompted to insert the Windows 98 CD-ROM or other specified disks.

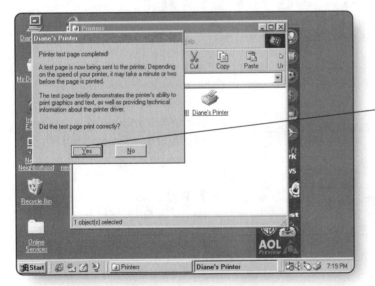

If you elected to print a test page, a dialog box opens, asking you if the test page printed correctly.

15. Click on **Yes** if the page printed correctly.

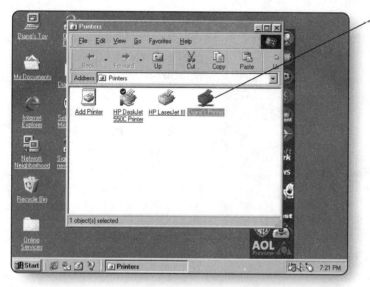

A new printer icon appears in the Printers window. A network printer is designated by what looks like a cable running underneath it.

MAKING A PRINTER THE DEFAULT

You might have several printers you can print to, including a fax or other device. One of these must be set as a default printer. The default printer is the one Windows assumes you want to print to unless you tell it otherwise.

1. **Right-click** on the **printer** to be the default printer. A shortcut menu will appear.

2. **Click** on **Set as Default**. The shortcut menu will close.

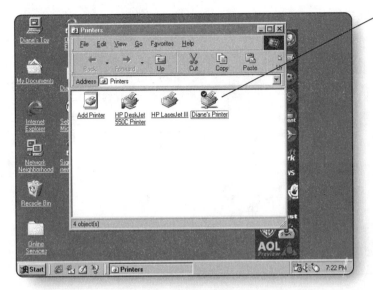

A ✔ appears on the printer icon to indicate it is the default printer.

CREATING A DESKTOP SHORTCUT TO THE PRINTER

Having a printer icon on the desktop allows for "drag-and-drop" printing.

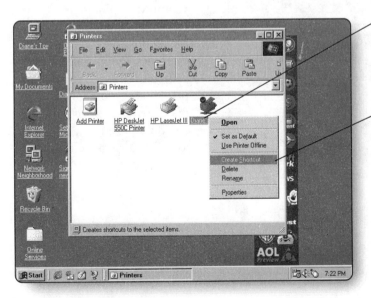

1. **Right-click** on the **printer** to which you want to create a shortcut. A shortcut menu will appear.

2. **Click** on **Create Shortcut**. The Shortcut dialog box will open.

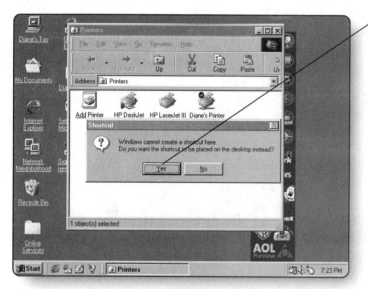

3. Click on **Yes**. The Shortcut dialog box will close.

4. Click on the **Close button** ([X]). The Printers window will close, and a printer shortcut will appear on your desktop.

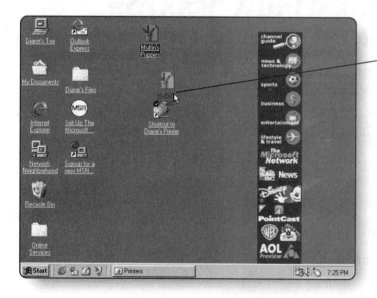

NOTE

To take advantage of drag-and-drop printing from the Windows desktop, Windows Explorer, or any Windows Open or Save File dialog box, click on the document you want to print and drag it to the printer shortcut icon. The document will print with any default settings installed for that printer.

PART IV REVIEW QUESTIONS

1. How can you turn off the Auto Arrange feature? *See "Moving and Deleting Icons" in Chapter 15*

2. When is a file permanently deleted? *See "Emptying the Recycle Bin" in Chapter 15*

3. What does Auto hide do to the Windows Taskbar? *See "Changing Taskbar Options" in Chapter 15*

4. When are mouse trails handy to use? *See "Changing Mouse Visibility" in Chapter 16*

5. Why should you have a Windows 98 startup disk? *See "Creating a Windows 98 Startup Disk" in Chapter 16*

6. What do MouseKeys do? *See "Using MouseKeys" in Chapter 16*

7. What types of documents can be displayed as Windows wallpaper? *See "Changing Backgrounds" in Chapter 17*

8. Which types of features do the Desktop Themes include? *See "Using Desktop Themes" in Chapter 17*

9. What is the name of the tool furnished with Windows 98 to assist you with installing a new printer? *See "Installing a New Printer" in Chapter 18*

10. How can you tell if your printer is shared? *See "Sharing a Printer" in Chapter 18*

PART V
Using the Internet

19 Connecting to the Internet

Whether you're planning on surfing the Internet or just need to send an e-mail message to a coworker, you need to get connected. Windows 98 provides several tools to assist you with your connectivity needs. In this chapter, you'll learn how to:

✦ Subscribe to an online service

✦ Create an Internet connection

✦ Start your Web browser

SUBSCRIBING TO AN ONLINE SERVICE

When you install Windows 98, the Online Services folder is placed on your desktop. This folder contains setup icons that connect to several different online services or Internet Service Providers (ISPs). By selecting an online service or ISP, you establish an account with that company directly.

Internet Service Providers included in the Online Services folder include:

✦ America Online

✦ CompuServe

✦ The Microsoft Network

✦ Prodigy Internet

✦ AT&T WorldNet

There is a fee for these services. The fee varies with the plan you subscribe to, but the average is between 10 and 30 dollars per month. Your payment arrangements are made directly with the online service or ISP. Many services also give a predetermined number of free trial hours.

NOTE

To setup an online service, you'll need a credit card to bill for the services. You won't be billed during the free trial hours, but you can't even get connected without a credit card number. If you decide to cancel an online service, you'll need to notify the service provider.

The set up process for each service is similar, but each will vary slightly from the others. In this book, you'll subscribe to The Microsoft Network (MSN).

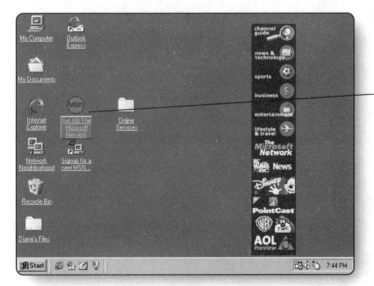

1. **Insert** the **Windows 98 CD-ROM** into the CD-ROM drive.

2a. **Click** on the **MSN icon**. The MSN Setup screen will appear. Skip to step 4.

OR

NOTE

Before you can connect to any of these services, you must have a modem in your computer that is connected to a telephone line.

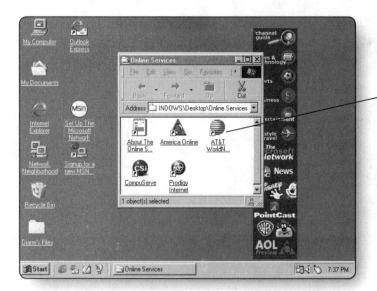

2b. **Click** on the **Online Services folder**. The Online Services window will appear.

3. **Click** on the **service** you want to set up. The online service's set up screen will appear.

4. **Click** on **Next**. You will continue to the next screen. MSN will check to make sure no other programs are currently running.

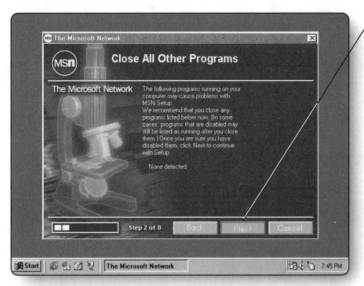

5. Click on **Next**. You will continue to the next screen. MSN will identify which country you are in.

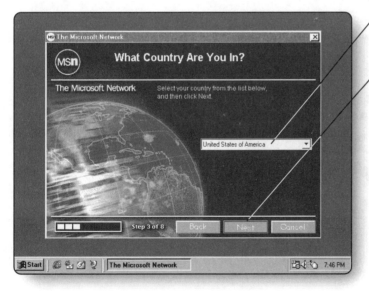

6. Select your **country** from the list box.

7. Click on **Next**. You will continue to the next screen. MSN will display the member agreement. Read it carefully.

8. Click on **I Agree**. MSN will be ready to start the installation.

9. Click on **Next**. You will continue to the next screen, and the software installation process will begin. Be patient. This process will take a few minutes.

Next, MSN wants to know if you have an existing MSN account and whether you want to dial in using MSN or an existing Internet connection.

10. **Click** on the appropriate **choices**. The options will be selected.

11. **Click** on **Next**. You will continue to the next screen.

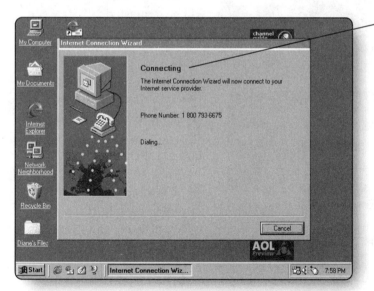

The Internet Connection Wizard connects you to MSN or your ISP.

The MSN Signup Wizard appears and prompts you for personal information, such as name, address, and phone number.

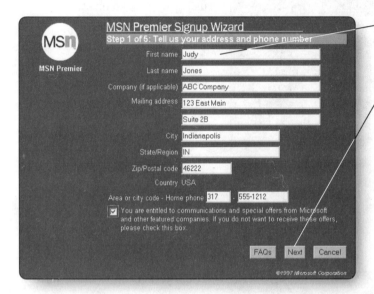

12. **Type** the requested **information** in the appropriate text boxes.

13. **Click** on **Next**. You will continue to the next screen. You will also be advised of the available membership plans and their fees.

14. **Click** on **Next**. You will continue to the next screen, and payment method information will be requested.

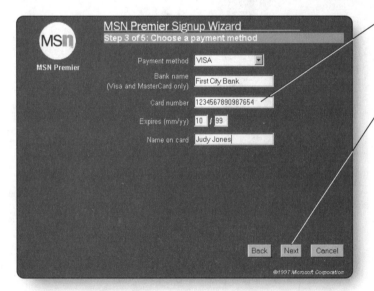

15. **Type** your **credit card information**. Don't put any dashes or spaces in the credit card number.

16. **Click** on **Next**. You will continue to the next screen. MSN will display information on the membership rules.

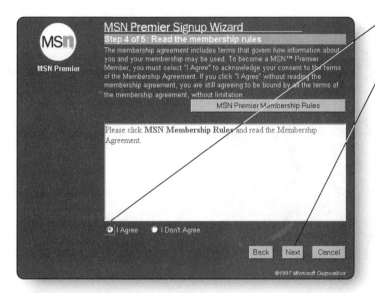

17. Click on **I Agree**. The option will be selected.

18. Click on **Next**. You will continue to the next screen.

19. Type a **user name** and **password**. You'll need to type the password twice. A series of asterisks will appear.

TIP

User names can be any combination of letters, numbers, or hyphens, but cannot contain spaces or other special characters.

20. Click on **Sign Me Up!** Your information will be validated, and a final signup screen will appear confirming your signup.

21. Click on **Exit**. You will return to the Windows desktop.

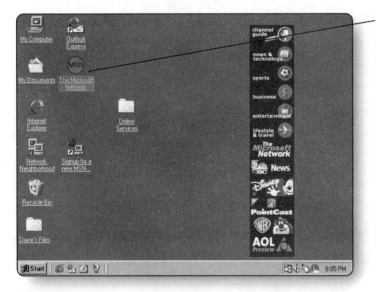

22. Click on the **Microsoft Network icon**. The MSN Sign-In window will appear.

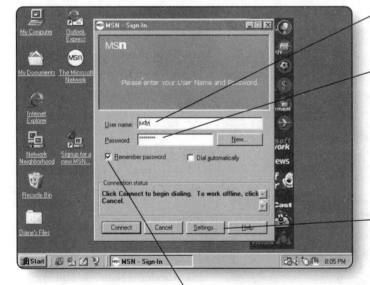

23. Type your **user name** in the User name: text box.

24. Type your **password** in the Password: text box. A series of asterisks will appear.

The first time you connect, you must select a phone number to dial.

25. Click on **Settings**. The Connection Settings dialog box will open.

TIP

Click on the Remember Password check box and you won't have to type your password each time; however, this also gives anyone who uses your computer free access to your Internet account.

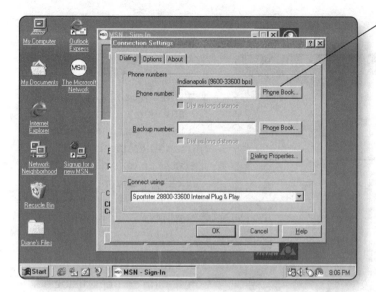

26. **Click** on **Phone Book**. The Phone Book dialog box will open.

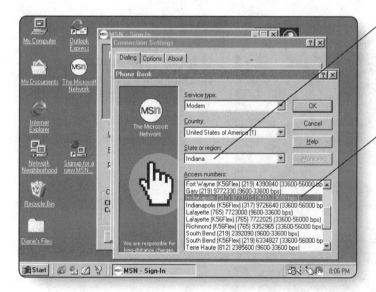

27. **Click** on your **state** in the State or region: list box. A list of access phone numbers will appear in the Access numbers: list box.

28. **Click** on the **access number** closest to you. The access number will be selected.

29. **Click** on **OK**. The Phone Book dialog box will close.

The access number appears in the Phone number: text box.

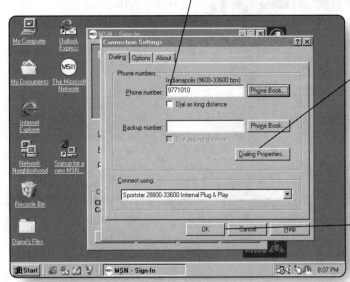

If you have the Call Waiting feature on your modem line, or if you need to dial 9 or another number to access an outside number, click on Dialing Properties and change any necessary settings.

30. Click on **OK**. The Connection Settings dialog box will close.

31. Click on **Connect**. The modem will dial in to The Microsoft Network.

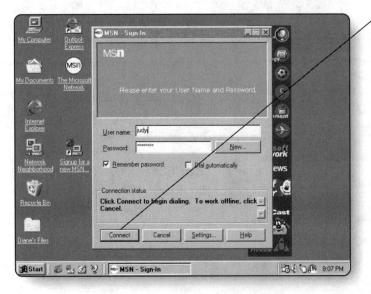

ESTABLISHING A DIAL-UP CONNECTION

If you already have a direct Internet Service Provider, you'll need to tell Windows 98 how to connect to the ISP. Information about your connections is stored in the Dial-Up Networking folder. Dial-Up Networking is sometimes referred to as *DUN* or *DUNS*.

1. Click on **My Computer**. The My Computer window will appear.

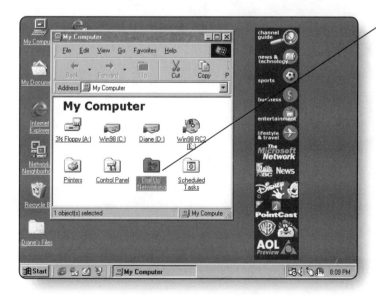

2. Click on **Dial-Up Networking**. The Dial-Up Networking window will appear.

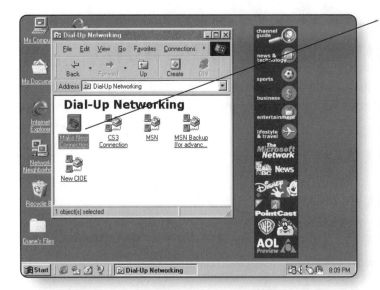

3. Click on **Make New Connection**. The Make New Connection Wizard will appear.

> ### TIP
>
> To delete a connection, right-click on the unwanted connection and click on Delete from the shortcut menu. Click on Yes to confirm the deletion.

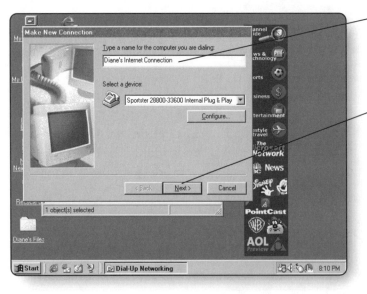

4. Type a **name** for the connection (one that you'll recognize as a connection to your ISP).

5. Click on **Next**. You will continue to the next screen.

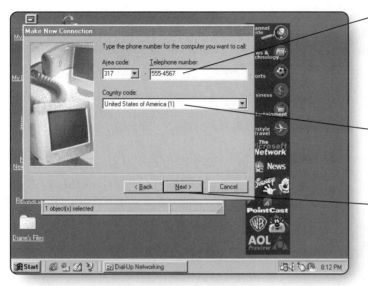

6. **Type** the **area code** and **telephone number** of the computer to which you are dialing. Your ISP will give this phone number to you.

7. **Select** your **country** from the Country code: list box. Your country will appear.

8. **Click** on **Next**. You will continue to the next screen.

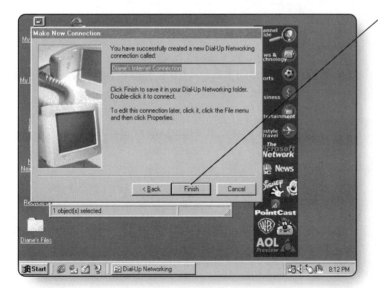

9. **Click** on **Finish**. The Make New Connection Wizard will close.

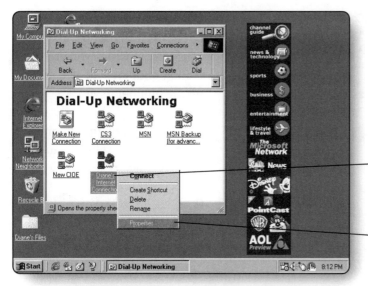

The connection information will be saved in the Dial-Up Networking folder, but you're not quite finished yet. Most ISPs have other information you'll need to enter that is appropriate to their operations.

10. **Right-click** on the **connection** you created. A shortcut menu will appear.

11. **Click** on **Properties**. The properties dialog box for your connection will open.

12. **Click** on the **Server Types tab**. The Server Types tab will move to the front.

The type of information you enter here varies between the different ISPs. If you don't have written instructions for these steps from your ISP, call them on the phone and have them talk you through the choices you need to make for their connection.

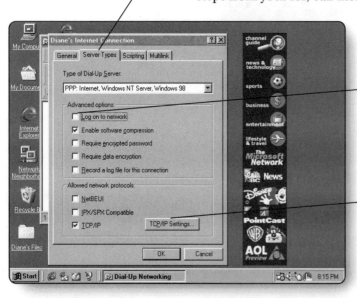

13. **Click** on any necessary choices. A ✔ will appear in the check boxes (the ✔ will disappear from check boxes that were already selected).

14. **Click** on **TCP/IP Settings**. The TCP/IP Settings dialog box will open.

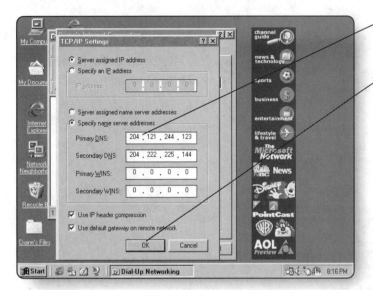

15. **Type** the **information** as specified by your ISP.

16. **Click** on **OK**. The TCP/IP Settings dialog box will close.

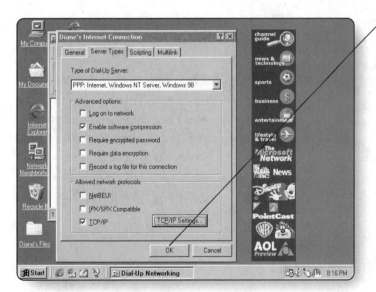

17. **Click** on **OK** when you have completed making any changes to your connection. The properties dialog box will close, and your connection will be ready to use.

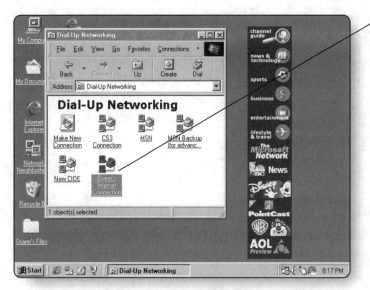

18. **Click** on your new **connection** to connect to your ISP. The Connect To dialog box will open.

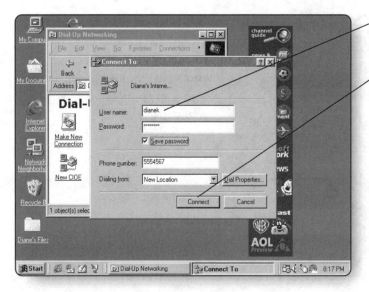

19. **Type** your **user name** and **password,** if prompted to do so.

20. **Click** on **Connect**. Your modem will dial in to your ISP. As it establishes a connection, you'll hear some screeching and strange noises from your computer. That's OK—it's one computer saying "hello" to the other.

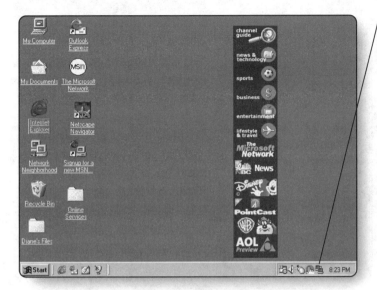

When you are connected, an icon representing two small computers appears on the Windows 98 System Tray.

TIP

To disconnect from your ISP, double-click on the connection icon in the System Tray and click on Disconnect.

STARTING YOUR WEB BROWSER

Now that you are connected to the Internet, you'll need a program to view the HTML documents that have been created for the World Wide Web. These programs are called *Web browsers*. There are several types of Web browsers on the market today, and the features that each one offers are updated frequently.

Two of the most popular Web browsers are Microsoft Internet Explorer and Netscape Navigator. Microsoft Internet Explorer is included with Windows 98. Netscape Navigator is also a free product. You can download it from http://www.netscape.com.

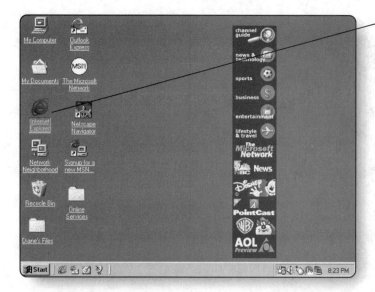

1. **Click** on the **browser** you want to use. The program will start and display a starting page. From here you can "surf the net."

2. **Click** on the **Close button** ([×]). The browser window will close. You may be prompted to disconnect from your ISP.

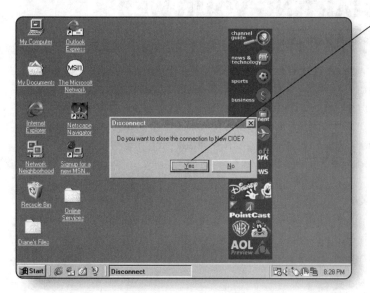

3. **Click** on **Yes** if you want to disconnect.

20 Looking at Internet Explorer

The Internet is a collection of millions of computers around the world. Learning opportunities and hours of fun are at your fingertips. But how do you get to these computers? Internet Explorer enables you to gain access to the vast stores of information on these computers. In this chapter, you'll learn how to:

✦ Browse the Web with Internet Explorer

✦ Set and use Favorites

✦ Set parental controls

✦ Discover channels

BROWSING THE WEB WITH INTERNET EXPLORER

Screens that are accessed on the Internet are called *Web pages* or *home pages*. A *home page* is the starting point of a series of connected Web pages. Web pages have *addresses*. A typical Web address usually starts with http://www. Then you'll need to specify an exact address such as microsoft.com or whitehouse.gov. Therefore, a completed Web address might look something like http://www.disney.com.

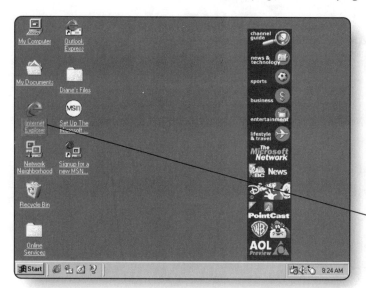

1. **Click** on **Internet Explorer**. The Dial-Up Connection dialog box will open.

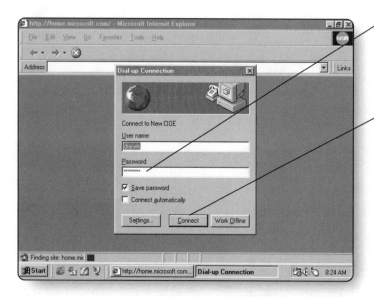

2. **Type** your **password**, if it is not already entered in the Password: text box. A series of asterisks will appear.

3. **Click** on **Connect**. A connection to your ISP will be established, and the Internet Explorer start page will appear.

TIP

A *start page* is the first page a browser looks at when it is launched.

You can type a specific address to go to, or you can search the Internet for specific information.

4. **Type** the specific **address** in the Address list box.

5. **Press** the **Enter key**. Internet Explorer will display the home page for the address you specified.

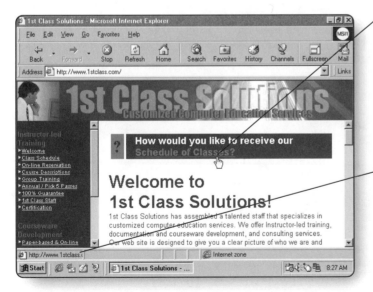

When you position your mouse on underlined text or pictures and the mouse turns into a hand, you are pointing to a hyperlink. You click on a *hyperlink* to go to another Web page in the site you are visiting.

When you point to a hyperlink, its Web address will appear at the bottom of the Internet Explorer window.

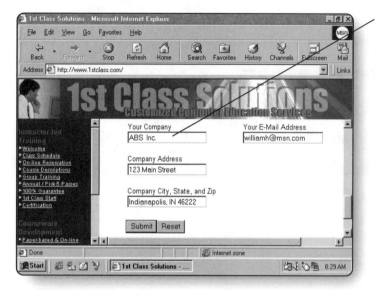

Many Web pages have forms that you can fill out and submit. You'll see these a lot if you request information or purchase something on the Web.

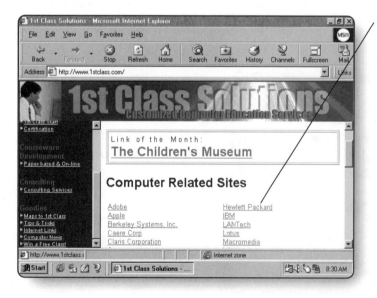

Many Web pages also have hyperlinks to other Web sites that might be of interest to you.

TIP

If the toolbar is not displayed, click on View, Toolbars, and then Standard Buttons.

EXPLORING THE INTERNET EXPLORER WINDOW

The Internet Explorer window has a toolbar with buttons to help you navigate the Web.

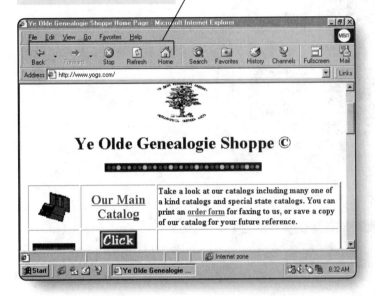

✦ **Back**. Sends Internet Explorer to the previously-viewed Web page.

✦ **Forward**. Returns Internet Explorer to the page you were on before you clicked the Back button.

✦ **Stop**. Stops the loading of the current Web page.

✦ **Refresh**. Reloads the current Web page.

✦ **Home**. Returns you to your start page.

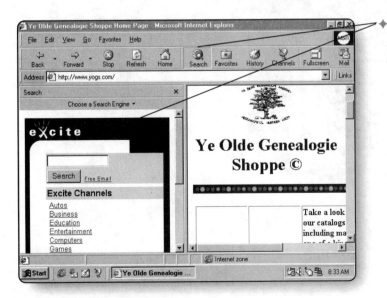

✦ **Search**. Displays a list of search engines to help you find a topic.

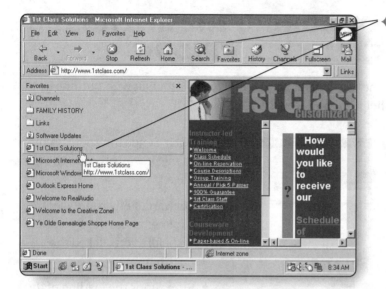

♦ **Favorites**. Displays a collection of Web sites you frequently access.

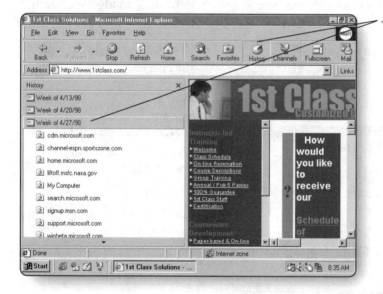

♦ **History**. Displays a list of Web sites you have previously viewed.

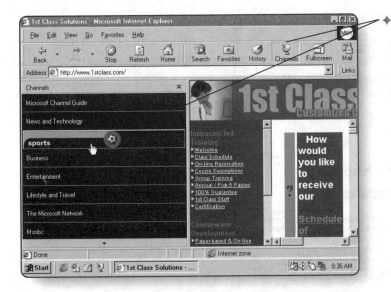

◆ **Channels**. Displays links to Web sites used to receive information from the Internet to your computer.

◆ **Full Screen**. Hides the Internet Explorer menu bar and makes the toolbar smaller for larger screen space in which to view a Web page.

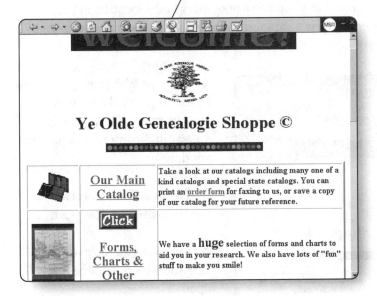

✦ **Mail**. Displays a shortcut menu with Internet mail options.

PLAYING FAVORITES

If you have a special poem in a book that you like to read often, you might place a bookmark at the location of that poem. Internet Explorer Favorites are like bookmarks to your favorite Web sites.

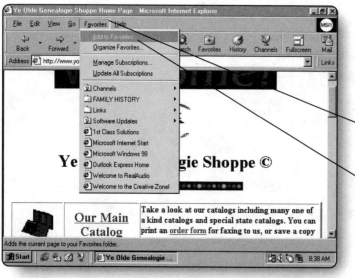

1. **Go** to the **Web page** you want to add to your collection of favorite pages. The page will appear in the Internet Explorer window.

2. **Click** on **Favorites**. The Favorites menu will appear.

3. **Click** on **Add to Favorites**. The Add Favorite dialog box will open.

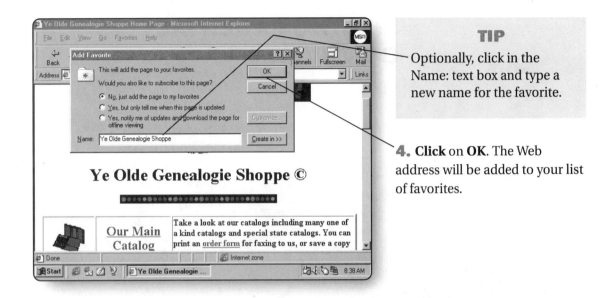

Optionally, click in the
Name: text box and type a
new name for the favorite.

4. **Click** on **OK**. The Web
address will be added to your list
of favorites.

Accessing Your Favorite Sites

By using bookmarks, you won't have to remember to type the
Web addresses of your favorite sites. Your favorite site is only a
mouse click away.

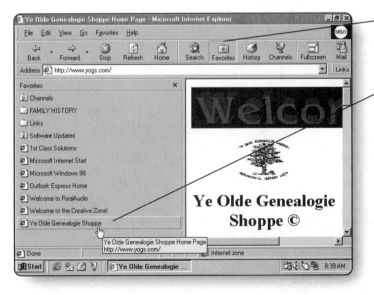

1. **Click** on the **Favorites
button**. The Favorites list will
appear.

2. **Click** on the **page** you want
to open. Internet Explorer will
jump to the specified Web page.

SETTING PARENTAL CONTROLS

NOTE

Not all Web pages are rated.

The Web is filled with information. Any topic you want to research, you'll find on the Web. However, you might want to monitor the information you or your children can access. With the Content Advisor, you can screen out objectionable or offensive content by using industry-standard ratings defined independently by the Platform for Internet Content Selection (PICS) committee.

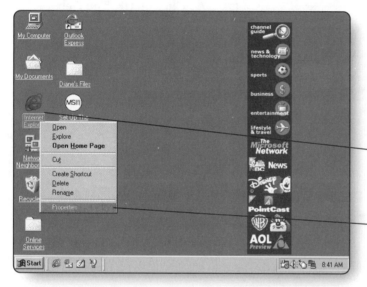

1. Right-click on **Internet Explorer**. A shortcut menu will appear.

2. Click on **Properties**. The Internet Properties dialog box will open.

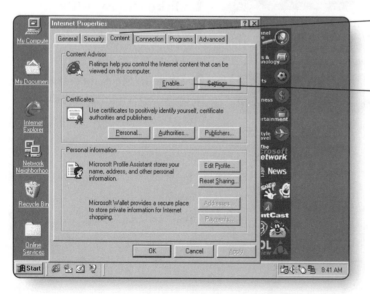

3. Click on the **Content tab**. The Content tab will move to the front.

4. Click on **Enable**. The Create Supervisor Password dialog box will open.

When you enable the Content Advisor, a supervisor password must be assigned to prevent others from changing the settings. The settings can be modified only by someone who knows the password.

5. **Type** a **password** in the Password: text box. Asterisks will appear in the text box.

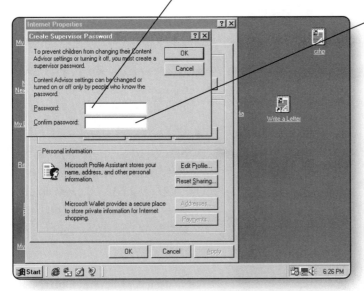

6. **Type** the same **password** in the Confirm password: text box. Asterisks will appear in the text box.

7. **Click** on **OK**. The Content Advisor dialog box will open. Here you can control the level of language, nudity, sex, and violence of the Web pages displayed.

> ### NOTE
> Each category has a five-level rating beginning with zero, the strictest rating, and going to four, which is the most lenient rating.

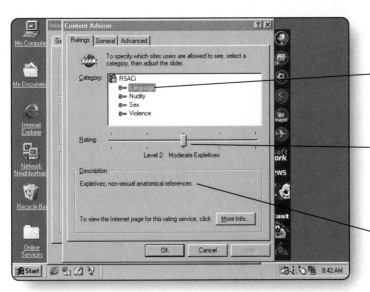

8. **Click** on the **category** you want to change. A Rating slide bar will appear.

9. **Slide** the **rating bar** to the desired level.

> ### NOTE
> A description of each rating is displayed under the Rating: slide bar.

10. **Repeat steps 8** and **9** for each category you want to restrict.

11. **Click** on the **General tab**. The General tab will move to the front.

The General tab has two more options from which you can select.

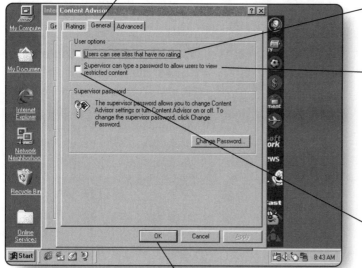

♦ **Users can see sites that have no rating**. Enables access to a site that is not rated.

♦ **Supervisor can type a password to allow users to view restricted content**. Enables access to a restricted Web site for anyone who has access to the supervisor password.

12. **Click** on the **check boxes**, if desired. A ✔ will appear in the box next to a selected item.

13. **Click** on **OK**. The Content Advisor dialog box will close.

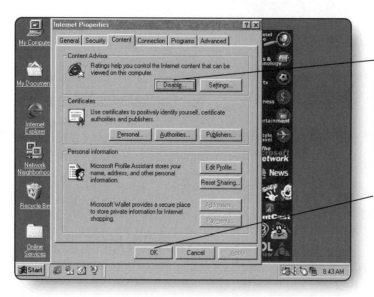

NOTE

If you want to disable ratings restrictions, return to the Content tab of the Internet Properties dialog box, click on Disable, and then click on OK.

14. **Click** on **OK**. The Internet Properties dialog box will close.

DISCOVERING CHANNELS

A *channel* is a Web site designed to deliver live content from the Internet to your computer. You can subscribe to a stock market channel or a news channel so you'll always be up to date with the latest information. Channels are some of the most colorful and dynamic pages you'll find. The Channel bar displayed on the Active Desktop has suggested categories for you to subscribe to, but you can customize it with the topics you use most.

> **NOTE**
>
> To view the Channel bar that comes with Windows 98, you must have the Active Desktop configured. See "Integrating Your Desktop with the Web" in Chapter 17 for information on activating the Active Desktop feature.

A few of the channel categories that come with Windows 98 include:

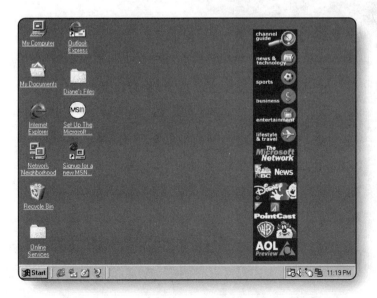

+ Entertainment channels, such as Comics, AudioNet, MTV, Hollywood Online, People, and NBC Daily

+ News and technology channels, such as CNN, NY Times, Time, and ZDNet

+ Sports channels, such as ESPN, MSNBC Sports, and CBS SportsLine

+ Travel and lifestyle channels, such as Discover and National Geographic

+ Disney and Warner Brothers channels

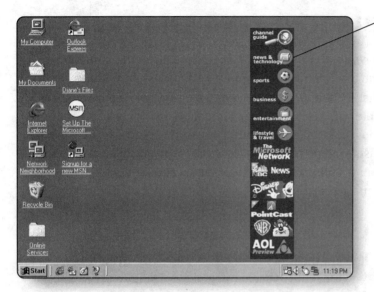

1. Click on a **category** on the Channel bar. The channel window will appear.

The first time you click on the Channel bar, a welcome message appears. You can choose an overview of channels if you want more information.

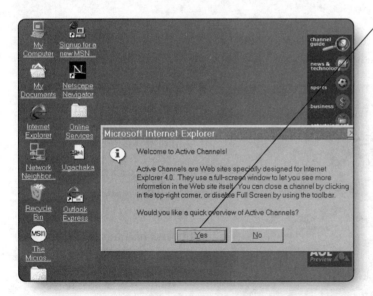

2. Click on **Yes** or **No**. If you choose yes, the Active Channel overview will appear.

NOTE

If you are not already connected to the Internet, you will be prompted to do so.

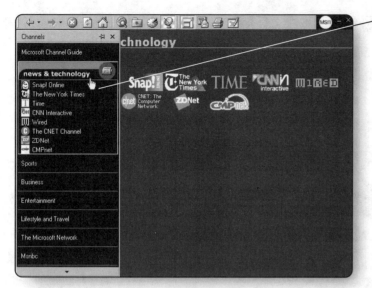

Position your mouse on the left side of the screen to see the Channel bar.

The channel categories are displayed. Some of the categories have subcategories; however, some are direct links to a specific Web site. If you choose a category, such as News & Technology, the Internet Explorer window shows a list of the channel sites available in that category.

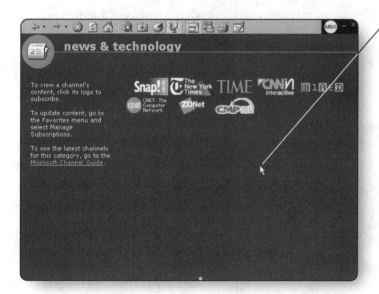

Move the mouse to the right to hide the Channel bar.

3. **Click** on the **channel** you want to view. The Web page will appear.

4. **Click** on **Add Active Channel**. The Modify Channel Usage dialog box will open.

There are three ways you can update an Active Channel:

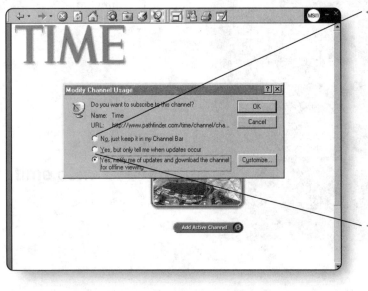

✦ **No, just keep it in my Channel Bar**. Specifies that you want to add this channel to your Channel bar, but you do not want to be automatically notified when the content changes on this channel. Also you do not want updated content automatically downloaded to your computer.

✦ **Yes, but only tell me when updates occur**. Specifies that you want Internet Explorer to make scheduled checks for changes to this channel and to notify you when the content changes.

✦ **Yes, notify me of updates and download the channel for offline viewing**. Specifies that you want to subscribe to the current channel. Internet Explorer automatically notifies you of changes to the channel and automatically downloads pages from the site according to the schedule set by the channel provider or you.

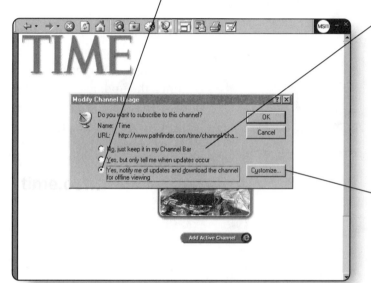

5. **Click** on an **option**. The option will be selected.

If you selected to be notified of updates to your subscribed channel, you can now advise Windows 98 when and how to do so.

6. **Click** on **Customize**. The Subscription Wizard will open.

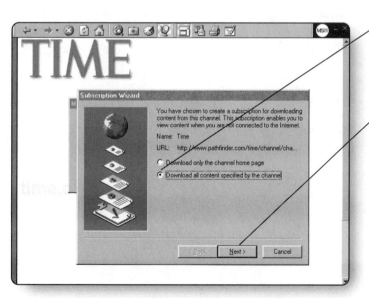

7. **Click** on **Download all content specified by the channel**. The option will be selected.

8. **Click** on **Next**. You will continue to the next screen.

Internet Explorer can notify you if the page has changed by adding a red dot to its icon; you can also be notified via e-mail.

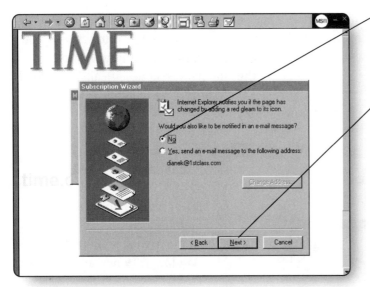

9. Click on **No** if you do not want to be notified by e-mail of any changes to the Web site. The option will be selected.

10. Click on **Next**. You will continue to the next screen.

Each channel publisher has a recommended update schedule. Depending on the type of channel, the update could be hourly, every four hours, or once a day. You can alternately choose to have it updated daily, monthly, or weekly.

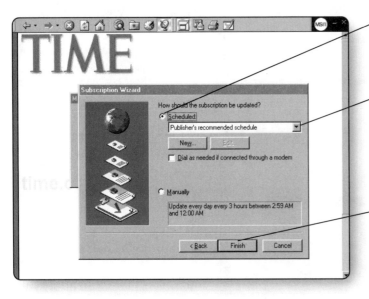

11. Click on the **option button** next to Scheduled. The option will be selected.

12. Click on the **down arrow** (▼) next to the Scheduled: list box and **select** the **scheduled time** you want the subscription to be updated.

13. Click on **Finish**. The Subscription Wizard dialog box will close.

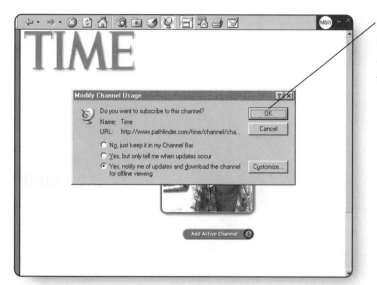

14. Click on **OK**. The Modify Channel Usage dialog box will close, and the channel Web site will appear.

Manually Updating a Channel Subscription

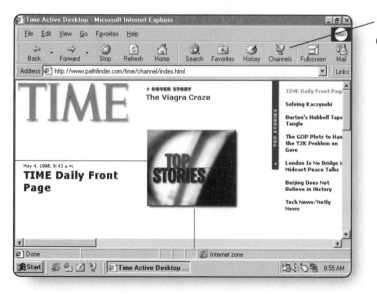

1. Click on **Channels**. The Channels folder will open.

2. Right-click on the **channel** you want to update. A shortcut menu will appear.

3. Click on **Update Now**. The channel information will be updated.

21 Working with Outlook Express

The capability to send and receive e-mail is one of the most important functions of a computer. What is e-mail? E-mail is defined as the exchange of text messages and computer files over a communications network, such as the Internet or a company network. Outlook Express is a full-featured e-mail and news reading client that comes with Windows 98. In this chapter, you'll learn how to:

✦ Create and send e-mail

✦ Attach a file to an e-mail

✦ Receive and manage e-mail

STARTING OUTLOOK EXPRESS

To send or receive e-mail or to access newsgroups, you must have a modem hooked up to your computer, and you must have access to some type of online service.

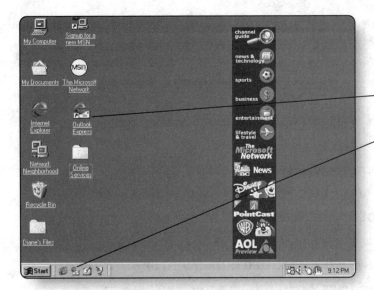

There are three ways you can start the Outlook Express program:

✦ Click on the Outlook Express icon on the desktop.

✦ Click on the Outlook Express icon on the Taskbar.

✦ Click on the Start button, and then Programs, Internet Explorer, and Outlook Express.

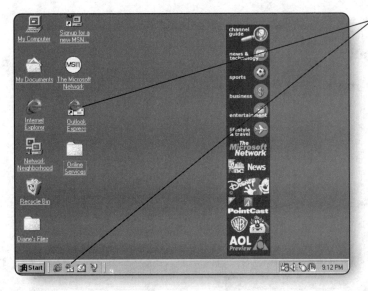

1. **Click** on **either** of the **Outlook Express icons**. The Outlook Express program will start.

USING OUTLOOK EXPRESS FOR E-MAIL

The first time you open Outlook Express, the Internet Connection Wizard appears to help you set up Outlook Express, and then it prompts you for basic Internet access account information. The information the Internet Connection Wizard asks for is a one-time-only setup choice.

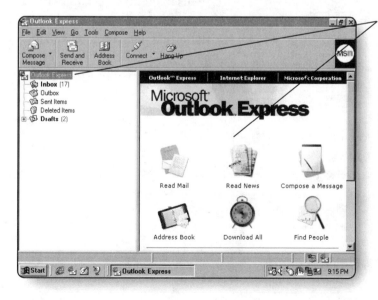

> **NOTE**
>
> See Chapter 19 for more information on the Internet Connection Wizard.

After Outlook Express has been configured, if you are not connected to your Internet Service Provider, Outlook Express will connect you.

After connecting, several folders appear in the folder list. The top item is Outlook Express with subfolders listed under it. Clicking on the Outlook Express folder displays the Start page on the right side.

The next folder in Outlook Express is the Inbox folder. When you are connected to your ISP, Outlook Express places any incoming mail in the Inbox folder. A number (in parentheses) on the right side of the Inbox folder indicates there are new messages.

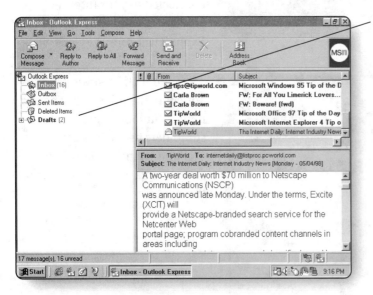

When you create e-mail messages, you have the option to send them immediately or send them at a later time. Any messages waiting to be sent are indicated in the Outbox folder.

Other folders created with Outlook Express include a Sent Items folder to keep copies of any e-mail you send, a Deleted Items folder to throw away e-mail, and a Drafts folder in which to keep unfinished messages.

Setting Up E-mail Accounts

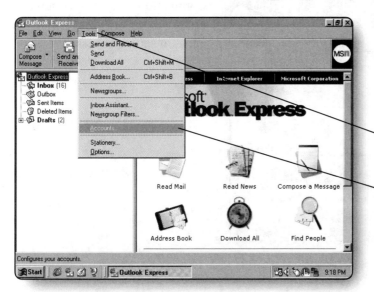

Outlook Express uses the Internet Connection Wizard to quickly lead you through the process of setting up a new e-mail account.

1. Click on **Tools**. The Tools menu will appear.

2. Click on **Accounts**. The Internet Accounts dialog box will open.

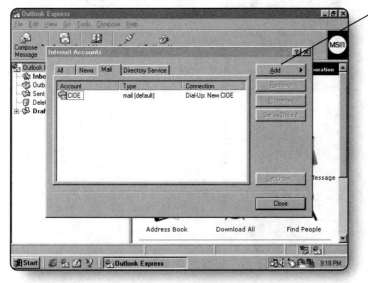

3. Click on **Add**. The Add menu will appear.

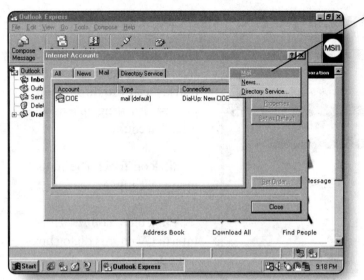

4. Click on **Mail**. The Internet Connection Wizard will open to assist you through the e-mail account setup process.

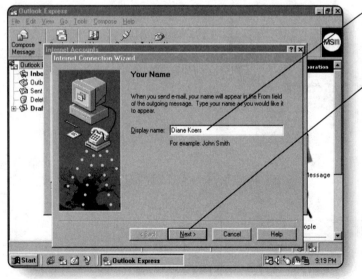

5. Type the **name** you want others to see when you send them a message.

6. Click on **Next**. You will proceed to the next screen.

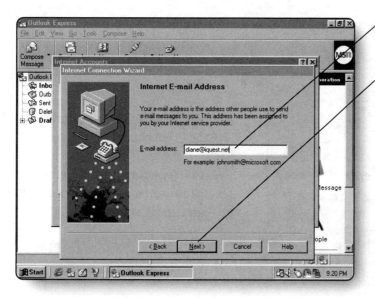

7. Type your **e-mail address** in the E-mail address: text box.

8. Click on **Next**. You will proceed to the next screen.

It gets a little trickier here. When you get to this screen, contact your ISP and ask for the information. They'll be happy to provide it to you.

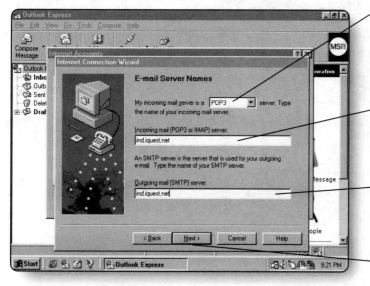

9. Click on the correct type of **mail server** (POP3 or IMAP). Your selection will appear in the list box.

10. Type the **incoming mail server name** in the Incoming mail server: text box.

11. Type the **outgoing mail server name** in the Outgoing mail server: text box.

12. Click on **Next**. You will proceed to the next screen.

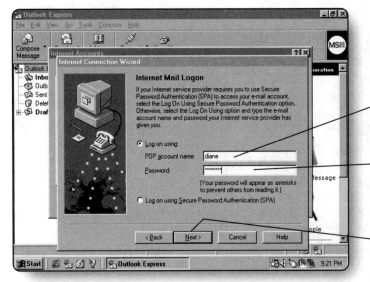

Most ISPs require you to log on with a password. You'll need to enter it here, as well as your log on name.

13. Type your **log on name** in the POP account name: text box.

14. Type your **password** in the Password: text box. Asterisks will appear in the text box.

15. Click on **Next**. You will proceed to the next screen.

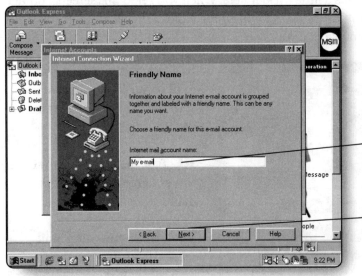

The next screen asks you to enter a "friendly name" for this e-mail account. Generally, the name of the ISP is used, such as CompuServe or Iquest, but you can call it anything you want.

16. Type a friendly **name** in the Internet mail account name: text box.

17. Click on **Next**. You will proceed to the next screen.

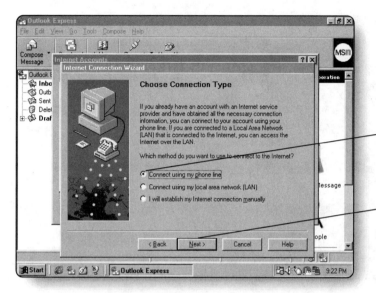

Now you must tell the Internet Connection Wizard what type of connection you have: a modem, a local area network (LAN), or a manual connection.

18. **Click** on the appropriate **option button**. The option will be selected.

19. **Click** on **Next**. You will proceed to the next screen.

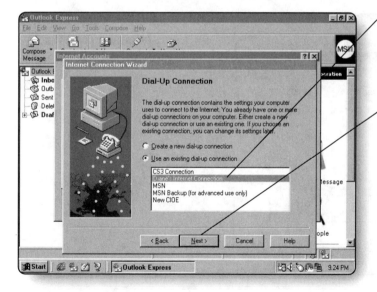

20. **Click** on the **dial-up connection** you want to use to access this mail. The selection will be highlighted.

21. **Click** on **Next**. You will proceed to the next screen.

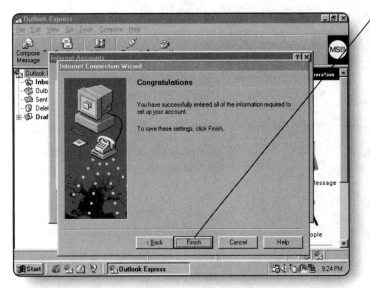

22. Click on **Finish**. The new mail connection will be displayed in the Internet Accounts dialog box.

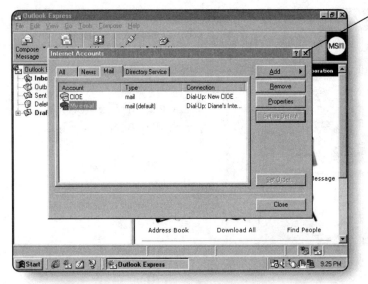

23. Click on the **Close button** (⊠). The Internet Accounts dialog box will close.

Creating an E-mail Message

If you want to communicate with someone quickly, send him an e-mail message. In Outlook Express, you can read, create, and send your e-mail messages.

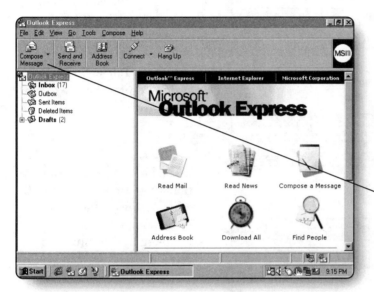

1. **Click** on the **Compose Message button**. The New Message dialog box will open.

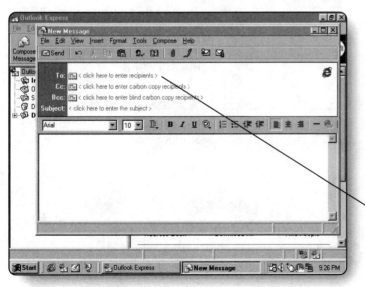

2. **Type** the **e-mail address** of the person to whom you want to send the message. The name will appear in the To: line.

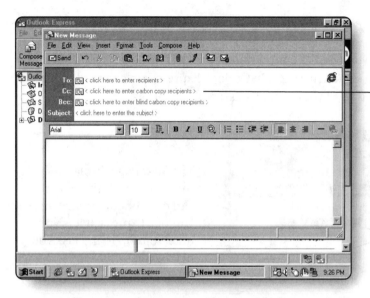

3. **Press** the **Tab key**. The insertion point will move to the Cc: line.

4. **Type** an **e-mail address** of anyone to whom you want to send a carbon copy (CC) of the message, if desired.

5. **Press** the **Tab key**. The insertion point will move to the Bcc: line.

TIP

If you have more than one person to list on any of the address lines, separate the e-mail name of each recipient by a comma or a semicolon.

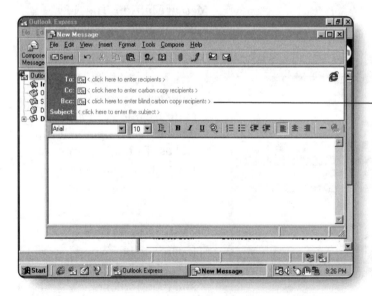

6. **Type** an **e-mail address** of anyone to whom you want to send a blind carbon copy (BCC) of the message, if desired. The e-mail address will appear on the BCC: line.

7. **Press** the **Tab key**. The insertion point will move to the Subject: line.

NOTE

Blind carbon copies allow you to send a copy of the message to someone without the names on the first two lines knowing about it.

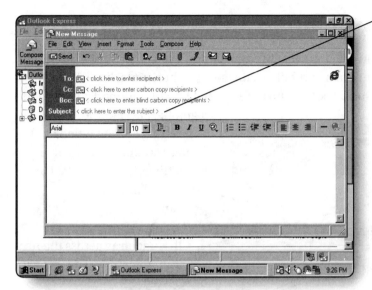

8. Type a **subject** for the message. The text will appear in the Subject: line.

9. Press the **Tab key**. The insertion point will move to the body of the message.

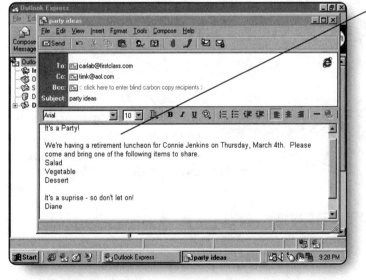

10. Type your **message** in the body of the message box. The typed text will appear in the lower half of the window.

Formatting an E-mail Message

You can dress up your e-mail messages. Instead of plain text, you can insert bullets, images, and horizontal lines. You can also add colors and styles with different fonts and sizes or add a graphic background. Formatting text in Outlook Express is almost identical to formatting text in WordPad or other word processing programs.

1. **Click** and **drag** across the **text** you want to modify. The text will be selected.

2. **Click** on the **Bold, Italics,** or **Underline button**. The text will become bold, italicized, or underlined.

3. **Click** on the **down arrows** (▼) to choose the font or font size. A selection of fonts or font sizes will appear.

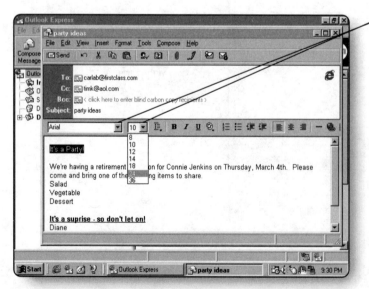

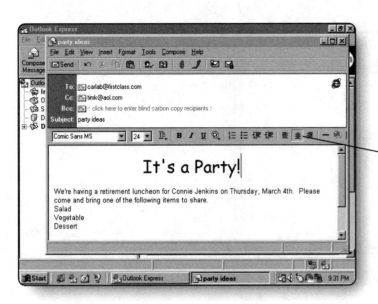

4. **Click** on the **font** or **font size** you want to use. The text will change to the new font selection.

TIP

Click on the Center button to center selected text.

5. **Click** and **drag** across the text to which you want to apply bullets or numbers. The text will be selected.

6. **Click** on the **Bullet button**.

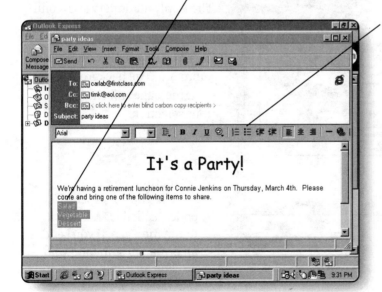

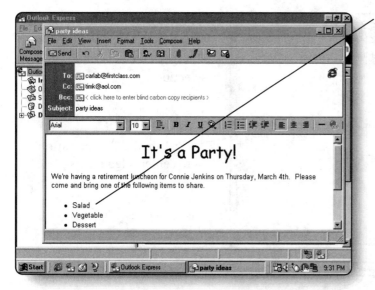

A bullet point is applied to the front of each line of the selected text.

7. **Click** on **Format**. The Format menu will appear.

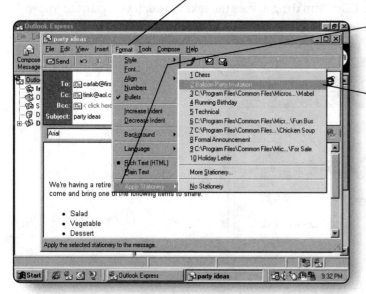

8. **Click** on **Apply Stationery**. The Apply Stationery submenu will appear.

9. **Click** on a **selection** from the submenu. The background of your message will change to your selection.

NOTE

Formatting an e-mail message applies special codes, called *HTML codes*, to the message. If you send an e-mail to someone who is using an e-mail program that doesn't support HTML, the recipient may see HTML coding in the message. The recipient can simply ignore the codes.

10. **Click** on the **Send button**. The message will immediately be sent to the recipients.

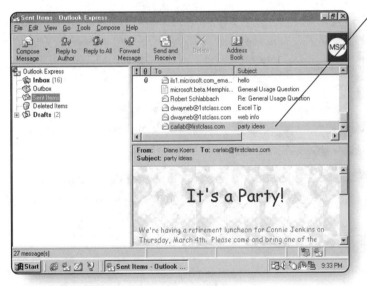

A copy of the message is placed in the Sent Items folder.

Attaching Files to E-mail

You might want to include a spreadsheet or other document with an e-mail message. Outlook Express can send files of any type—pictures, documents, spreadsheets, or any text or binary files.

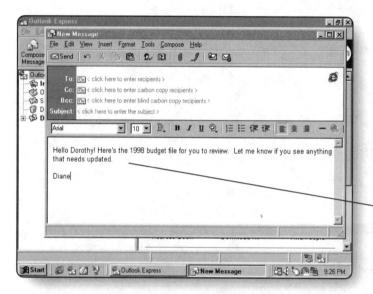

In order to open the additional document, the recipient must have a program that supports the file format you are sending. For example, if you send an Excel file, the recipient must either have Excel on their system, or a spreadsheet application that can read Excel files.

1. **Create** the **e-mail message**.

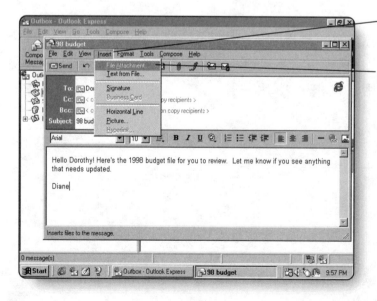

2. **Click** on **Insert**. The Insert menu will appear.

3. **Click** on **File Attachment**. The Insert Attachment dialog box will open.

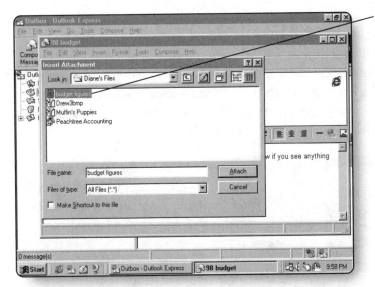

4. Locate and **double-click** on the **file** you want to attach to the message. The Insert Attachment dialog box will close.

An icon representing the attached file is displayed at the bottom of the new message box.

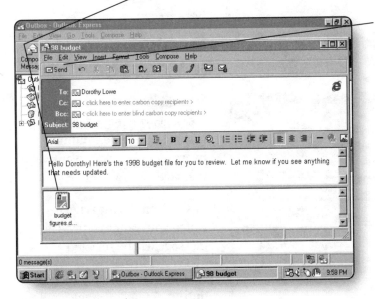

5. Click on **Send**. The file will be sent along with the message.

Retrieving Incoming E-mail

TIP

You can print any message by pressing Ctrl+P.

Outlook Express tells you when you have new messages by putting the number of new messages in parentheses next to the Inbox. If you are online, Outlook Express will check for new messages at specified intervals. You will hear a light tone when a new message is received.

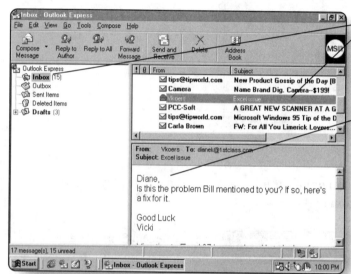

1. **Click** on the **Inbox**. A list of new messages will appear on the right side of the screen. One of the messages will be selected.

2. **Read** the **message** in the Preview pane.

3. **Click** on the **next message**. The next message will appear in the Preview pane.

Replying to a Message

Now that you've read the message, you might want to reply to the sender. Outlook Express enables you to answer a message.

1. **Click** on the **message** to which you want to reply. The message will be selected.

2. **Click** on the **Reply to Author button**. A mail message window will appear with the sender's e-mail address and subject already entered.

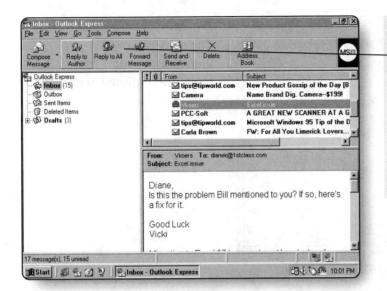

TIP

If the original message was sent to more than one person, you can click on Reply to All instead of Reply to Author. Your reply will be sent to each person who received the original message.

In the body of the new e-mail message, the original message is displayed. The original message has a carat sign (>) in front of it.

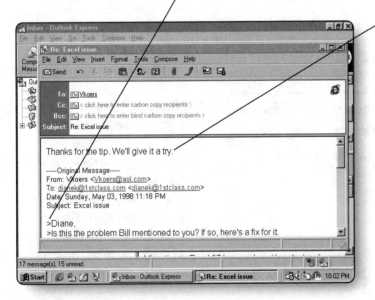

3. Type the **reply** in the message body. The text will appear in the bottom half of the window.

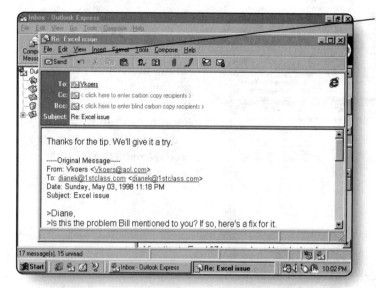

4. Click on the **Send button**. The reply will be sent immediately, and a copy of the reply will be placed in the Sent Items folder.

Forwarding a Message

You can send a received message on to another person by forwarding it. You can even add your own message along with it.

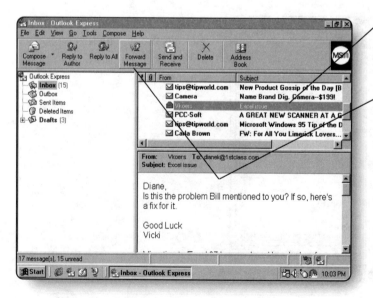

1. Click on the **message** you want to forward. The message will be selected.

2. Click on the **Forward Message button**. A new mail message window will appear and the e-mail address will be blank in the To: line. The Subject: line will contain the same subject as the mail you received, and the original message will be in the body of the new e-mail message.

3. Type the **recipient's e-mail address** in the To: line.

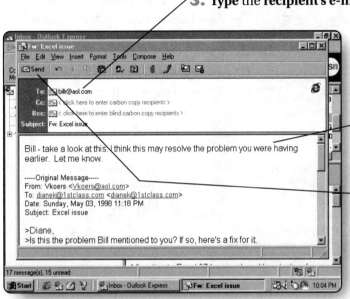

4. Click in the **body** of the e-mail message. The insertion point will flash in the bottom half of the window.

5. Type the **message** you want to send. The text will appear in addition to the original message.

6. Click on the **Send button**. The message will be sent to the new recipient immediately, and a copy will be placed in the Sent Items folder.

Creating an E-mail Folder

Incoming messages are stored in the Inbox until you do something with them. As more and more e-mail arrives, the Inbox can get very full. You can create new folders to organize your mail.

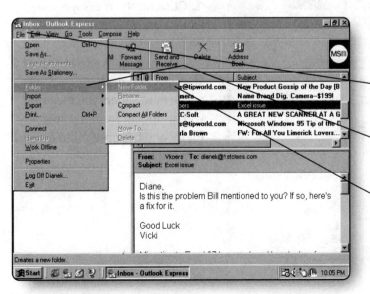

1. Click on **File**. The File menu will appear.

2. Click on **Folder**. The Folder submenu will appear.

3. Click on **New Folder**. The Create Folder dialog box will open.

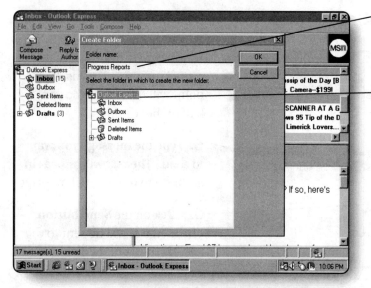

4. Type a **name** for the new folder in the Folder name: text box.

5. Click on the **folder** in which you want to place the new folder. The selected folder will be highlighted.

6. Click on **OK**. The new folder will be created and displayed in the Folder list.

Moving an E-mail Message

Any e-mail from the Inbox can be moved to any existing folder. This is done in the same manner as moving files in Windows Explorer.

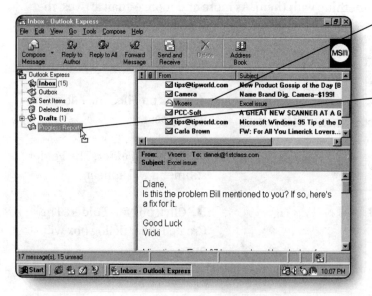

1. Click on the **message** you want to move. The message will be selected.

2. Click and **drag** the **message** to the new folder. The message will disappear from the current folder and be moved into the new folder.

Deleting an E-mail Message

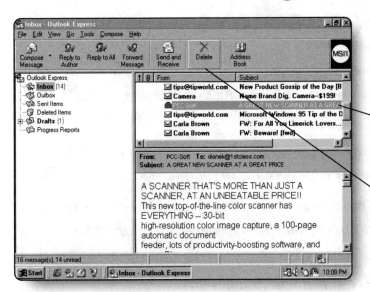

Deleted messages are not permanently deleted until you exit the Outlook Express program.

1. **Click** on the **message** you want to delete. The message will be selected.

2. **Click** on the **Delete button**. The message will be moved to the Deleted Items folder.

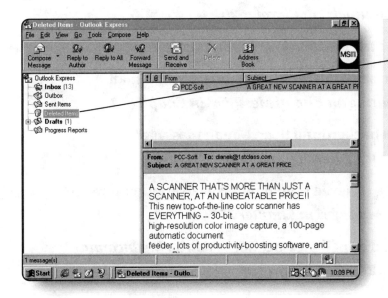

TIP

If you want to "undelete" a mail message, click on the Deleted Items folder and drag the message to a different folder.

PART V REVIEW QUESTIONS

1. **What piece of equipment must your computer have in order to connect to the Internet?** *See "Subscribing to an Online Service" in Chapter 19*

2. **User names can be any combination of what three characters?** *See "Subscribing to an Online Service" in Chapter 19*

3. **What are two of the most frequently-used Web browsers on the market today?** *See "Starting Your Web Browser" in Chapter 19*

4. **What types of content can you control with parental control?** *See "Setting Parental Controls" in Chapter 20*

5. **What type of desktop setting must be activated to use Channels?** *See "Discovering Channels" in Chapter 20*

6. **What is e-mail?** *See the introduction in Chapter 21*

7. **What do you use to separate multiple names on an e-mail message?** *See "Creating an E-mail Message" in Chapter 21*

8. **How can you add a background to an e-mail message?** *See "Formatting an E-mail Message" in Chapter 21*

9. **How can you send a received e-mail message to another person?** *See "Forwarding a Message" in Chapter 21*

10. **How do you print an e-mail message?** *See "Retrieving Incoming E-mail" in Chapter 21*

A Upgrading to Windows 98

If you go out today and buy a new computer, most likely it will have Windows 98 preinstalled on it. But if you're upgrading from an earlier version of Microsoft Windows, you'll be pleasantly surprised with the ease of installing Windows 98. In this appendix, you'll learn how to:

✦ **Install Windows 98**

EXPLORING THE SETUP PROCESS

Setup is a very simple process with Windows 98 and requires very little interaction between you and the computer. During the setup process, Windows 98 recognizes your current configuration on the PC and retains those settings. It easily detects your hardware and existing software and it has a built-in setup recovery system. If the setup process should fail in the middle, Windows 98 remembers where it left off and begins at that step. This feature saves time because you won't have to redo the successful installation steps.

Windows 98 can be installed on or over a network. It offers the same networking capabilities as Windows 95 but also has added provisions for better support of networks.

INSTALLING THE WINDOWS 98 UPGRADE

Installation of the Windows 98 upgrade requires six basic parts, all of which are run almost automatically by the setup program. Part 1 starts the setup program and checks for your existing system information.

1. **Insert** the **Windows 98 CD-ROM**. A Windows 98 dialog box will open.

Windows detects that the version of software on the CD-ROM is newer than the existing operating system. The Windows 98 Setup program asks if you want to upgrade now.

2. **Click** on **Yes**. The Windows 98 installation process will begin.

Windows first checks out your existing system; you can track the process with the progress bar. On the left side of your screen, a display lists the steps to be done during the upgrade and the estimated time remaining to accomplish it. The current step is displayed in yellow. The exact time depends on the speed and configuration of your machine.

Part 2 asks for your agreement to Microsoft licensing terms and prepares you for uninstallation, if necessary. First, read through the agreement. You can press the Page Down key to see more of it.

3. **Click** on **"I Accept This Agreement."** The option will be selected.

4. **Click** on **Next** to continue to the next screen.

Now, the Setup Wizard begins collecting information about your computer, including the components that are already installed in your existing operating system. Next, it will check for available disk space. If you don't have enough, a dialog box will advise you that Setup cannot continue. Then, the Setup Wizard asks you about saving the existing system files so you can uninstall Windows 98, if necessary. This step requires an additional 50MB of disk space.

5a. **Click** on **Yes** if you want to save the existing files.

OR

5b. **Click** on **No** if you don't want those files saved. You will not be able to uninstall Windows 98 if you choose No.

6. **Click** on **Next** to continue to the next screen.

The CD key code that Setup asks for pertains to your license to use Windows 98. This code could be located in one of two places. First, look on the CD-ROM case. Second, look on the certificate of authenticity included with the paperwork that came with your Windows 98 upgrade.

7. **Type** the **CD code**. It will appear in the text box.

8. **Click** on **Next** to continue to the next screen.

The Setup Wizard asks about which Internet Channels you want to use. Internet Channels enable you to get region-specific news and other information through Channels. *Channels* are Web sites designed to deliver content from the Internet to your computer.

9. **Click** on the **down arrow [▼]**. A list of available countries will appear.

10. **Click** on your **country**. Your country will appear in the list box.

11. **Click** on **Next** to continue to the next screen.

Part 3 creates a startup disk. The Setup Wizard can create a startup disk for you to use if you later have trouble starting Windows 98. Creating a startup disk isn't mandatory, but I highly recommend it.

12. **Click** on **Next** to continue to the next screen.

13. **Insert** a floppy **disk** into the floppy disk drive. If the floppy disk has existing files on it, those files will be erased.

14. **Click** on **OK**. Setup will transfer the necessary startup files to a floppy disk.

TIP

If you do not want to create a startup disk, click on Cancel.

A message box appears when the startup disk is complete. Remove the disk from the disk drive and label the disk "Emergency Windows 98 Startup Disk." Store this disk in a safe, convenient place.

15. **Click** on **OK** to continue the setup process.

NOTE

Be patient, part 4 may take a little while. Read the screens displayed onscreen for information on Windows 98's new features and enhancements. These screens change periodically. On the left side of the screen, a progress indicator keeps you up-to-date on the status of the upgrade.

In part 4, the Setup Wizard has enough information about your systems and is ready to start copying Windows 98 files to your hard drive.

16. **Click** on **Next**. The Welcome to Windows 98 screen will appear.

At several different points, the Setup Wizard will restart your machine. It does so automatically, so you don't have to do anything. As your machine is restarting, you'll see a message, "Please Wait While Setup Updates

Your Configuration Files. This May Take a Few Minutes." The Windows opening screen appears with a message that it is getting ready to run Windows for the first time. Then, the Setup program jumps back to the black screen that appears when you first turn on your computer and advises you that it has completed updating files and is continuing to load Windows 98.

Part 5 detects the hardware on your machine. The Windows 98 Setup Wizard reappears and begins looking for hardware attached to your machine.

Again, Setup will restart your computer, and you will see the same type of updating messages that were displayed the last time Windows 98 restarted. Windows may ask you to please insert the Windows 98 CD-ROM. If it's not still in the CD-ROM drive, put it back in and click on OK. The hardware detection process continues.

Part 6 detects your current configuration and matches it with Windows 98. Setup now configures Control Panel, Start menu items, Help, DOS program settings, system configuration, and other settings. It is also looking for the various software programs you have installed on your machine and configures them to work with Windows 98. A small box announces that Windows 98 is updating system settings, and Windows restarts one more time.

When Windows restarts this time, it finishes building a driver database and sets up personalized settings for other Windows components, such as Internet Explorer 4, Multimedia, Channels, and Accessories. The dialog box displayed as Windows sets up each component appears several times. Finally, Windows 98 is installed, and ready to use!

Glossary

Access number. The telephone number used to dial into an online service, such as The Microsoft Network, America Online, or CompuServe, or an Internet Service Provider such as AT&T.

Active Desktop. A feature to customize your desktop to display information you can update from the Internet. A term that is synonymous with viewing your desktop as a Web page.

Active window. The window that is currently open for use. The active window is designated by a different color title bar than other open windows.

Alignment. The arrangement of text in relation to the margins of a document or the edges of a table cell. Also called *justification*.

AOL (America Online). A widely used online service offering access service to the Internet as well as proprietary information created by AOL. This proprietary information includes news, financial planning, homework help for students, chat lines, and much more.

Application. Computer program designed to enable users to perform specific job functions. Word processing, accounting, and engineering programs are examples of applications.

AT&T WorldNet. A widely used online service.

Attributes. Items that determine the appearance of text, such as bolding, underlining, italics, or point size.

Back up. The process of making additional copies of data to protect them from unexpected disaster.

Bitmap. A graphics file format made up of small dots.

Block. To highlight text that will be affected by the next action.

Bold. A font attribute that makes text thicker and more prominent.

Border. A line or graphic surrounding paragraphs, pages, or objects.

Browser. A software program specifically designed for viewing Web pages on the Internet.

Bullet. A symbol, such as a filled circle, that precedes items in a list.

Button. A graphical representation of an option or a command that activates the option.

Byte. The amount of space needed to store a single character, such as a number or a letter. 1,024 bytes equals one kilobyte (1 KB).

Card. A removable circuit board that is plugged into an expansion slot inside the computer (such as a graphics card, sound card, or fax card).

Cascading menu. An additional list of menu items opening from a single menu item. Sometimes called a *submenu*.

CD-ROM. Compact Disk-Read Only Memory. Means of data storage using optical storage technology. A single CD-ROM can hold more than 650 MB of information, or one-half billion characters of text.

Channels. A link to Web sites used to receive information from the Internet to your computer.

Check box. A small box next to an option in a dialog box. Clicking an empty check box selects the option; clicking a marked check box deselects the option.

Choose. To use the mouse or the keyboard to pick a menu item or dialog box option that initiates an immediate action.

Click. To push and release the mouse button.

Clip art. A piece of artwork that can be inserted into a document.

Clipboard. An area of computer memory where text or graphics can be temporarily stored. It is a holding place for items that have been cut or copied. The item remains on the Clipboard until you cut or copy an additional item or until you turn off the computer.

Close. To shut down or exit a dialog box, window, or application.

Command. An instruction given to a computer to carry out a particular action.

Command button. A button in a dialog box, such as Open, Close, Exit, OK, or Cancel, that carries out a command. The selected command button is indicated by a different appearance, such as a dotted rectangle or another color.

CompuServe. A widely used online service that offers access to the Internet and proprietary content and information.

Connect charge. The fee a user must pay for the privilege of having access to an online service or Internet access. Generally, a connect charge is based on a monthly rate.

Conversion. A process by which files created in one application are changed to a format that can be used in another application.

Copy. To take a selection from the document and duplicate it on the Clipboard.

Cursor. A symbol (usually a blinking horizontal or vertical bar) that designates the position on the screen where text or codes will be inserted or deleted.

Cut. To take a selection from the document and move it to the Clipboard.

Data. The information to be entered into a spreadsheet.

Default. A setting or action predetermined by the program unless changed by the user.

Deselect. To remove the ✔ from a check box, or menu item, or to remove highlighting from selected text in a document.

Desktop. The screen background and main area of Windows where you can open and manage files and programs.

Destination disk. A disk to which data is written. Traditionally used when making a copy of a disk.

Dialog box. A box that opens and lets you select options, or displays warnings and messages.

Dimmed. Describes the appearance of an icon, a command, or a button that cannot be chosen or selected.

Document. A letter, memo, proposal, or other file that is created in a software application.

Double-click. Pushing and releasing the left mouse button twice in rapid succession.

Drag and drop. To move text or an object by positioning the mouse pointer on the item you want to move, pressing and holding the mouse button, moving the mouse, then releasing the mouse button to drop it into its new location.

Driver. A computer software program that runs a certain device. For example, a printer needs a driver to communicate with the computer.

Ellipses. A punctuation mark consisting of three successive periods (...). Choosing a menu item or command button with an ellipsis opens a dialog box.

E-mail. The exchange of text messages or computer files over a local area network or the Internet.

Endnote. Reference information that prints at the end of a document.

Exit. To leave a program.

Extranet. An inter-company network designed to distribute information, documents, files, and databases. Similar to the Internet except it is limited to a certain number of companies that share information.

FAT. File Allocation Table. A table, or list, within the operating system that keeps track of a user's files and their locations. The system uses this table as users create and modify files.

Fax modem. An internal or external modem that enables documents to be sent directly from the computer to another fax modem or to a standard facsimile machine.

File format. The arrangement and organization of information in a file. File format is determined by the application that created the file.

File. Information stored on a disk under a single name.

Filename. The name given to a file that a user uses to identify the contents of that file, or that a program uses to open or save a file.

Fill. The background color or pattern of an object, such as a cell of a table or a paragraph.

Folder. An organizational tool used to store files.

Font. A group of letters, numbers, and symbols with a common typeface.

Format. The arrangement of data. For example, word processing programs offer commands for modifying the appearance of text with fonts, alignment, page numbers, and so on. An alternate use of format relates to the preparation of a disk with sectors so it can be used for storing data.

Function keys. A set of keys, usually labeled Fl, F2, F3, and so on, used by themselves or with the Shift, Ctrl, or Alt keys to provide quick access to certain features in an application.

Gigabyte (GB). Approximately one billion bytes.

Group. A set of related options in a dialog box, often with its own subtitle.

Handle. Small black squares that appear when you select an object that enable you to resize the object.

Header. Text entered in an area of the document that will be displayed at the top of each page of the document.

Help. A feature that gives you instructions and additional information on using a program.

Help topic. An explanation of a specific feature, dialog box, or task. Help topics usually contain instructions on how to use a feature, pop-up terms with glossary definitions, and related topics. You can access Help topics by choosing any command from the Help menu.

Highlight. To change to a reverse-video appearance when a menu item is selected or an area of text is blocked.

Hypertext link. Used to provide a connection from the current document to another document or to a document on the World Wide Web.

Icon. A small graphic image that represents an application, command, or a tool. An action is performed when an icon is clicked or double-clicked.

Inactive window. A window that is not currently being used. Its title bar changes appearance, and keystrokes and mouse actions do not affect its contents. An inactive window can be activated by clicking on it.

Indent. To move a complete paragraph one tab stop to the right.

Input. The process of entering data into a computer from a keyboard or other device.

Internet. An international computer network connecting businesses, government agencies, universities, and other organizations for the purposes of sharing information.

Internet Explorer. A browser made by Microsoft used to view documents on the World Wide Web.

Intranet. An inter-company network designed to distribute information, documents, files, and databases. Similar to the Internet except it is contained within an organization.

Kilobyte (KB). 1,024 bytes of information or storage space.

Link. A connection between two objects that allows data to be passed between them.

List box. A box that displays a list of choices. When a list is too long to display all choices, it will have a scroll bar, so that you can view additional items.

Log in or Log on. The process a user goes through to begin using a computer system. Usually involves entering some type of identification, followed by a password.

Log out or Log off. The process a user goes through to end a session on the computer.

Mailbox. An area of memory or disk that is assigned to store any e-mail messages sent by other users.

Margin. The width of blank space from the edge of the page to the edge of the text. All four sides of a document have a margin.

Maximize. The step of making a window take up the entire screen.

Megabyte (MB). Approximately one million bytes or 1,024 kilobytes (1,048,576 bytes) of information or storage space.

Memory. A generic term for storage areas in the computer. The area in a computer where information is stored while being worked on. Information is only temporarily stored in memory.

Menu. A list of options displayed onscreen from which you can select a particular function or command.

Menu bar. The area at the top of a window containing headings for pull-down menu items.

Message box. A type of dialog box that appears with information, a warning, an error message, or a request for confirmation to carry out a command.

Microsoft Network. A widely used online service offering access to the Internet and propriety content and information.

MIDI. Musical Instrument Digital Interface. A format that allows communication of musical data between devices, such as computers and synthesizers.

Mnemonics. Underlined, bolded, or colored letters on menu commands or dialog box options indicating keystroke access for that item or option.

Modem. A device used to connect a personal computer with a telephone line so that the computer can be used for accessing online information or communicating with other computers.

Mouse Pointer. A symbol that indicates a position onscreen as you move the mouse around on your desk.

Movement keys. Keys that control cursor movement within a document, including the arrow keys, Page Up, Page Down, Home, and End.

Multimedia. A generic term for computer applications and files that combine standard computer capabilities with other media, such as video and sound.

Multitasking. The capability of a computer to perform multiple operations at the same time.

My Briefcase. A special folder on the Windows desktop used to keep documents up to date when shared between computers.

Netiquette. Short for *network etiquette*. Internet rules of courtesy for sending e-mail and participating in newsgroups.

Netscape Navigator. A popular browser made by Netscape to view documents on the World Wide Web.

Network. An information system based on two or more computers connected through hardware and software for the purpose of sharing files and resources.

Newsgroups. An Internet forum of discussions on a range of topics. They consist of articles and follow-up messages related to specific subjects.

Object. A picture, map, or other graphic element that you can place in a document.

Open. To start an application, to insert a document into a new document window, or to access a dialog box.

Operating system. Software that controls how a computer does basic operations and interfaces between the hardware and software.

Option. A choice inside a dialog box.

Option button. One of a set of buttons found before options in a dialog box. Only one option button in a set can be selected at a time. Sometimes called *radio buttons*.

Orientation. A setting that designates whether a document will print with text running along the long or short side of a piece of paper.

Page break. A command that tells an application to begin a new page.

Password. A secret code word that restricts access to a file. Without the password, the file cannot be opened.

Paste. The process of retrieving information stored on the Clipboard and inserting a copy of it into a document.

Path. A pattern of folders used to designate the location of a file.

Pixel. Short for "picture element." A pixel is the smallest dot that can be represented on a screen or in a paint (bitmap) graphic.

Plug & Play. A set of hardware standards followed by computer manufacturers to allow for better compatibility between computers and software. Also known as *PnP*.

Pop-up list. A list of options that appears when a pop-up button is selected. Most pop-up buttons are marked by double arrows or triangles and display mutually exclusive options. The button itself shows the selected option. Other pop-up lists, marked by single arrows or triangles, show the feature name rather than the selected option.

Pop-up term. A box that appears when you click on an underlined word in a Help topic. Pop-ups contain additional information or glossary definitions.

Port. A connection device between a computer and another component, such as a printer or modem. For example, a printer cable is plugged into the printer port on the computer so information can be sent to the computer.

Print Preview. Enables you to see a preview onscreen of how your printed document will look before you print it.

Print queue. The list of print jobs waiting to be sent to a particular printer.

Print spooling. The process of sending documents to a storage area on a disk, called a buffer, where they remain until the printer is ready for each one in turn.

Printer driver. The software that enables a program to communicate with the printer so the program's information can be printed.

Prodigy. A widely used online service offering access service to the Internet and proprietary content and information.

Program. A set of instructions for a computer to execute. Software designed for a certain use, such as word processing, e-mail, or spreadsheet entries. Sometimes called an *application*.

Queue. A waiting or holding location, usually for printing or e-mail messages.

Quick Launch bar. A toolbar on the Taskbar that provides shortcuts to frequently-used features, such as the desktop, the Web browser, Outlook Express, and channels.

Radio button. See options button.

RAM. Random Access Memory. The main memory that holds programs and data that are currently being used.

Recycle Bin. An icon on the desktop that represents a temporary holding place for files that are deleted.

Redo. Reverses the last Undo action.

Registry. A central file that Windows 98 uses to store information about the hardware, software, and preferences on a specific computer.

Restore. Copies files from a backup storage device to their normal location or changes the size of a program window.

ROM. Read Only Memory. The part of a computer's main memory that contains the basic programs that run the computer when it is turned on. ROM cannot be erased.

Ruler. Used to change page format elements, such as tabs and margins.

Save As. Saves a previously saved worksheet with a new name or properties.

Save. The process of taking a document residing in the memory of the computer and creating a file to be stored on a disk.

Scroll bar. The bars on the right side and bottom of a window that let you move vertically and horizontally through a document.

Select. To identify a command or option (from menus or dialog boxes) to be applied to an object or block of text.

Selection cursor. The highlighted text, dotted rectangle, or cursor that shows you where the next keystroke or mouse action will apply in a dialog box or window.

Serial port. A port on a computer through which data is sent and received one bit at a time.

Shortcut. An icon that represents a quick way to start a program or open a file or folder.

Shortcut key. A keystroke or keystroke combination that gives you quick access to a feature.

Shut down. The process of saving all settings before a computer is physically turned off. Accessed from the Start menu.

Sizing handle. The small solid squares that appear on the borders of a graphics box or a graphics line that has been selected. You can drag these handles to size the box and its contents.

Software. The instructions created from computer programs that direct the computer in performing various operations. Software can also include data.

Sort. To arrange data in a specified order. For example, data can be sorted in ascending or descending alphabetical order.

Source disk. A disk from which data is read. Traditionally used when making a copy of a disk.

Spin box. A button in a dialog box that lets you specify program-selected amounts by clicking the mouse instead of typing numbers.

Start button. The button in the lower-left corner of the Taskbar that is used to access programs.

Status bar. The line at the bottom of a window that shows such information as the path, page information, or location of the insertion point.

Submenu. An additional list of menu items opening from a single menu item. Also called a *cascading menu*.

Subscribe. The capability to receive updated information from a channel on a regular basis.

System Tray. The icons displayed in the lower-right corner that represent programs running in the background. Formerly referred to as TSRs.

Taskbar. The bar (usually at the bottom of the screen) that lists all open folders and active programs.

Telephony. A general term for the technology of the telephone, including the conversion of sound into signals that are transmitted to other locations and then converted back into sound. A modem uses telephony.

Template. A document file with customized format, content, and features. Frequently used to create faxes, memos, and proposals.

Temporary file. A file that a program creates when it is running. Temporary files are deleted when the program is exited properly.

Text file. A file saved in ASCII file format. It contains text, spaces, and returns, but no formatting codes.

Tile. A display format for open windows. Tiled windows are displayed side by side, with no window overlapping any other window.

Toggle. A term used to refer to something (such as a feature) that turns on and off with the same switch (such as a keystroke).

Toolbar. Appears at the top of the application window and is used to access the features available in an application.

Trackball. A pointing device consisting of a small platform with a ball resting on it, similar in size to a mouse. The platform remains stationary, while the user manipulates the ball with his or her hand, and thus moves the cursor or arrow on the screen.

Undo. Reverses the last editing action.

Upgrade. To install a new release of a software program so that the latest features are available for use.

Views. Ways of displaying documents to see different perspectives of the information in that document.

Virus. A computer program that infects computer files by inserting into those files copies of itself. Although not all virus programs are damaging, some can be very destructive, such as destroying a computer hard disk.

Wallpaper. A photograph, drawing, or pattern displayed on the background of the Windows 98 desktop.

Wildcard. The character used to replace one character (?) or any number of characters (*) in a search string. These two characters are conventions in most applications.

Window. A method of displaying a document so that many of its elements appear graphically and many features are immediately available as onscreen choices. The place where you type your documents is called a document window.

Wizards. The interactive programs supplied with Windows 98 to assist users through a project or problem by asking a series of questions.

World Wide Web. A series of specially designed documents, all linked together, to be viewed on the Internet.

WYSIWYG. What You See Is What You Get. Refers to a computer screen display that approximates the printed page, showing fonts and graphics in correct proportions.

Zoom. Used to enlarge or reduce the way text is displayed onscreen. It does not affect how the document will print.

Index

B

C

Send Us
YOUR COMMENTS

Dear Reader:

Thank you for buying this book. In order to offer you more quality books on the topics *you* would like to see, we need your input. At Prima Publishing, we pride ourselves on timely responsiveness to our readers needs. If you'll complete and return this brief questionnaire, *we will listen!*

Name: (first) _____ (M.I.) _____ (last) _____

Company: _____ Type of business: _____

Address: _____ City: _____ State: _____ Zip: _____

Phone: _____ Fax: _____ E-mail address: _____

May we contact you for research purposes? ❑ Yes ❑ No

(If you participate in a research project, we will supply you with your choice of a book from Prima CPD)

❶ How would you rate this book, overall?

❑ Excellent ❑ Fair
❑ Very Good ❑ Below Average
❑ Good ❑ Poor

❷ Why did you buy this book?

❑ Price of book ❑ Content
❑ Author's reputation ❑ Prima's reputation
❑ CD-ROM/disk included with book
❑ Information highlighted on cover
❑ Other (Please specify): _____

❸ How did you discover this book?

❑ Found it on bookstore shelf
❑ Saw it in Prima Publishing catalog
❑ Recommended by store personnel
❑ Recommended by friend or colleague
❑ Saw an advertisement in: _____
❑ Read book review in: _____
❑ Saw it on Web site: _____
❑ Other (Please specify): _____

❹ Where did you buy this book?

❑ Bookstore (name)_____
❑ Computer Store (name) _____
❑ Electronics Store (name) _____
❑ Wholesale Club (name) _____
❑ Mail Order (name) _____
❑ Direct from Prima Publishing
❑ Other (please specify): _____

❺ Which computer periodicals do you read regularly? _____

_____

_____

❻ Would you like to see your name in print?

May we use your name and quote you in future Prima Publishing books or promotional materials?

❑ Yes ❑ No

❼ Comments & Suggestions: _____

_____

_____

9 How do you rate your level of computer skills?

- ☐ Beginner
- ☐ Advanced
- ☐ Intermediate

11 I would be interested in computer books on these topics

- ☐ Word Processing
- ☐ Database:
- ☐ Networking
- ☐ Spreadsheets
- ☐ Desktop Publishing
- ☐ Web site design
- Other _____

8 Where do you use your computer?

	100%	75%	50%	25%
Work	☐	☐	☐	☐
Home	☐	☐	☐	☐
School	☐	☐	☐	☐

Other _____

10 What is your age?

- ☐ Under 18
- ☐ 18-24
- ☐ 25-29
- ☐ 30-39
- ☐ 40-49
- ☐ 50-59
- ☐ 60-over

PRIMA PUBLISHING
Computers & Technology
3875 Atherton Road
Rocklin, CA 95765

OTHER BOOKS FROM PRIMA PUBLISHING
Computers & Technology

ISBN	Title	Price
0-7615-1363-9	Access 97 Fast & Easy	$16.99
0-7615-1175-x	ACT! 3.0 Fast & Easy	$16.99
0-7615-1412-0	ACT! 4.0 Fast & Easy	$16.99
0-7615-1348-5	Create FrontPage 98 Web Pages In a Weekend	$24.99
0-7615-1294-2	Create PowerPoint Presentations In a Weekend	$19.99
0-7615-1388-4	Create Your First Web Page In a Weekend, Revised Edition	$24.99
0-7615-0428-1	The Essential Excel 97 Book	$27.99
0-7615-0733-7	The Essential Netscape Communicator Book	$24.99
0-7615-0969-0	The Essential Office 97 Book	$27.99
0-7615-0695-0	The Essential Photoshop Book	$35.00
0-7615-1182-2	The Essential PowerPoint 97 Book	$24.99
0-7615-1136-9	The Essential Publisher 97 Book	$24.99
0-7615-0967-4	The Essential Windows 98 Book	$24.99
0-7615-0752-3	The Essential Windows NT 4 Book	$27.99
0-7615-0427-3	The Essential Word 97 Book	$27.99
0-7615-0425-7	The Essential WordPerfect 8 Book	$24.99
0-7615-1008-7	Excel 97 Fast & Easy	$16.99
0-7615-1534-8	FrontPage 98 Fast & Easy	$16.99
0-7615-1194-6	Increase Your Web Traffic In a Weekend	$19.99
0-7615-1191-1	Internet Explorer 4.0 Fast & Easy	$19.99
0-7615-1137-7	Jazz Up Your Web Site In a Weekend	$24.99
0-7615-1379-5	Learn Access 97 In a Weekend	$19.99
0-7615-1293-4	Learn HTML In a Weekend	$24.99
0-7615-1295-0	Learn the Internet In a Weekend	$19.99
0-7615-1217-9	Learn Publisher 97 In a Weekend	$19.99
0-7615-1251-9	Learn Word 97 In a Weekend	$19.99
0-7615-1296-9	Learn Windows 98 In a Weekend	$19.99
0-7615-1193-8	Lotus 1-2-3 97 Fast & Easy	$16.99
0-7615-1420-1	Managing with Microsoft Project 98	$29.99
0-7615-1382-5	Netscape Navigator 4.0 Fast & Easy	$16.99
0-7615-1162-8	Office 97 Fast & Easy	$16.99
0-7615-1186-5	Organize Your Finances with Quicken Deluxe 98 In a Weekend	$19.99
0-7615-1405-8	Outlook 98 Fast & Easy	$16.99
0-7615-1513-5	Publisher 98 Fast & Easy	$19.99
0-7615-1192-X	SmartSuite 97 Fast & Easy	$16.99
0-7615-1138-5	Upgrade Your PC In a Weekend	$19.99
1-55958-738-5	Windows 95 Fast & Easy	$19.95
0-7615-1007-9	Word 97 Fast & Easy	$16.99
0-7615-1316-7	Word 97 for Law Firms	$29.99
0-7615-1083-4	WordPerfect 8 Fast & Easy	$16.99
0-7615-1188-1	WordPerfect Suite 8 Fast & Easy	$16.99

TO ORDER BOOKS

Please send me the following items:

Quantity	Title	Unit Price	Total
_____	_____	$_____	$_____
_____	_____	$_____	$_____
_____	_____	$_____	$_____
_____	_____	$_____	$_____
_____	_____	$_____	$_____

	Subtotal	$_____
	Deduct 10% when ordering 3–5 books	$_____
	7.25% Sales Tax (CA only)	$_____
	8.25% Sales Tax (TN only)	$_____
	5.0% Sales Tax (MD and IN only)	$_____
	Shipping and Handling*	$_____
	TOTAL ORDER	$_____

Shipping and Handling depend on Subtotal.

Subtotal	Shipping/Handling
$0.00–$14.99	$3.00
$15.00–29.99	$4.00
$30.00–49.99	$6.00
$50.00–99.99	$10.00
$100.00–199.99	$13.00
$200.00+	call for quote

Foreign and all Priority Request orders:
Call Order Entry department for price quote
at 1-916-632-4400

This chart represents the total retail price of books
only (before applicable discounts are taken).

By telephone: With Visa, Mastercard, or American Express, call 1-800-632-8676. Mon.–Fri. 8:30–4:00 PST.

By Internet e-mail: sales@primapub.com

By mail: Just fill out the information below and send with your remittance to:

PRIMA PUBLISHING
P.O. Box 1260BK
Rocklin, CA 95677-1260

www.primapublishing.com

Name_____ Daytime Telephone_____

Address _____

City _____ State _____ Zip_____

Visa /MC#_____Exp. _____

Check/Money Order enclosed for $_____ Payable to Prima Publishing

Signature_____

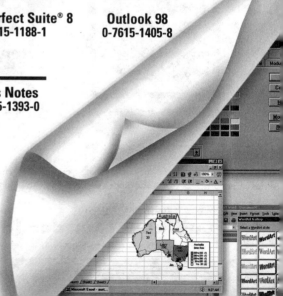